COLLABORATIVE ONLINE
GAME CREATION

NANU SWAMY AND NAVEENA ASWADHATI

COURSE TECHNOLOGY
CENGAGE Learning

Collaborative Online Game Creation

Nanu Swamy and Naveena Aswadhati

Publisher and General Manager, Course Technology PTR:
Stacy L. Hiquet

Associate Director of Marketing:
Sarah Panella

Content Project Manager:
Jessica McNavich

Marketing Manager: Jordan Casey

Acquisitions Editor: Heather Hurley

Project/Copy Editor:
Karen A. Gill

Technical Reviewer: Danny Vink

Editorial Services Coordinator:
Jen Blaney

Interior Layout: Jill Flores

Cover Designer: Mike Tanamachi

Indexer: Kevin Broccoli

Proofreader: Mike Beady

2009 Course Technology, a part of Cengage Learning.

ALL RIGHTS RESERVED. No part of this work covered by the copyright herein may be reproduced, transmitted, stored, or used in any form or by any means graphic, electronic, or mechanical, including but not limited to photocopying, recording, scanning, digitizing, taping, Web distribution, information networks, or information storage and retrieval systems, except as permitted under Section 107 or 108 of the 1976 United States Copyright Act, without the prior written permission of the publisher.

For product information and technology assistance, contact us at
Cengage Learning Customer & Sales Support, 1-800-354-9706.

For permission to use material from this text or product, submit all requests online at **cengage.com/permissions.**
Further permissions questions can be e-mailed to
permissionrequest@cengage.com.

Adobe Flash is a registered trademark of Adobe, Inc. All rights reserved. All other trademarks are the property of their respective owners.

Library of Congress Control Number: 2008929224

ISBN-13: 978-1-58450-560-0

ISBN-10: 1-58450-560-5

Course Technology, a part of Cengage Learning
20 Channel Center Street
Boston, MA 02210
USA

Cengage Learning is a leading provider of customized learning solutions with office locations around the globe, including Singapore, the United Kingdom, Australia, Mexico, Brazil, and Japan. Locate your local office at:
international.cengage.com/region.

Cengage Learning products are represented in Canada by Nelson Education, Ltd.

For your lifelong learning solutions, visit **courseptr.com.**

Visit our corporate Web site at **cengage.com.**

Printed in the United States of America
1 2 3 4 5 6 7 11 10 09

Dedication

To Planet Earth, with thanks!

Acknowledgments

Nanu Swamy would like to acknowledge the following people:

- Gregory Clayton, Heather Hurley, and Jen Blaney, for giving me this opportunity.
- All the stakeholders at Digital Brix, for the financial support to make the GameBrix technology a reality.
- Karen Gill, for bringing it all together, having boundless patience, offering encouragement and support, and going above and beyond at all times.
- Danny Vink, for the wonderful suggestions and providing great feedback.
- Jessica McNavich, Jordan Casey, Jill Flores, Mike Tanamachi, Kevin Broccoli, and Mike Beady, for their assistance in the publishing process.

Naveena Aswadhati would like to acknowledge the following people:

- Gregory Clayton, Heather Hurley, and Jennifer Blaney, for giving me this opportunity.
- Dorothy Shamonsky, Nathan Felde, and Richard Phung, faculty members of Art Institutes, for their feedback on GameBrix technology for *Collaborative Online Game Creation* in the classroom that was a key driver in taking up the monumental effort to get this book completed.
- All the Digital Brix stakeholders and coworkers, for their support and encouragement for the project.
- Danny Vink, for keeping us straight on all the game terminology and feedback.
- Karen Gill, for providing razor-sharp attention to detail, whipping chapters into shape, and offering encouragement and support, without which this book would not have gotten done.
- Jessica McNavich, Jordan Casey, Jill Flores, Mike Tanamachi, Kevin Broccoli, and Mike Beady, for their assistance in the publishing process.

- To all the enthusiastic supporters of this project: Ian Smith, Nick Eaton, Andrew Eaton, Collin Smith, Susanna Harrison, Vijay Aswadhati, Shriram Costlow, Brian Traumuller, Dan Weiss, Melissa Burrows, Rohit Swamy, Susan Frenette, Stewart Noyce, Tom Dusenberry, Sheli Petersen, Colin Greenhill, Karthick Balakrishnan, Manjith G., Rajesh Kannan, and Visu K.

- Special thanks to Frank Ferguson, the greatest cheerleader of GameBrix technology. Also, thanks to Morton E. Goulder, Richard Corley, Pat Walsh, Ben Williams, Jean Hammond, Devin Berger, George Schwenk, David Patrick, Ajoy Aswadhati, Carol Mcguire, and Dan McGuire for their support.

- My daughter, Ramya Swamy, a high school junior, who came up with the concepts of purchasing assets with Brix and having a store and sacrificed many weekends to review the flow of content in each chapter.

- My mom, Sujaya, for all her prayers and long-distance voice mails from Silicon Valley encouraging me to find the inner strength to complete the book.

- To my dog, Olly, for his constant cheerful disposition.

About the Authors

Nanu Swamy is an experienced hands-on software engineer with several years of experience building commercially successful applications in a variety of software organizations. During his academic pursuits, his interests were in assembly language, microprocessors, and software security. His first large projects were at the server engineering group at Sybase, where he worked on heterogeneous database access products. He has worked for more than 15 years in different companies since then in areas such as Internet commerce, network management, J2EE, Adobe Flex, Web 2.0, and databases, and he is now working on semantic technologies that will power the next Internet revolution. Nanu has an M.S. and B.Tech from Indian Institute of Technology (IIT). In his free time, Nanu enjoys hacking hardware and software as a hobby roboticist and volunteering at the Technology Learning Center of the Museum of Science, Boston.

Naveena Aswadhati is an experienced product manager and the coauthor of *Basic Game Creation for Fun and Learning.* Her first projects were in building optical communications systems at Indian Institute of Technology (IIT) for startups and Fortune 500 organizations. She has worked for more than 15 years in Fortune 500 companies since then in the areas of application-specific integrated circuit (ASIC) design, electronic design automation tools, next-generation networks, animation, game technology, and robotics. Naveena has also spoken at many user conferences, including the Game Developers Conference, SigmaXi, Electronic Design Automation, and Robotic Trends. She holds an M.S. and an M.B.A., and she has pursued research at IIT in voice and data networks. Naveena is also involved in developing programs on emerging technologies at RoboTech Center (http://www.robotechcenter.com). In her spare time, she enjoys outdoor activities. Naveena resides in Nashua, New Hampshire, with her husband Nanu, their two children, Ramya and Rohit, and their dog, Olly.

Contents

Introduction

This is the first edition of *Collaborative Online Game Creation*, offering all the material to create graphics, animations, and Flash games. The concepts for this book came out of our experimentation with many game development tools. The need for a comprehensive tool suite for building custom Flash graphics, animations, and games on the Web made this project compelling. This book allows you to create Flash games without the need for ActionScript programming.

In addition to the material that covers the process of building games, you have access to a 30-day free trial to the GameBrix portal. The GameBrix Web technology server is supported by the authors as a hobby platform. We welcome your suggestions to improve the product. At the expiration of the 30-day trial, you will be prompted to pay a subscription fee that covers the hosting, storage, and support costs. Once the trial period ends, the trial data will be removed.

WHAT YOU'LL FIND IN THIS BOOK

Digital Brix's GameBrix platform is a Web-based rich media application that provides avenues for beginners to explore the process of creating Flash games without the need for downloadable software, installation, or knowledge of ActionScript programming. The technology works on any computer with Internet Explorer or Firefox. The book facilitates anyone with a curiosity in game creation and publishing to use the simple step-by-step instructions to create Flash games. The majority of this book introduces you to building different types of simple Flash games. Following are some of the main concepts in this book:

- Setup of your online account at http://www.gamebrix.com
- Introduction to the Web portal for creating Flash graphics, animations, and games
- Purchasing of assets using Brix to create games described in the book

- Step-by-step instructions to create games
- Introductory ActionScript programming concepts
- A detailed reference to all the states and tasks in the Appendix

WHO THIS BOOK IS FOR

In general, this book can be used by various people but is geared toward any hands-on learner with a curiosity and interest in building Flash games. There are no prerequisites for using the book other than a basic working knowledge of the computer. The examples, step-by-step instructions, and game templates in this book are intended to be general and can be applied to many Flash games. We envision students, animators, illustrators, programmers, professional Web site developers, game designers, and advertisers using this book to create quick proto-types to communicate ideas on their creations.

HOW THIS BOOK IS ORGANIZED

Each chapter has relevant visual aids such as screenshots, graphics, and game templates to guide you through the game creation process. You'll also find special sections to call your attention to items of note, tips and tricks, and areas of caution that we have found particularly relevant. Finally, each chapter ends with a summary of concepts learned.

WHAT YOU CAN DO WITH THIS BOOK

This book offers a comprehensive tool suite to build Flash games on the Web. Learn to create graphics, game objects, and intelligence to make complete games that can be played on any computer with an Internet browser or on any device that supports the Flash Player. Use your own graphic style and customize the graphics to make them your own. This book provides a hands-on approach to learn the process of building games. In addition, the book details the framework of sharing assets, purchasing assets from the store, managing your assets, or sharing through an online store. Have fun creating a game club and building games with your social network.

UPDATES AND COMMUNICATION

Despite the care we took while writing and editing this book to make it complete and accurate, it is possible that you will discover minor issues with code or that future versions or bug fixes of GameBrix will produce changes in Builder requiring modifications of the book contents. When this happens, all efforts will be made to post updates and corrections on a special page located at http://www.courseptr.com/collaborativegamecreation. You can also go to this page to learn how to contact the authors and the publisher.

HAVE FUN

Our hope as authors is that you can learn something from this book that furthers your aspirations to build games for fun and learning. Playing games is a lot of fun; our hope is that you will find the same joy in building games.

1 Building Flash Games Online

In This Chapter

- What Is Flash?
- Flash Games' Reach and Portability
- Why Build Flash Games Online?
- Monetizing Flash Games
- Careers and Opportunities

Over the past decade, the creative design community has embraced technologies that have enabled them to express their creativity. Adobe Flash technology is tightly coupled with people looking for new ways to express their creative ideas. Flash technology has enabled the creation of animations, multimedia presentations, video players, audio players, presentation graphics, games, and Web pages. Flash technology is available on more than a half billion mobile devices and more than one billion computers worldwide.

WHAT IS FLASH?

Flash technology and the digital design community have experienced a rich connection for more than a decade. With Flash technology, creative artists have enjoyed a new avenue to express their creativity. Artists use Flash to create stunning graphical and interactive content for the Web. Because of the global nature of the Web, countless artists and designers worldwide have been inspired by Flash content and set out to create their own animations and graphics using this powerful technology. People have created great work with this technology, spurring on its ever-growing popularity across the Internet. The connection between Flash and the creative community has been solidified by the love and joy that comes from using and building beautiful digital content. The design community wasn't driven by the commercial successes that have shaped many other technologies, but rather by the sheer happiness and excitement they were able to inspire in themselves and others using their skills. Adobe and the creative community have built a strong and mutually beneficial symbiotic ecosystem around Flash technology. This relationship has led to more and more Web sites adopting Flash.

The term *Flash* can have many different meanings, depending on its context. Typically, it refers to one of the following three things:

- Adobe Flash, the application used to create Flash content
- Flash content, which is distributed as files in the SWF format
- Flash player or browser plug-in, which is used to view content created with the Adobe Flash application

Adobe Flash CS3 is the current version of the Flash application, Flash 9 is the current file format produced by Flash, and Flash Player 9.0 is the most up-to-date version of the player. Recently, Adobe published the Flash file format on its Web site, which enables third-party vendors to create other applications that can directly produce Flash content. You can find the Flash 9.0 file format at http://www.adobe.com/devnet/swf/pdf/swf_file_format_spec_v9.pdf.

The Flash Player plays Flash content with the SWF file extension. This includes multimedia content, animations, audio, video, games, interactive advertisements, special effects on Web sites, and even complete Web applications. Flash applications with online capabilities and the look and feel of a desktop application are known as *rich Internet applications*. In the context of this book, *Flash* refers to the content that is created on the GameBrix portal in Adobe's published Flash 9.0 file format.

Although Flash was not originally intended as an engine for game creation, it has evolved into a platform for creating casual games. Examples of Flash games include *Bejeweled*, *AniBrix*, and *MomoNinja*. You can play many Flash games on a Web browser from any computer connected to the Internet. Flash games run consistently on Mac OS, Microsoft Windows, Linux, and various other UNIX systems. You can also play Flash games on game consoles with Internet capabilities, such as the Nintendo Wii, PlayStation 3, Xbox 360, and handhelds, like the Sony PSP.

Frontiers are constantly opening up for Flash developers to create new types of content. As of the publication of this book, Adobe has released a technology called AIR (Adobe Integrated Runtime) that provides avenues for Flash developers to create desktop applications that harness the power of the desktop computer and access the Internet to create a new breed of application, known as *hybrid applications*. GameBrix technology offers a new frontier of its own, allowing anyone to create interactive Flash games directly from his Web browser with or without programming knowledge.

FLASH GAMES' REACH AND PORTABILITY

Games built using Flash technology have tremendous reach. Game developers everywhere on the planet aspire to release games to the widest audience they can. Games are distributed not only for entertainment, fame, and money but also for social and political causes, advertisement, and even establishing career paths into well-known game studios. Having established itself as the standard for delivering high-impact, rich Web content, Flash is one of the most popular tools for game creation. Flash games can be played on all platforms, browsers, handhelds, and consoles. This diversity is part of what makes it such a powerful and popular tool among amateur and professional game developers alike.

Games deployed across multiple browsers and platforms deliver a consistent, rich Web experience. Flash Player supports a scripting language called ActionScript 3.0, which is compliant with the European Computer Manufacturers Association-Script (ECMAScript) language specification, Third Edition (ECMA-262). ECMA is an international industry association that is based in Geneva and was founded in 1961. It is dedicated to the standardization of information and communication technology (ICT) and consumer electronics (CE). Work on the ECMA programming language is not complete. The organization's technical committee is working on significant enhancements, including mechanisms for scripts to be created and used across the Internet, and tighter coordination with other standards bodies such as groups within the World Wide Web Consortium (W3C) and the Wireless Application Protocol (WAP) Forum.

Using ActionScript 3.0, Flash programmers can develop rich cross-platform games that users can enjoy on their desktop computers as well as on their PDAs and

Flash Lite–enabled mobile phones. 98.8 percent of desktops worldwide connected to the Internet have the Flash plug-in installed. This makes the Flash Player ubiquitous on all operating systems.

WHY BUILD FLASH GAMES ONLINE?

Traditionally, applications for building games have been confined to the desktop. Game development requires game designers to come up with concepts and create systems, creative artists to produce game graphics (commonly known as *game sprites*), and programmers to write and develop code. All of these people must work together as a team to create a game. It is common to find game development teams working together from different locations. Game development tools designed for the desktop do not facilitate collaboration among developers separated by physical distance. They are machine dependent and are accessible only from individual computers. Such tools are managed by license keys, which prevent the software from being used on multiple machines without the user purchasing a new copy.

Creativity and inspiration happen in bursts and have been known to be non-linear. When you are working on enterprise applications like payroll, accounting, and banking, such applications have in common a set of rules that can be logically and systematically processed and executed in a methodical linear approach. The thinking process is different for creating any type of art; the artist goes through a multitude of iterations before arriving at the final product.

This creative effort is never really complete because there is no definite end-point for creativity. Because creative ideas can occur anywhere at any time, it is ideal to use Web browser–based applications that enable creating graphics, animations, or games from any computer. This eliminates the need for multiple software licenses that are specific to a single computer.

In addition to problems associated with desktop applications creating vertical silos of content, distribution of content such as games and animations requires the use of traditional media like CDs and USB hard drives. Today, game developers have new avenues to publish content on portals that are supported by ad revenue or through agreements with hosting sites that have a large audience. However, this exposure requires the game to be fully developed to ensure acceptance by users, publishers, and retailers. The GameBrix portal provides simple avenues for all kinds of users to publish and showcase their content on the Web, without going through the hassle of publishers and retailers or the limitations of desktop software. Because game design and development is a collaborative process that requires multiple iterations, the logical and ideal platform to build games on is the Web. GameBrix is Web software that allows game creators and players to unite and form communities to review, play, provide feedback, and then get the attention of the media moguls. This enables developers to showcase a portfolio that attracts the attention of industry leaders such as Adobe, Yahoo, Google, and Microsoft. It is the dream of every game designer and developer in the world.

Applications in SWF format are typically small, allowing for fast download and installation and easy distribution over the Internet. They can even be run inside an Internet browser so that anyone can use them. The Web browser is becoming a digital bridge that connects human beings with information. It is not uncommon to see children move a mouse and use a computer before they can even read and recognize the 26 letters of the English alphabet. Clearly, the transition to the digital world does not require a person to be technologically savvy. The large-scale adoption of the browser as a medium of communication has led to the transformation of several desktop applications into Web-based applications. Using rich Internet applications created with Flash, artists and programmers can harness the following advantages:

- Content is shared on the Internet.
- Collaboration is rapid.
- Applications are accessible from anywhere, allowing content creation from anywhere.
- Browser-based applications are platform independent.
- You can publish content at the push of a button.

DigitalBrix Inc. created the world's first online platform that allows users to create Flash games online. With this platform, known as GameBrix, games can be created from anywhere and published to the Internet. GameBrix hosts a set of Web applications for game developers to collaborate and build Flash games of all kinds. You can distribute Flash games you create on GameBrix to mass audiences.

GameBrix has an easy-to-learn drag-and-drop interface for creating games. You can create and distribute custom Flash games without the need for complex programming skills. Furthermore, experts can use ActionScript, an industry standard scripting language, to enhance their game mechanics.

MONETIZING FLASH GAMES

Video games have emerged as a mainstream entertainment medium that generates worldwide revenues through new hardware and software sales. Surpassing box office revenues, movie rentals, and book and music sales, the PC video game market is poised to reach global revenues of $13 billion by 2009. According to the outlook posted by PricewaterhouseCoopers report on the global video game industry, new Internet-enabled consoles and growing broadband penetration will spur growth in the online game market, whereas next-generation wireless devices will drive demand for wireless games. Globally, video game spending is expected to rise from $32 billion in 2006 to $49 billion in 2011. The integration of online games across all hardware platforms has resulted in the emergence of advertising as a significant revenue driver for the games industry.

Revenue accrual through interactive advertisements in Flash games is a reality that has brought enterprises and independent (affectionately known as *indie*) game developers into the digital economy. Building Flash games, integrating them with advertisements, and distributing them freely allow millions of people to play the game and see the embedded ads. Games do not have to feature top-of-the line graphics or advanced programming. Even silly games, like the World Cup soccer head-butt game, were played several million times. Such games can be built and published within a few hours of time investment using GameBrix online applications. The most important thing with monetizing Flash games is to find simple ideas that can engage millions of people worldwide.

The Interactive Advertising Bureau (IAB), founded in 1996, represents interactive companies that actively engage in and support the sale of interactive advertising. IAB has predefined sizes and formats for integrating advertisements into Web sites and games. IAB members are responsible for selling more than 86 percent of online advertising in the United States.

Different types of advertisements can be displayed before, during, and after gameplay, as shown in Table 1.1. *Around game advertising* refers to the traditional display of digital video units before and after the game. These ads can be shown as companion ads, prerolls, interlevel, pregame, or postgame. *Skinning advertisements* brand the gameplay area but not necessarily the game elements.

Flash game developers worldwide have used Google's innovative IAB standardized advertisement services platform for revenue generation. It has allowed the ad-serving process to enable any Web portal in the world to serve IAB standard advertisements for revenue generation. The format of choice for creating interactive ads served on Web portals is Flash SWF. *Advergames* are games that include an interactive advertisement in them. *Anti-advergames* are games that delineate or satirize bad features of a product or service. Advergames have generated significant revenues on large Web portals.

For ease of distribution, Flash advertisements must comply with one of the following four ad sizes: 728×90 pixels, 300×250 pixels, 160×600 pixels, or 180×150 pixels. The ads can reach a majority of audiences this way.

TABLE 1.1 ADVERGAME FORMATS

Advertising Format	Description
Advergames	Custom-made games designed specifically for a product or service
Dynamic in Game	Ads displayed inside a game that can be dynamically changed
Interlevel Ads	Ads displayed between levels in a game
Game Skinning	Custom branding integrated into the game
Postgame	Ads shown after the game
Pregame	Ads shown before the game
Pre-/Postroll	Ads shown while a game is loading or ending
Product Placement	Sponsored products placed inside the game
Static in Game	Advertisements hard-coded into games

Developers can easily create Flash advertisements with GameBrix online for the Web marketplace. With GameBrix Builder or GameBrix Express, developers can now develop and deliver rich media to reach and engage consumers.

Flash game developers have multiple options for profiting from their games. Their knowledge of building Flash games allows them to construct a rich, compelling portfolio that can lead to a rewarding career. In addition, the Internet has awarded multiple cash incentives to game developers. They can host Flash games on Web sites with single-level teasers that players can play for free. If players enjoy the game, they can then pay a one-time fee to play additional levels. Developers can also sell games that promote products to clients. Flash games can be distributed on multiple host sites. The host sites or content aggregators in turn share advertising revenue with the developers of the game.

CAREERS AND OPPORTUNITIES

The entertainment and media industry provides numerous opportunities for Flash game developers. Skills required include proven interactive design and development skills and the ability to complete a variety of projects. It is important to keep an online portfolio with finished games, interactive animations, and artwork.

Previously, game designers without programming knowledge were forced to display their expertise through written design documents. Now they can design and develop playable digital games to show to potential employers. GameBrix users can create graphical elements like characters and backgrounds with the online Game-Brix Animator, and they can build games and interactive components with Game-Brix Express or GameBrix Builder. Users with programming experience can include ActionScript code to extend the game mechanics and to demonstrate their expertise. In addition to seeking employment with media organizations, GameBrix users can host a Web portfolio on their own and profit through Google Ads or by publishing their games to portals such as Atom Entertainment, Kongregate, New Grounds, and other Web sites that publish user-generated content.

SUMMARY

This chapter explored the diversity and functionality of Flash technology and provided reasons to pursue career paths in the game industry by using GameBrix technology. The next chapter describes the GameBrix portal.

2 Introduction to GameBrix

In This Chapter

- The GameBrix Menus
- The GameBuilder Interface
- The Animator Interface
- The Express Interface
- Getting Started
- Playing Games

Creating games requires a unique combination of creative and programming skills. The GameBrix portal enables creative people with little or no programming knowledge to collaborate online and create platform-independent Flash games. The online game development platform enables people to publish their own games, collaborate with others, and deploy the games on Web sites of their choice. No prerequisite knowledge is required to start using the GameBrix portal and its associated set of online tools to build games.

Game creation can be fun. For many years, creative artists have been frustrated with tools and technologies offered for game creation. With GameBrix Game-Builder, the game creation process is broken down into simple steps that people with minimal computer skills can follow.

The GameBrix portal truly democratizes game creation and empowers anyone to build and publish user-generated, casual online games for browser-based entertainment. GameBrix is built on top of Adobe's Flash technology. Although not a requirement, it would be advantageous to have prior knowledge of Adobe's Flash technology. It enables you to leap ahead and jump into the hot new technology area encompassing creation of casual games for the Web.

THE GAMEBRIX MENUS

GameBrix is a collaborative portal that provides a suite of technologies for building, sharing, and playing casual online games. Figure 2.1 shows you the login page, and Figure 2.2 shows you the menus available to users after login.

People of all types can collaborate, build, share, publish, and play games online using the portal. GameBrix allows anyone, anywhere with reach to a computer or a portable device that is connected to the Internet through broadband to open a Web browser to build, play, and publish Flash games. It uses the Web browser as a platform that provides applications to create graphics, animate graphics, and build interactive Flash games. Interactive applications like GameBrix that use the Internet browser as a platform to collaborate, create, and share are known as Web 2.0 applications.

FIGURE 2.1
The GameBrix home page.

The GameBrix community shares the following online applications:

- **The Builder.** A Web 2.0 browser-based application that enables community members to build games
- **The Animator.** A Web 2.0 application that enables the creation of both graphics and simple animations
- **The Express.** A high-level, template-based development application that speeds up game development
- **The Script and Path Editors.** Designed for the ActionScript developers

Using GameBrix technology, an artist in Korea, working with a musician in Florida and an animator in Japan, can share resources and build a collaborative game. The Animator application enables artists to develop and post graphics and animated sprites for use within the Builder application. These applications together provide a one-stop solution for game creation.

Registered users of the GameBrix portal can see their inventory of games and resources, their profile and library of tutorials—everything that can be used to learn and develop strategies, meet with new friends, share resources, and publish games.

Inside GameBrix, you'll see three rows of menu selections available, as shown in Figure 2.2.

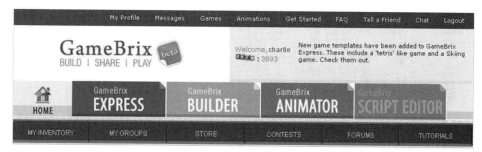

FIGURE 2.2
The main menu.

The menu items from the top row are listed in Table 2.1.

TABLE 2.1 TOP MENU

This...	Enables You To...
MyProfile	Change your profile
Games	Access all the games made by the GameBrix community
Animations	Access animations published by other community members
Getting Started	Follow basic explanations of games and learn how the GameBrix features work
FAQ	Get answers to some of the more general, common questions and issues
Tell a Friend	Send an e-mail message from your GameBrix account to a friend
Logout	Exit from your GameBrix session

The menu items in the middle row contain all the GameBrix applications, as shown in Table 2.2.

TABLE 2.2 SECOND-LEVEL MENU

This...	Enables You To...
Express	Use templates that speed up your game development
Builder	Learn and build games from scratch
Animator	Create graphics and animations for use in your games and the games of others
Script Editor	Edit the code used within GameBrix Builder

The menu items in the last row contain all the workspace features, as shown in Table 2.3.

TABLE 2.3 WORKSPACE MENU

This...	Enables You To...
My Inventory	Manage all your images, animations, music, intelligence, and game files
My Groups	Create, manage, join, and share assets with friends and groups
Store	Manage your store and trade assets with others
Contests	Enroll, submit entries, and watch contests
Forums	Discuss issues with community members and share ideas
Tutorials	Access guides and references

Along with your inventory, groups, and other selections, after login, the My Profile page and its editing features are shown in Figure 2.3.

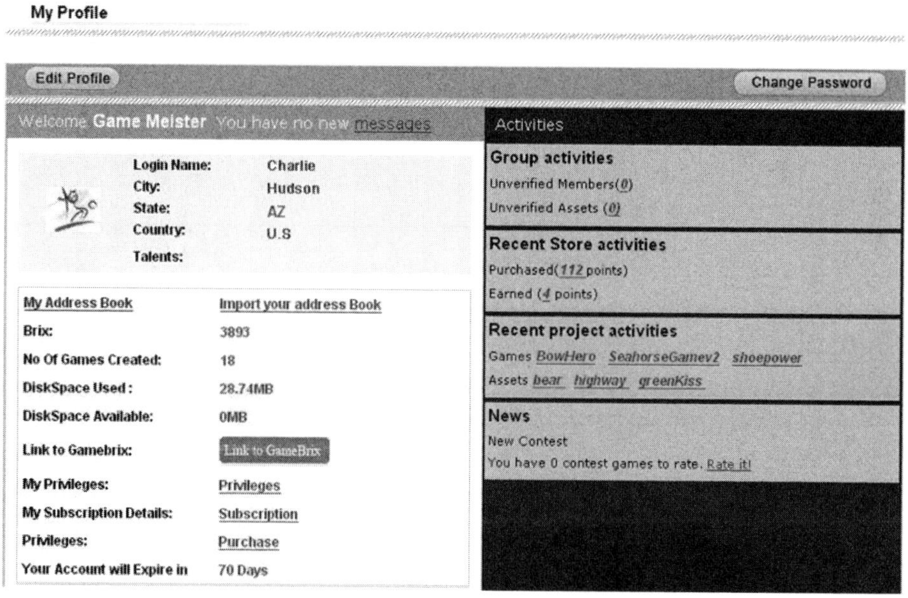

FIGURE 2.3
The My Profile page.

Some of the personal information fields within the profile can be edited by clicking on the Edit Profile button. The fields that can be edited are shown in Figure 2.4.

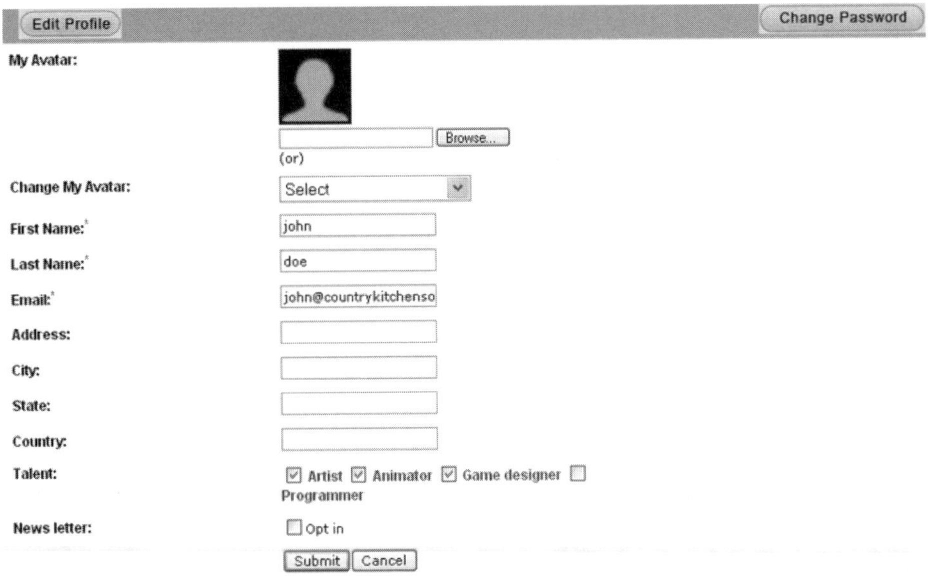

FIGURE 2.4
Editing your profile.

THE GAMEBUILDER INTERFACE

Now that you have an understanding of the basic navigation menus within Game-Brix, it's time to take a peek at the GameBuilder user interface. Click on the green GameBrix Builder menu button that is on the middle set of menus. It may take a few moments for the engine and your profile information to load. The Game-Builder screen is shown in Figure 2.5.

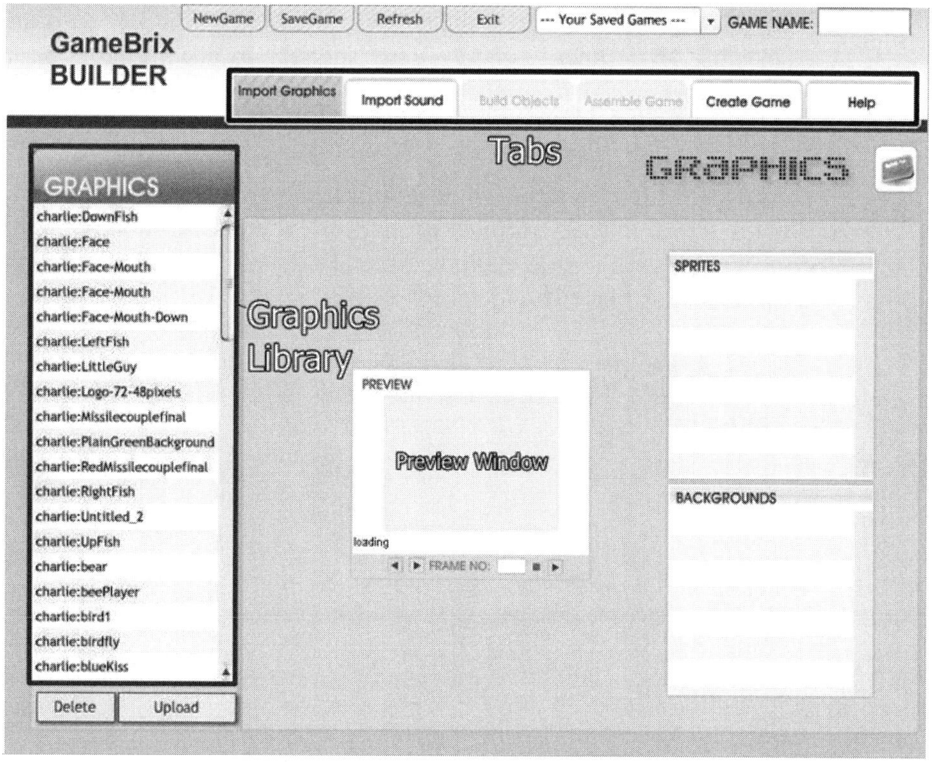

FIGURE 2.5
The GameBuilder start screen.

The Builder's start screen has a set of library images, a preview screen, and two small areas that list the selected images to be used as sprites and backgrounds for the game. There are a few tabs within the GameBuilder:

- **Import Graphics.** Used for selecting images and animations to be used in the game.
- **Import Sound.** Used for selected music files for use in the game.
- **Build Objects.** Used for creating intelligent objects. This tab is disabled until you have chosen graphics from the Import Graphics tab.
- **Assemble Game.** This is the place where you assemble your game objects into game levels.
- **Create Game.** The Preview Game button on this tab creates the game for you.
- **Help.** The Preview Game button on this tab creates the game for you.

For the senior developers—those who are familiar with more advanced tools used in game development—there are two special buttons: the Path Editor and the Object Editor. You can access these by clicking on the Build Objects tab. The Build Objects tab is enabled only after you have selected either sprites or backgrounds from the Import Graphics tab.

A sample screen from the Object Editor is shown in Figure 2.6. As you can see, this is the screen that experienced game developers use to modify programming scripts. If you have an in-depth knowledge of Adobe's ActionScript programming, you can use your skills to build complex objects.

FIGURE 2.6
The Object Editor screen.

A sample screen from the Path Editor is shown in Figure 2.7. The Path Editor is used for creating paths along which an object can move.

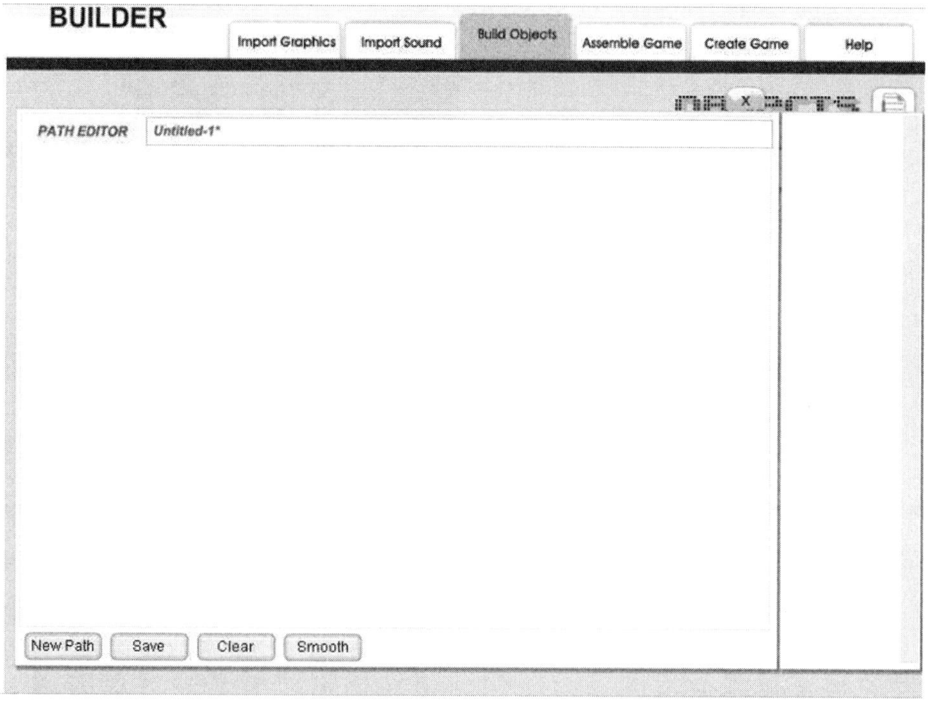

FIGURE 2.7
The Path Editor screen.

THE ANIMATOR INTERFACE

The Animator is used to create images and animations. With it, you can paint, draw, and create images that you can use in games created by GameBuilder. You can create simple frame-by-frame animations with ease. Figure 2.8 shows you a glimpse of the Animator interface.

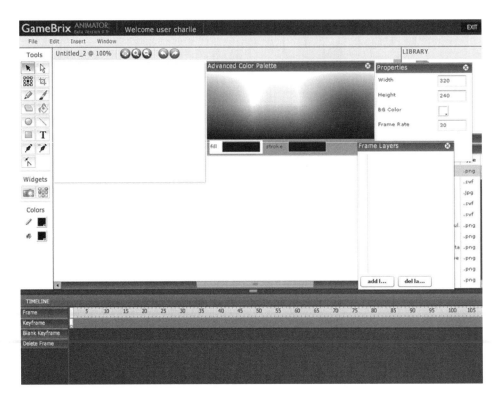

FIGURE 2.8
The Animator interface.

THE EXPRESS INTERFACE

GameBrix Express is a high-speed, template-driven engine for game creation. Game templates are added to Express periodically. Users can modify these templates using their own assets to create new games with the same mechanics but different visuals. Different categories of games can be created, including platform and greeting card games. Figure 2.9 shows you a glimpse of the Express interface.

FIGURE 2.9
The Express interface.

GETTING STARTED

Clicking on the Getting Started link on the top menu takes you to the Getting Started page, as shown in Figure 2.10. Each of these links takes you to a page that describes how each game can be built. Once you have read through them, the system automatically remembers that you have read the page and inserts a check mark in the first column.

Getting started with GameBrix is an easy process. Here's how to create an account. First, open your browser and go to http://www.gamebrix.com. On the top-right side, click on the link labeled Join Now. There are two options for registering, as shown in Figure 2.11. You will be using the free trial subscription option, shown on the right, which does not require a license key.

After you click the Proceed button, detailed features available with different subscription types are shown, as in Figure 2.12.

GET STARTED WITH

GameBrix™
BUILD I SHARE I PLAY

| GameBrix **EXPRESS** | GameBrix **BUILDER** | GameBrix **ANIMATOR** | GameBrix **SCRIPT EDITOR** |

☐ *GameBrix™ Express Tutorial*

This explores the features of GameBrix™ Express, a quick, easy way to create a range of games. Based on the idea of templates and an easy to use interface, Express takes you through the steps of building a game, and enables you to personalize your game from a range of choices GameBrix™ Express presents to you..

Tools Required

☐ *Make a Break Out Game*

This is another tutorial in the series that explores the features of GameBrix™ Builder. Each is an example of a fun, simple game; a guide to take you into the realm of game design; a step towards your imagination.

Tools Required

☐ *Bouncing Ball Tutorial*

By following these steps you will create a simple game where balls appear, bounce around in a room, and it's up to you to get rid of them -- and win.

Tools Required

☐ *How to Create a Platform Game.*

Platform games are named because the players jump from one platform to another, avoiding or fighting enemies while collecting objects or points, and it's here you'll get started on creating your own platform game.

Tools Required

☐ *Create a simple animation*

This explores the features of the GameBrix™ Animator, a multi-featured tool that enables you to paint and animate images. Each image can then be placed into the GameBrix™ Builder Image Library and used with Web-based games.

Tools Required

☐ *Basic Graphics*

This explores the basic graphic features of the GameBrix™ Animator, a multi-featured tool that enables you to paint and animate images. Each image can then be placed into the GameBrix™ Builder Image Library.

Tools Required

FIGURE 2.10
Getting Started page.

 Click here **if you have a**
LICENSE KEY

 Click here **if you <u>don't</u> have a**
LICENSE KEY

Click this choice if you have a License Key. License Keys are typically issued to colleges and schools requiring multiple subscriptions to privileged accounts on GameBrix. License keys are usually sold in bulk and each license key issued can be used by one user. So for a classroom of 30 students, 30 license keys are required. Each license key can be used by the user to whom it assigned. License keys are tied to a user and not to the computer they are working on.

Click this choice if you <u>do not</u> have a license key. You could opt for a 15 day trial subscription or go for a premium subscription that grants you additional privileges. Free trial subscribers do not have access to game templates and premium game creation tutorials. Free users also do not have the privileges to download their games and artwork or customize messages displayed in their games or sell items in the GameBrix store.

Proceed

Proceed

FIGURE 2.11
License options.

Membership features	Free Trial	Monthly Subscription	Annual Subscription
cost	$0	$9	$99
DiskSpace(MB)	25MB	50 MB	50 MB
Duration(Days)	90	30	365
Forum	✖	✔	✔
Builder	✔	✔	✔
Express	✔	✔	✔
Animator	✔	✔	✔
Download Game	✖	✔	✔
Download swf	✖	✖	✖
Download Png	✖	✖	✖
Custom Message	✖	✔	✔
Premium Tutorials	✖	✔	✔
Game Templates	✖	✔	✔
Join GameBrix	join now!	join now!	join now!

FIGURE 2.12
Subscription options.

Click on the Join Now button in the Free Trial column. You will see a description of all the tools and features available with your selection, as shown in Figure 2.13.

Free Trial

Description:

This free account allows you to try out the GameBrix tools to build Flash games online for 90 days.

Product Feature	Allowed/DisAllowed
Ability to download games to your local computer – (html & swf file included)	×
Ability to download swf animations created with GameBrix Animator to your local computer	×
Ability to download png files created with GameBrix Animator to your local computer	×
Ability to customize messages for each game created	×
Ability to launch contests	×
Gold support (answers to questions in 24 hours)	×
Access to selected tutorials for game creation	×
Access to selected game templates	×
500 additional GameBrix	×
Access to GameBrix Builder	✓
Access to GameBrix Express	✓
Access to GameBrix Animator	✓
Access to GameBrix Object Editor	✓
Forums posting capability	×
Access to Chat	✓
Public profile page - page displaying account holders games	×
Access to sell items on the GameBrix Store	×

This is a trial subscription.

| Continue |

FIGURE 2.13
Subscription features.

Click Continue. You will see a form with several fields that need to be entered, as shown in Figure 2.14. Some of them are mandatory. As you fill in the E-Mail Address and Create Username fields, the system automatically lets you know if the entries are valid. Duplicate accounts with the same e-mail address or usernames are not allowed. The e-mail address you enter is important, because the GameBrix portal uses it to send you a confirmation link. Confirmation e-mail is sent to the e-mail address provided with an activation link to validate your account. Until you receive this e-mail and click on the Validation link, your account will not be activated. If you have not received a confirmation email, please check in your junk mail folder. It should be there. Alternatively, you can click on the Get New Verification E-Mail link button, located in the upper-right corner of the portal.

Registration

E-mail Address :*

Please provide a valid email address.
You will need this to activate your account.

Confirm Email Address :*

First Name :*

Last Name :*

Username :*

Password :*

Confirm Password :*

Date of Birth:*   June ▼ 04 ▼ 2008 ▼

Security question :*   Choose your question ▼

Your answer :*

Security Check :   Enter the characters below. What's This?
Can't read this? Try another.
Characters are case sensitive.

7khc9

Characters in the box:*

Register   Cancel

FIGURE 2.14
Registration page.

PLAYING GAMES

If you want to play the games made by other members of the GameBrix community, click on the blue button labeled Play Games Online. This takes you to the page shown in Figure 2.15.

You have six different mechanisms to find games that are of interest:

- If you know the name of a game, fill in the Search box with the name of the game you are looking for and click Search.
- Click Top Rated Games to see what the GameBrix community has rated the best.
- Click Latest Games to see the most recent postings of games created by the community.

- Click Popular Games to play the games that the majority of community gamers are trying out.
- Click on a game title displayed to play that game.
- Wander through the various page results by clicking page links just to see what the community has posted.

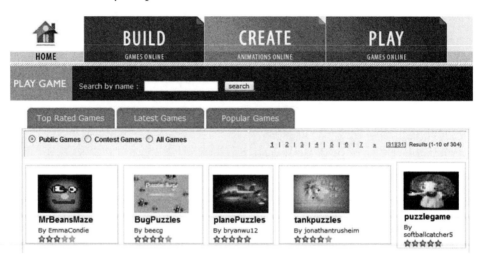

FIGURE 2.15
Play Games page.

SUMMARY

This chapter looked at the different components that make up the GameBrix portal. The next chapter builds on these tools and techniques to create games, graphics, and animations.

3 Creating Flash Games with GameBrix Express

In This Chapter

- Starting GameBrix Express
- Selecting the Game
- Using the Animator
- Selecting Images
- Selecting Sounds
- Building and Publishing Your Game

This chapter explores the features of GameBrix Express—a quick, easy way to create a range of games. Based on the idea of templates and an easy pick-and-choose interface, Express takes you through the steps of building a game and enables you to personalize your game from a wide range of choices.

Express also enables you to import game assets developed outside of Game-Brix, as well as assets developed collectively by friends or community developers and gamers.

STARTING GAMEBRIX EXPRESS

To get started with GameBrix Express, type your username and password into text boxes on the top-right corner of the login page (see Figure 3.1). Then click the Submit button.

FIGURE 3.1
The GameBrix login page.

On the next screen, click the button labeled Express. This opens the GameBrix Express online application (see Figure 3.2). Building and publishing a customized game with GameBrix Express is a five-step process. The steps are

1. Select the game.
2. Select the images.
3. Select the sounds.
4. Personalize your game.
5. Build and publish your game.

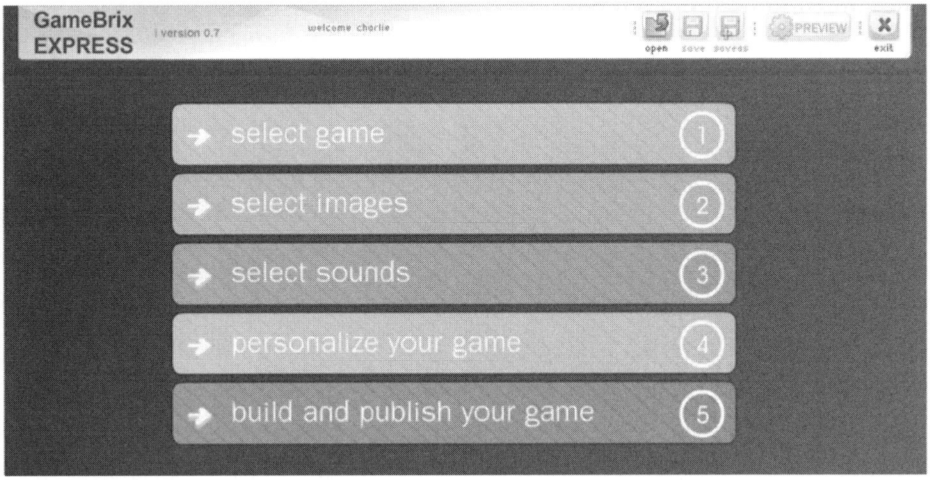

FIGURE 3.2
The GameBrix Express start page.

SELECTING THE GAME

The purpose of GameBrix Express is to make you successful in creating games using very simple steps. The first step is selecting the type of template your game will be based on. Click on the first horizontal tab labeled Select Game, and you will see a game selection screen (see Figure 3.3).

This shows you the game categories you can choose from:

- Action
- Puzzle
- Greetings

Action and Puzzle games are well-known categories. The Greetings category is shown in Figure 3.4.

As you can see, the Greetings category enables you to make a custom greeting card, just as you would create your own game—the Express way! To create an action game, click on the Action category button.

FIGURE 3.3
The Select Game screen.

FIGURE 3.4
The Greetings category.

Within the Action games category, click the Dots game—a classic arcade game. You can use Express as a template to create your own version of the classic. After you choose the game, Express opens a game description screen, as shown in Figure 3.5.

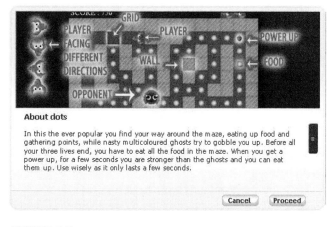

FIGURE 3.5
Game description screen.

Click the Proceed button to go to the next step. This brings you to the Select Images screen, as shown on Figure 3.6.

Notice that there are four different versions of the player in the image selection screen: one facing right, one facing left, one facing down, and one facing up. To put a custom player character into the game, you must replace all the images.

On this screen, you can

- Upload your own custom images from your computer
- Choose an image from your personal online library
- Use the default

If you are not using a default image, be sure to click and select the correct thumbnail. If there are many images, you may need to use the slide bar to see them.

Now you can use the Animator to modify a custom image, save it in your personal online library, and use it as the player character in the Dots game.

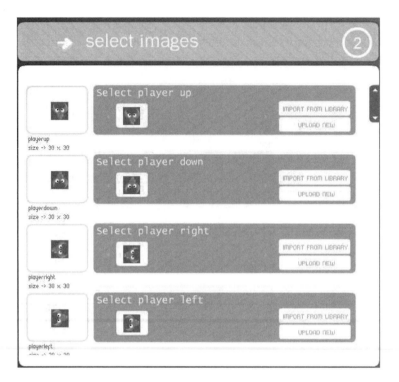

FIGURE 3.6
The Select Images screen.

Using the Animator

Start the Animator by clicking on the blue button labeled GameBrix Animator. The blue Animator button is active for logged in users.

Notice that the player character needs four images that face four different directions. To simplify the process, you can use two images: one image facing right and one image facing left. The image facing right will be used when the player moves up or right. The image facing left will be used when the player moves down or left. The transform tool can be used for flipping images.

After the Animator opens, locate the image labeled fish1 from the image library, as shown in Figure 3.7. This will be the player character. Alternatively, you could use any other image from the list or create your own using the drawing tools.

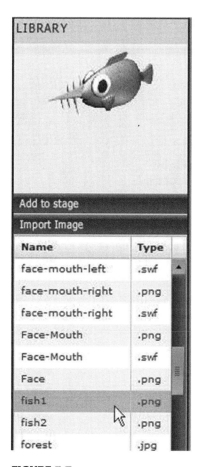

FIGURE 3.7
The Animator's image library.

Click on the Add to Stage button found under the displayed image within the image library, as shown in Figure 3.7. This is the left fish. For use in GameBrix Express, this image has to be exported. To export the image, click on File, Export Image. Name the image LeftFish, and then click OK.

To create the other image, select the Transform tool and flip the fish horizontally using the left center handle, as shown in Figure 3.8.

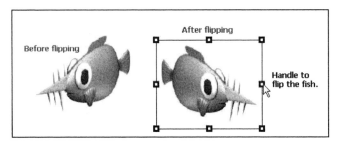

FIGURE 3.8
The flipped fish.

Again, for use in GameBrix Express, you need to export this image. To export the image, click on File, Export Image. Name the image RightFish, and then click OK.

Now you are ready to replace the character in the Dots game with your own fish images.

You may need to close the Animator and Express, reopen Express, and choose the Dots game before it recognizes your new images.

NOTE

SELECTING IMAGES

Now it's time to start replacing the images for the Player object in the Dots game. On the Select Images tab, there should be four rows labeled Select Player Up, Select Player Down, Select Player Right, and Select Player Left. You will use the Import from Library button found on each row to change the default image.

Start by clicking on the Import from Library button found on the row labeled Select Player Up, as shown in Figure 3.9. Next, select the fish image labeled RightFish, as shown in Figure 3.10. After the image is loaded, click on the newly loaded image to select it for use in the game, as shown in Figure 3.11. You need to repeat this procedure for all the other player images—Player Left, Player Right, and Player Down—found on the Select Image tab.

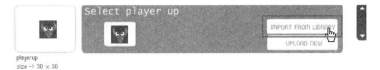

FIGURE 3.9
Import from the library.

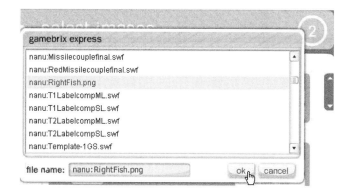

FIGURE 3.10
Select from the library.

FIGURE 3.11
Change the default image.

At this point, GameBrix Express displays a pop-up menu on the top-right corner of the window. You can now save or build the game, but you are not done incorporating your changes into the game.

Next, change the image of the food by clicking on the Import from Library button found next to it. Use the slider and pick up a different image to replace the food. Figure 3.12 shows a sample image selection screen. Clicking the OK button loads the new image and shows it as an alternate selection item, as shown in Figure 3.13. Now click on the icon representing the newly loaded image, as shown in Figure 3.14.

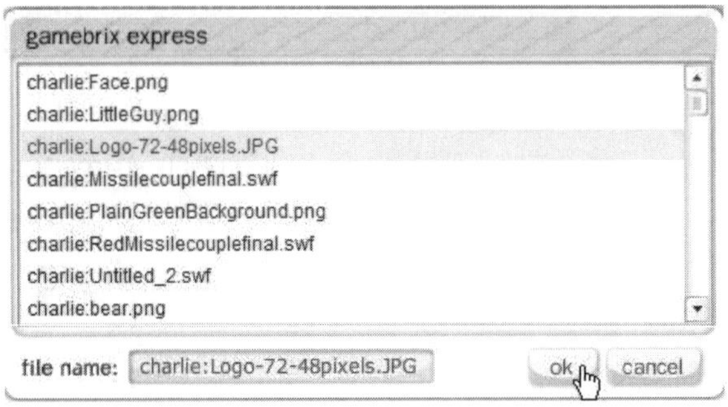
gamebrix express
charlie:Face.png
charlie:LittleGuy.png
charlie:Logo-72-48pixels.JPG
charlie:Missilecouplefinal.swf
charlie:PlainGreenBackground.png
charlie:RedMissilecouplefinal.swf
charlie:Untitled_2.swf
charlie:bear.png
file name: charlie:Logo-72-48pixels.JPG
ok
cancel

FIGURE 3.12
Select from the library.

select powerup
IMPORT FROM LIBRARY
UPLOAD NEW
strawberry
size -> 13 x 13

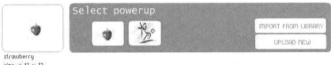

FIGURE 3.13
Alternate image loaded.

select powerup
IMPORT FROM LIBRARY
UPLOAD NEW
strawberry
size -> 13 x 13

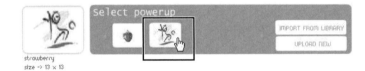

FIGURE 3.14
Change the default image.

SELECTING SOUNDS

The next customizable part is optional. GameBrix Express allows you to customize sounds played at different points of the game. Clicking the Select Sounds tab opens choices, as shown in Figure 3.15.

As with the images, you can select the sounds by either importing them from your library or uploading a new sound. Click on the Import from Library button to add a sound from your library. Figure 3.16 shows a sample selection. Click OK.

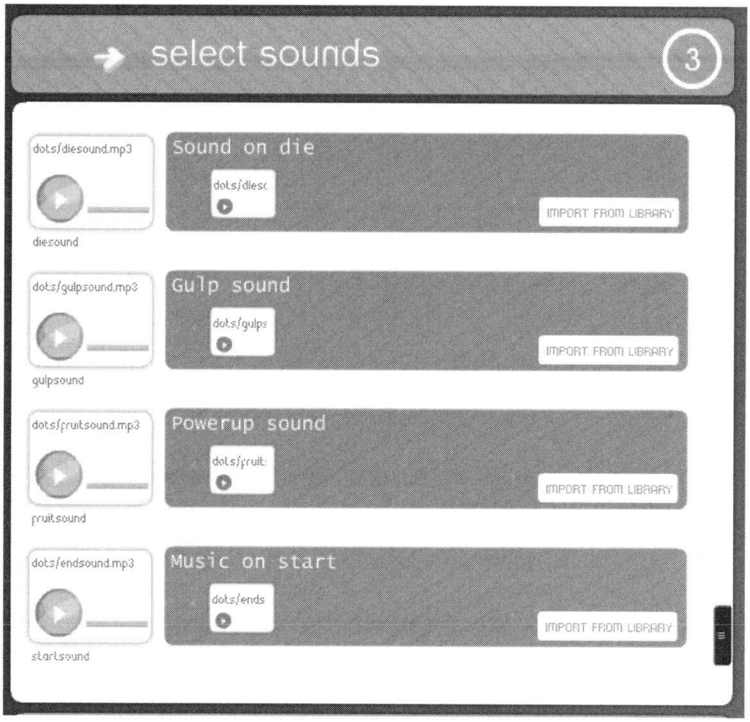

FIGURE 3.15
Select sounds.

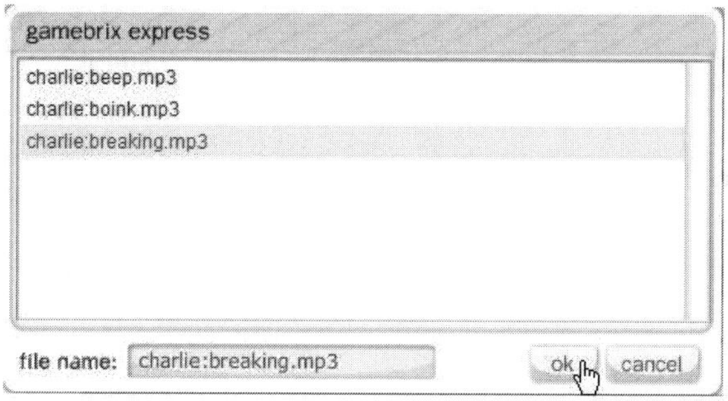

FIGURE 3.16
Selecting sounds from the library.

Click on the large horizontal tab labeled Personalize Your Game. You will see a list of customizable options. Modify the text boxes to reflect the messages you like, as shown in Figure 3.17. You can also change the font characteristics.

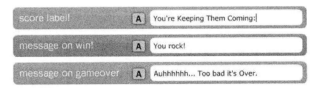

FIGURE 3.17
Customizing messages.

BUILDING AND PUBLISHING YOUR GAME

Click on the tab labeled Build and Publish Your Game. On the window that loads (see Figure 3.18), you have the choice of saving your game, building your game, or sending it to your friend. You could send it to all your buddies on Yahoo, AOL, or Google groups. After making your choice, click the Submit button to complete your operation. Well done! You have built and published your game to the Web!

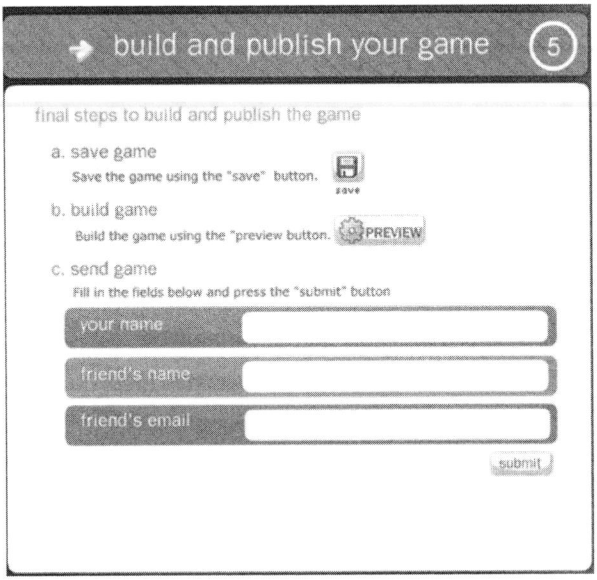

FIGURE 3.18
Publishing options.

SUMMARY

This chapter looked at how to build games using GameBrix Express. The next chapter takes an in-depth look at building more complex games with GameBrix Builder.

4 Creating Flash Games with GameBrix Builder

In This Chapter

- Entering the Builder
- Building Objects
- Assembling the Game
- Generating the Game
- Adding Gameplay

In this chapter, you learn to build simple Flash games. As you build more games, you travel deeper into the realm of game design and learn new skills.

In this chapter, you are introduced to the GameBrix Builder, a powerful Web-based application that you can use to create virtually any kind of Flash game.

So that you can understand the basic principles in game creation, this chapter starts with a simple game. You will create a game that has fish bouncing around inside a room. Your aim is to get rid of the bouncing fish. When you click on a fish, it disappears, adding 10 points to your score. When all the fish are gone, you win!

In Chapter 2, "Introduction to GameBrix," you had a peek at GameBrix Builder. In this chapter, you will be delving into GameBrix Builder to create the Bouncing Fish game. It is here where you assemble the graphics and animated sprites that you or other community members created. You can also embed sounds and music in your game using Builder.

ENTERING THE BUILDER

To enter the Builder, go to http://www.gamebrix.com, enter your username and password, and then click on the Submit button. If you are not a registered user of GameBrix, review Chapter 2 for a detailed description of the registration process. Click the Join Now link found on the top-right corner of the Web page and follow the directions. After the new user registration process is complete and you have logged into Gamebrix.com, you can continue from there.

At the welcome page, shown in Figure 4.1, click on the GameBrix Builder tab. A pre-loader bar shows the loading progress of the GameBrix Builder Web application.

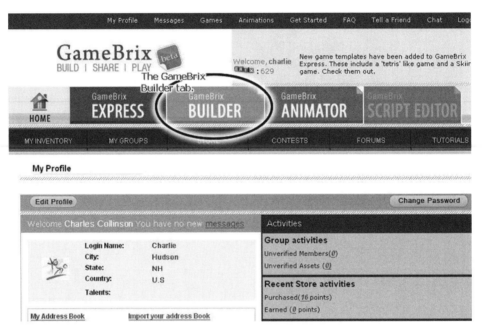

FIGURE 4.1
The GameBrix welcome page.

After the application is loaded, you will be presented with a GameBrix initialization widget, as shown in Figure 4.2, which displays your username and performs a set of background tasks to set up your machine for game creation. After initialization is complete, you will be presented with the Builder's Graphics window, as shown in Figure 4.3. This is where your creative journeys begin.

FIGURE 4.2
GameBrix initialization widget.

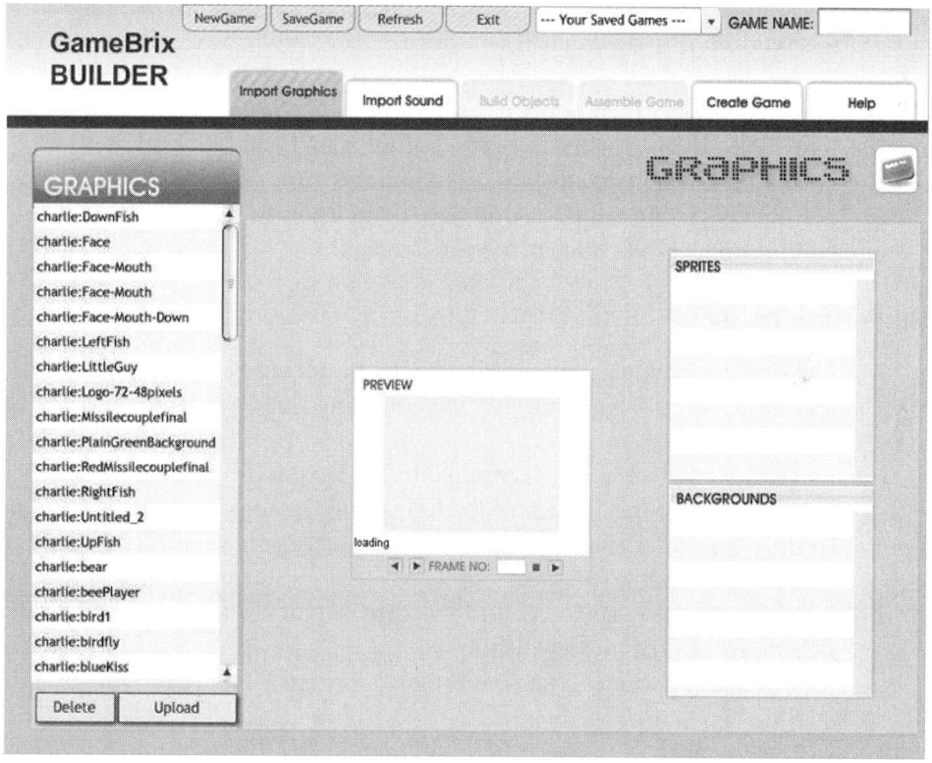

FIGURE 4.3
Builder's Graphics window.

BUILDING OBJECTS

Each game has one or more *objects*. Objects are pretty much anything that plays an active role in the game. Whether the objects are characters to be controlled by the player or enemies attacking the player character, they need to be able to take actions. Some objects need to respond to the player's keyboard and mouse activity. Others need to do things such as automatically attack when the player character is within its attack range. Still other objects simply need to be there for the player character and other objects to stand on. These behaviors are known as *intelligence*, and building these intelligent objects is central to creating a game.

Each object is made up of two parts: an image and a set of behaviors. When different "events" occur within an object, the object switches between different "states." This is similar to the concept of cause and effect. For example, the object moves into the "collision" state when it collides with another object. This state change can trigger a set of tasks to be performed. Another example is when an object is clicked. The object could then perform tasks such as FollowMouse, StartMoving, and many more listed in the Appendix, "Object States and Tasks."

Building objects is all about describing the series of tasks that will be performed when an object moves from one state to another. In this section, you will learn to build simple objects, such as a bouncing fish.

THE FISH AND THE BRICK

The first object you need to create for the Bouncing Fish game is the fish. You will also need a brick object for creating enclosing walls, which will be discussed after the fish is created.

You need to select a picture for your fish. Do this by importing a graphic from the Graphics list, on the left side of the builder. An image used in a game is known as a sprite. When you click on the name of a graphic, a preview of that graphic appears in the preview window.

Select the item labeled fish1 from the Graphics list, as shown in Figure 4.4. The fish appears in the preview window.

And as you can see, the Graphics window lets you

- Add a sprite
- Add a background
- Upload a new image or animation
- Remove sprites and backgrounds from their corresponding lists

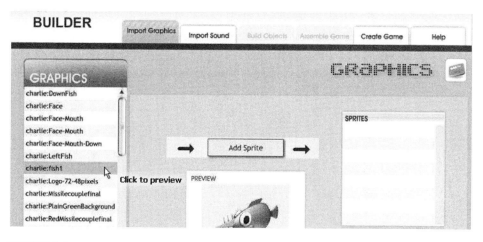

FIGURE 4.4
Selecting the fish image.

NOTE

Did you notice that the Import Graphics tab is raised and highlighted using hatched yellow lines? This indicates that the Graphics window is active.

The next step is to tell the Builder whether the graphics image you have chosen is a sprite or a background. Sprites are used for objects that will have intelligence assigned to them, while backgrounds are simply passive images that appear in the game. The fish image that has been chosen will play an active part in the game and will become part of an intelligent object, so it is added as a sprite.

Click the Add Sprite button with the fish1 image selected in the Graphics list. This moves the fish image into the list of active sprites on the right, as shown in Figure 4.5.

Now select the other graphic you'll need for the game. You'll need a brick, so select it from the Graphics list. The brick will also be a sprite, so add it to the Sprites list, as you did with the fish image.

Now you will have two sprites in your Sprites list, as shown in Figure 4.6.

Having chosen the images (sprites) for the objects required in your game, you need to start creating the objects and then embed intelligence into them. For example, you need to allow the fish to move. You do this in the Build Objects window.

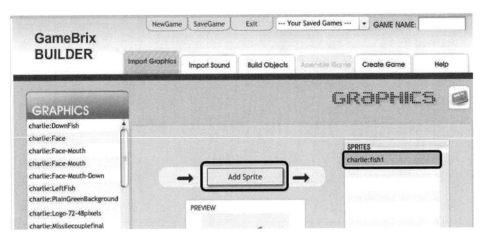

FIGURE 4.5
The fish is now one of your selected sprites.

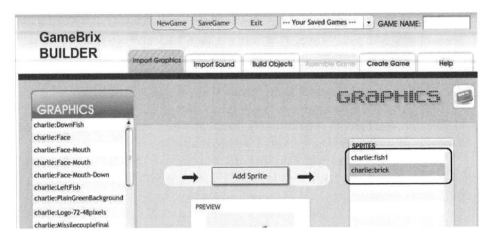

FIGURE 4.6
You have selected your sprites.

STATES AND TASKS

Click on the Build Objects tab. This should open the window shown in Figure 4.7.

Because you want to create two new objects, start by clicking on the New Object button. This opens the New Object Creation screen, as shown in Figure 4.8.

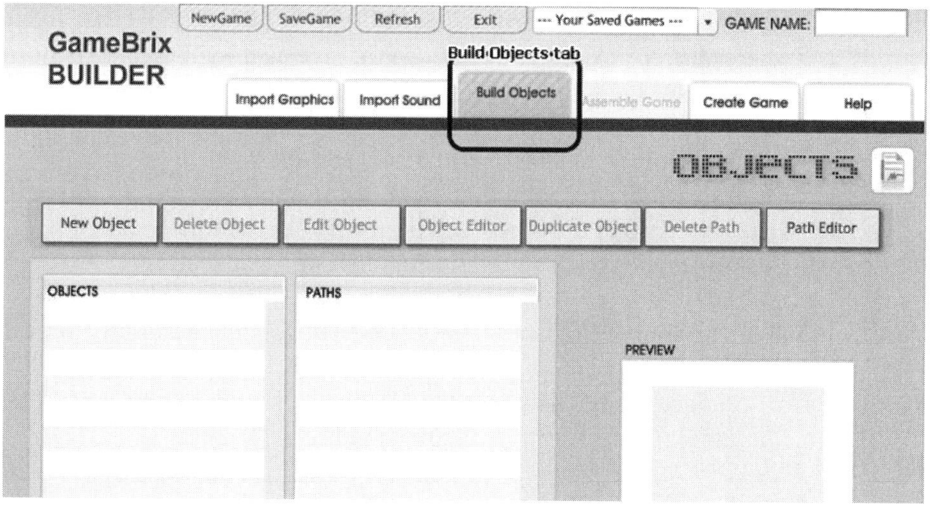

FIGURE 4.7
The Build Objects window.

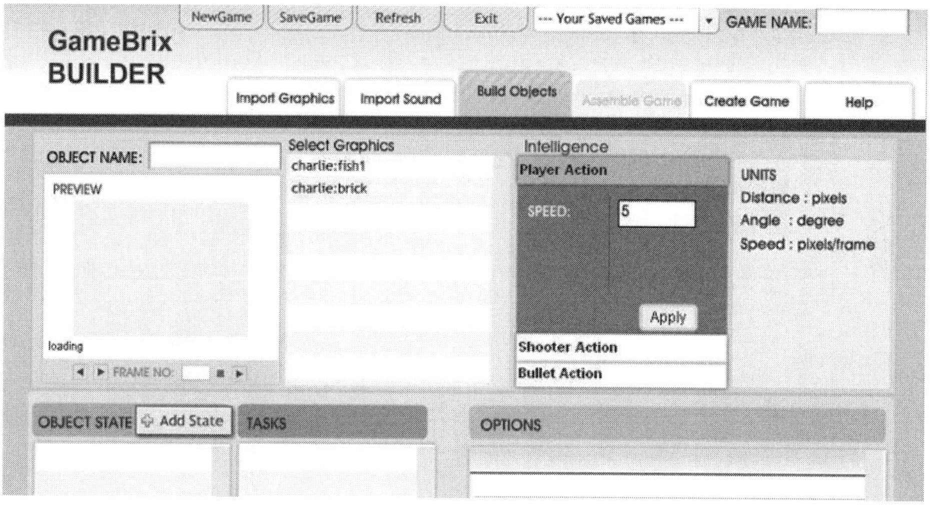

FIGURE 4.8
The New Object Creation screen.

It is in the Build Objects screen that objects are assigned intelligence and behaviors. It is where objects are programmed to do the tasks you want them to perform. In this screen, you will

- Define the object's name and attached sprite
- Choose the object's states that are of interest to you
- List the tasks that the object will perform in each of these states
- Customize each of these tasks using their optional features

First you must define your objects so that Builder can use them in the game. Start with the fish.

1. Builder needs a name for the fish object, so call it Fish1. Enter Fish1 in the Object Name text box, as shown in Figure 4.9.

It is important for the object name to be different from the sprite name. Note that the sprite is named fish1, with a lowercase "f," and the object is named Fish1, with an uppercase "F." It would be best to add the suffix obj to all your object names.

2. Attach a sprite to the fish object to give it a visible appearance in the game. From the Select Graphics list, click Fish1. The image of the fish appears in the preview window, as shown in Figure 4.9.

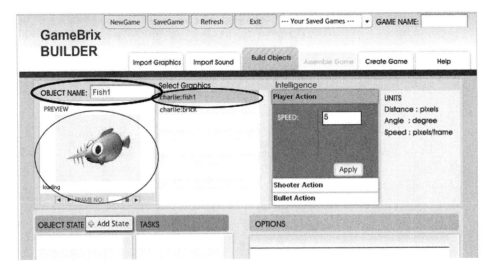

FIGURE 4.9
Building the Fish1 object.

3. The fish needs to move as soon as it is created in the game. A `Create` state and a `StartMoving` task are required to accomplish this. Click the New button beneath the Object State box.

4. From the list of states displayed, click on the one labeled Create, and then click Add.

Next, assign the tasks that the fish has to perform in the `Create` state.

Choose a new task by clicking on the New button at the bottom of the Tasks box. From the pop-up list that appears, select the `StartMoving` task. Click it, and then click Add. The fish object has now been instructed to start moving as soon as it is created in the game. The `StartMoving` task has two customizable options, labeled `Dirn` and `Speed`, which refer to the direction and speed of movement, respectively. To customize the direction, click on the default value of 0 assigned to the direction option, as shown in Figure 4.10.

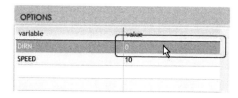

FIGURE 4.10
Changing the direction of the `Fish1` object.

This will open a small circular widget with a moveable handle (see Figure 4.11). You can grab the handle with the mouse and rotate it to define a finite angle of motion. However, for this game, you need the fish to move about in random directions. You do this by typing the text `random(360)` in the input box and clicking the Apply button. Your screen should be similar to that of Figure 4.12.

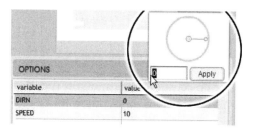

FIGURE 4.11
The angle definition widget.

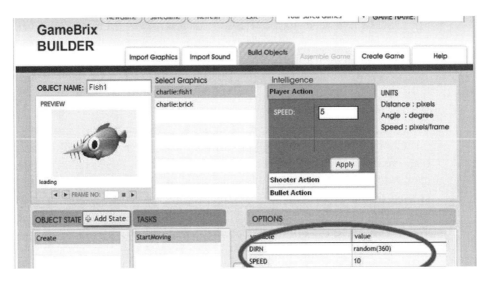

FIGURE 4.12
The Fish1 object thus far.

Look at the other option in the StartMoving task, Speed. The default speed of 10 for the fish object is relatively fast and should be okay. However, if you are feeling adventurous and want to make it faster or slower, you can do that by clicking on the default value and changing it.

Once you have changed the speed, click the Done button found beneath the Options box to save the fish objects settings and go back to the Objects tab.

The screen should look like that shown in Figure 4.13.

You need to assign states and tasks to the other objects in the game. There is only one other object in this game: the brick object.

Click the New Object button once again. This takes you to the New Objects window. Start creating this new brick object by assigning it a name, Brick. Type this into the Object Name field, and then select the brick sprite to be attached to it, as shown in Figure 4.14.

In the game, the brick object simply acts as a wall to let the fish bounce. It does not need special behaviors assigned to it, so you don't need to assign any states or tasks to it. Click the Done button to bring you back to the Objects window.

You have two objects in your game. Now that there is a brick object in the game, the fish object needs additional behaviors defined to describe what happens when it collides with the brick. In the Objects window, click on Fish1 from the objects list, and then click Edit Object, as shown in Figure 4.15.

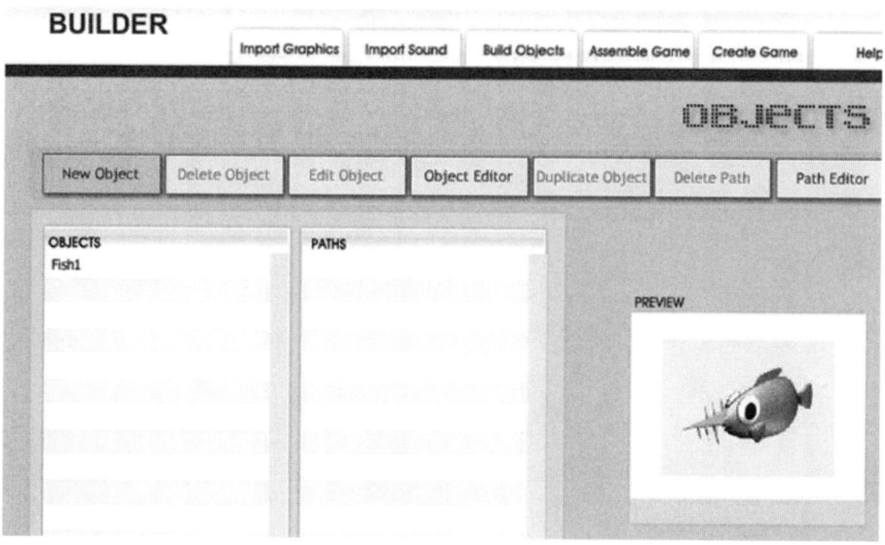

FIGURE 4.13
The saved and completed Fish1 object.

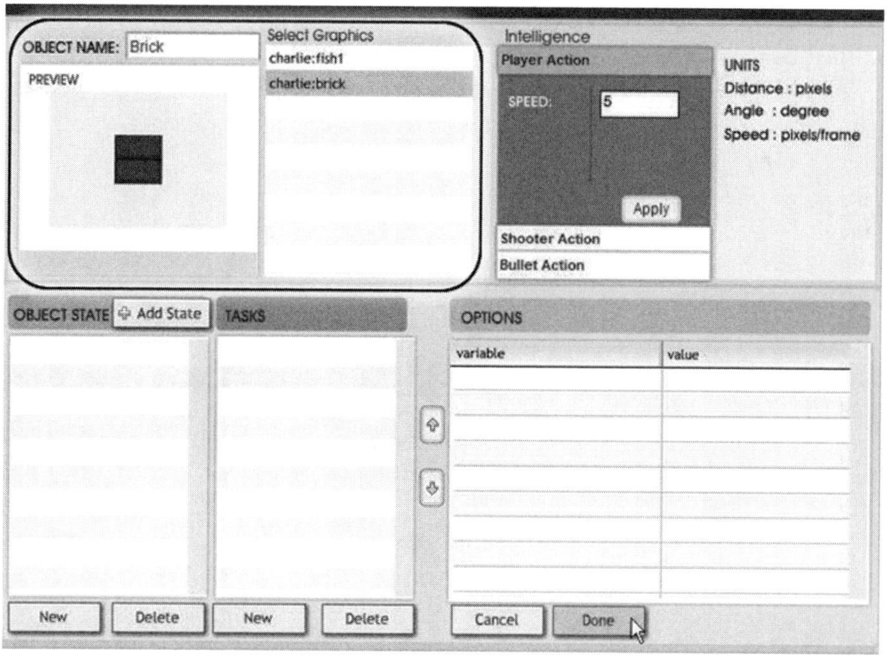

FIGURE 4.14
Building the Brick object.

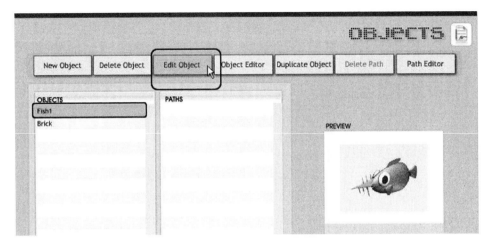

FIGURE 4.15
Selecting Edit Object.

Create a new object state by clicking the New button under the Object State column shown in Figure 4.16. Choose the collision state from the pop-up window, as shown in Figure 4.16. Then click the Add button to add the collision state for the fish object.

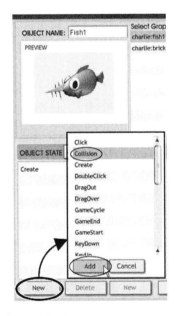

FIGURE 4.16
Adding a `collision` state for the fish object.

Click on the CollidingObject option to define the object that the fish will be colliding against, as shown in Figure 4.17. A pop-up box displays all the available objects. From this list, select the brick object, and then click the Apply button.

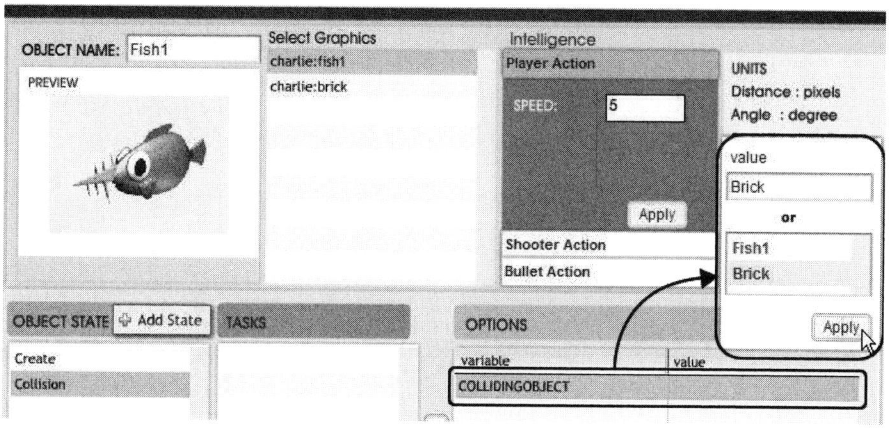

FIGURE 4.17
Selecting the colliding object.

Next, define the tasks to be performed when the fish object collides with the brick object. Click the button labeled New in the Tasks column, select Bounce from the list, and then click Add. You have essentially provided instructions to the fish to bounce when it collides with a brick.

You need no other functionality for the Fish1 object, so click Done. You will return to the Objects window, shown in Figure 4.18.

So far, the functionality created for the game is as follows: When the fish is created and first appears on the screen, it randomly moves in any direction (360 degrees), with a speed of 10 pixels per frame. When the fish collides with the brick, it is programmed to bounce. The next section describes the process of assembling the game and building it. It is a good time to save your work.

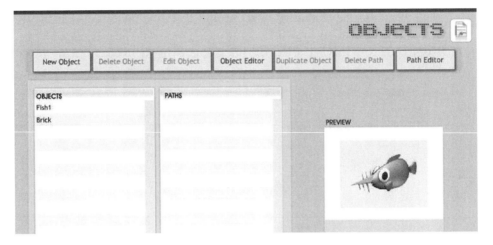

FIGURE 4.18
Return to the Build Objects window.

ASSEMBLING THE GAME

Click on the Assemble Game tab. This opens the Levels window, as shown in Figure 4.19, which allows you to assemble the objects of the game in a game room. Think of it as the play area where all the toys (game objects) are brought together and allowed to interact with each other.

Note the text box labeled Level 1 above the work area. This is the default name of the first level. You can change this name if you like. The Bouncing Fish game has only one level. Other games may have multiple levels.

The fish object and the brick object are two objects listed under the Objects section on the left side of the work area. They are the Fish1 object and the Brick object. To place objects in the game room, click on one and drag it to the empty level on the right. The object in the level is an instance of the original object. It is essentially a clone of the object. There can be many different instances of the same object in a game. To remove an instance from the level, right-click the instance and click Delete.

Place an instance of the Fish1 object into the game by clicking and dragging it into the level. Do the same with the Brick object. Place an instance of the Brick object in the game level, as shown in Figure 4.20.

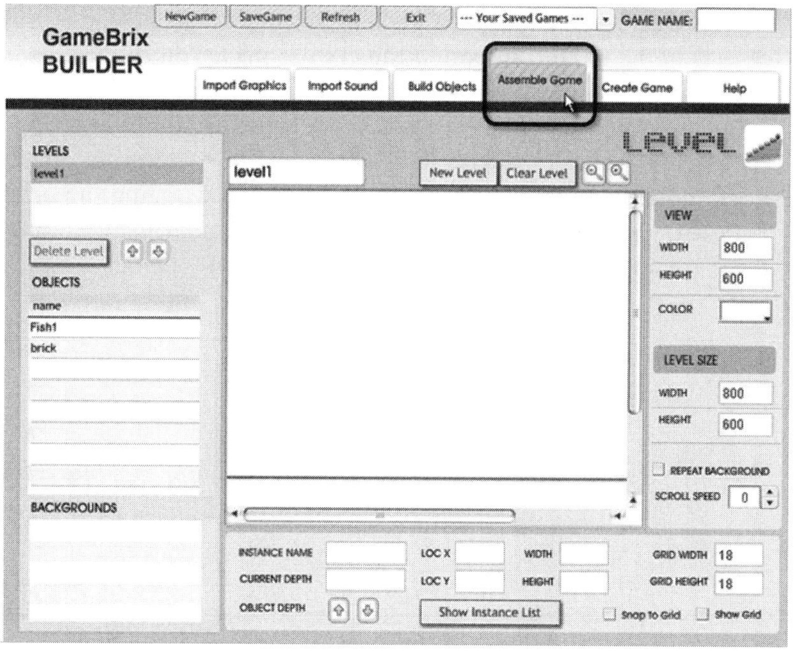

FIGURE 4.19
The Levels window.

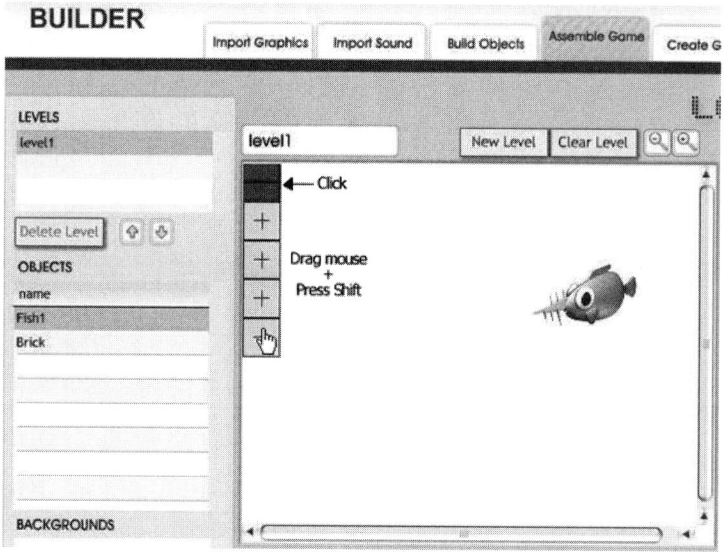

FIGURE 4.20
A brick and a fish instance on the first level.

To create a boundary with bricks around the game room, place more brick objects in the level to surround the Fish1 object. You can use a shortcut for this; just click on the brick, hold down the Shift key, and drag the brick vertically. This lays a series of tiled bricks vertically (see Figure 4.21). Now repeat the process to lay a series of bricks horizontally. You do this by clicking on the bottommost brick, holding down the Shift button, and then dragging the brick horizontally. Repeat the process to create a wall of bricks around the Fish object. Make sure there are no gaps in the walls.

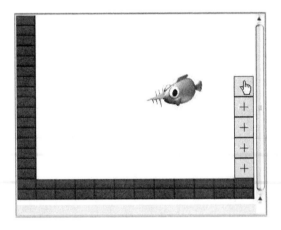

FIGURE 4.21
Creating brick walls around the fish.

To make the game more interesting, select and drag more fish into the brick room. Also, if you would like, resize the fish. You do this by clicking on a fish instance in the game level and then using the manipulators to rotate and scale the instance, as shown in Figure 4.22. To remove a fish, highlight it, right-click, and select Delete.

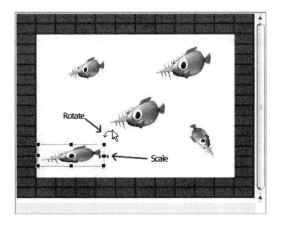

FIGURE 4.22
Rotating and scaling the fish.

GENERATING THE GAME

Now you can test the game! Click the Create Game tab to open the Create Game window shown in Figure 4.23.

Click the Preview Game button. A dialog box will pop up prompting you to save your game. Fill out the box with the desired name for your game and enter a short description of the game if you like. Click Save and Play, and Builder will generate your game. This may take a few moments. The preview will open in a new window. You should see a screen similar to the one shown in Figure 4.24.

Saving a game writes down (saves) a description of the game. Generating a game creates a version of the game that can be played inside the browser.

Congratulations! You have learned to use GameBrix Builder and the ease with which you can get started to create a Flash game.

However, note that at this point you don't have a game. It is more of an animation. Remember that you began with the idea of building a game where you could remove a fish by clicking on it. You also wanted to score 10 points each time you removed a fish. To build the Bouncing Fish game, you need to make additional modifications. It's time to get started.

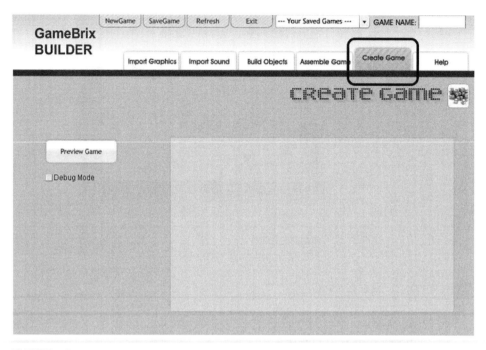

FIGURE 4.23
The Create Game window.

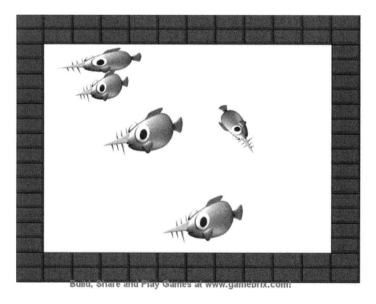

FIGURE 4.24
The game.

ADDING GAMEPLAY

At this point it may be prudent to note that if you are using the browser in the tabbed mode, a new tab is created every time you generate a game. You could close all these browser tabs that hold games that you are not playing.

Now you can get back to modifying your fish object. Click on the Build Objects tab to edit any object. That will bring you to the screen shown in Figure 4.25, which has a fish and a brick object. You'll continue building from here.

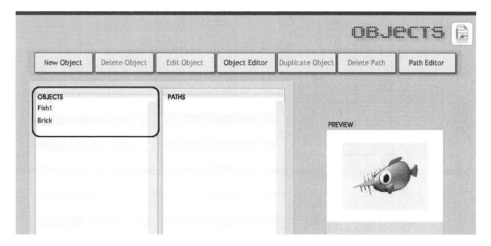

FIGURE 4.25
The Object list.

You first need to add a set of tasks to be performed when the Fish1 object enters the mouse-clicked state. One task would be the addition of 10 points to the score. Edit the Fish1 object by clicking on the Fish1 label followed by clicking the Edit Object button. This takes you to the Build Objects window, shown in Figure 4.26.

Under the Object State box, click on the New button to create a new state. Select the Click state, and then click the Add button, as shown in Figure 4.27.

Note that the Options box now has a Button option. Currently, this option is set to a value of Left, meaning that you want something to happen when the object is left-clicked. Add a SetScore task when the Fish1 object is in the Click state. You want the player's score to increase by 10 points when the fish sprites are left-clicked. Also, you want the fish to disappear after receiving the score, so leave this option as it is. Click the New button under the Tasks box. In the pop-up box, scroll down until you find the SetScore label, and then click on it. After that, click the Add button.

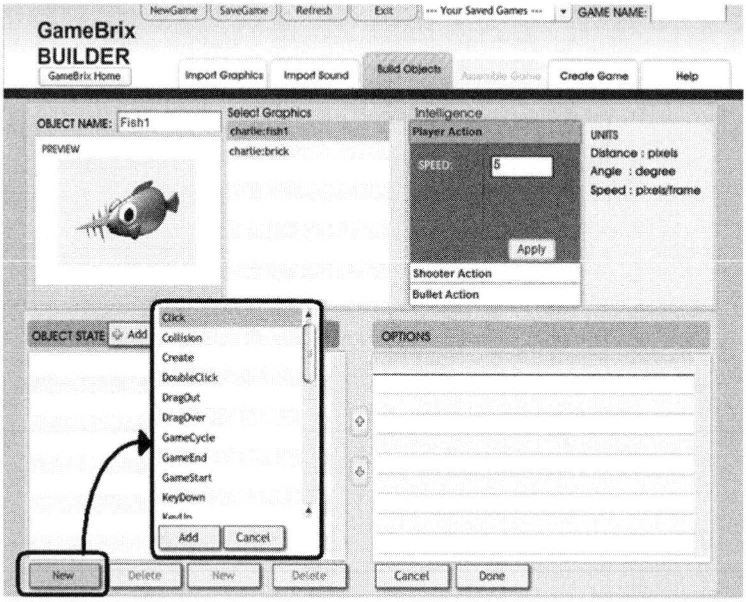

FIGURE 4.26
The Build Objects window.

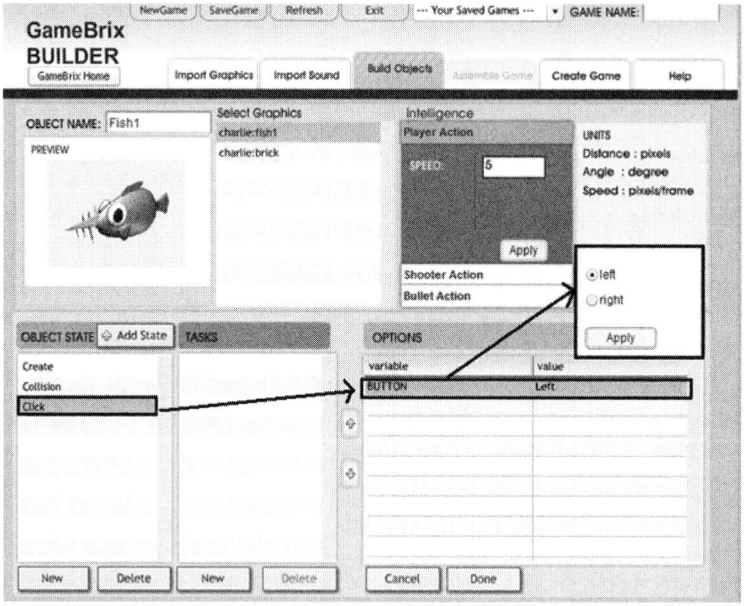

FIGURE 4.27
Adding the Click state.

A `Value` option now appears in the Options box. To set your score, click 0 under the Value section of the Options box. This opens a pop-up box. Type a value of 10 in the Value dialog box, and then click the Apply button, as shown in Figure 4.28. Make sure that the `Relative` option is set to `true`. This means that 10 points will be added to the player's existing score instead of setting the score to an absolute value of 10 points every time a fish is clicked.

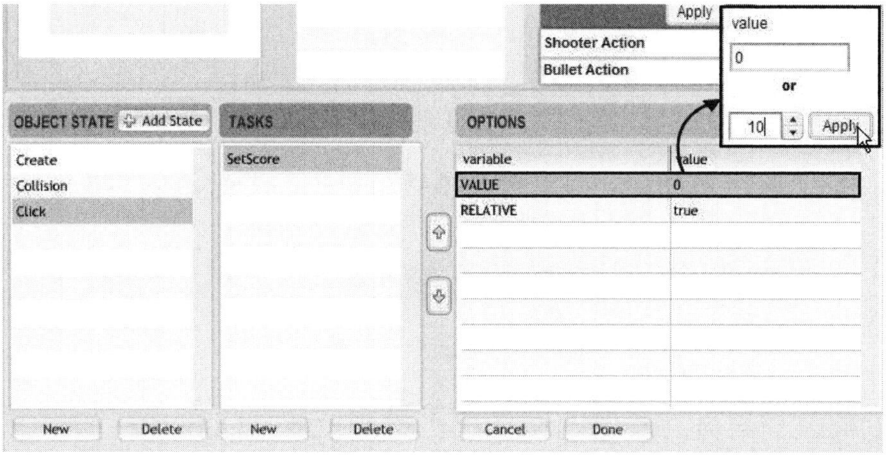

FIGURE 4.28
`SetScore` task.

As per the design, when a fish is clicked, you should destroy it with the `Destroy` task. Under Tasks, click New, select Destroy, and click Add, as shown in Figure 4.29. The Options box now has an `Instance` option, which is currently set to `This`, meaning that the object that is clicked will be destroyed. The alternate option is `Other`, meaning another object will be destroyed when the object is clicked. You want the fish to be destroyed when it is clicked, so leave this option set to `This`.

When you have destroyed all the fish in a game, you need to display a winning message. This is done using the `IfInstanceCount` task.

From the menu that pops up, select `IfInstanceCount` and click Add. In the Options box, you see three options: `Value`, `Object`, and `Operation`.

Set the `Value` option to `0`, because you want the `You Win!` message to be displayed when there are no more (zero) fish left.

The `Object` should be set to `Fish1`, as shown in Figure 4.31.

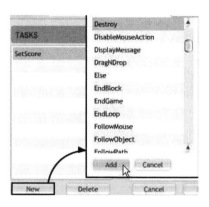

FIGURE 4.29
`Destroy` task.

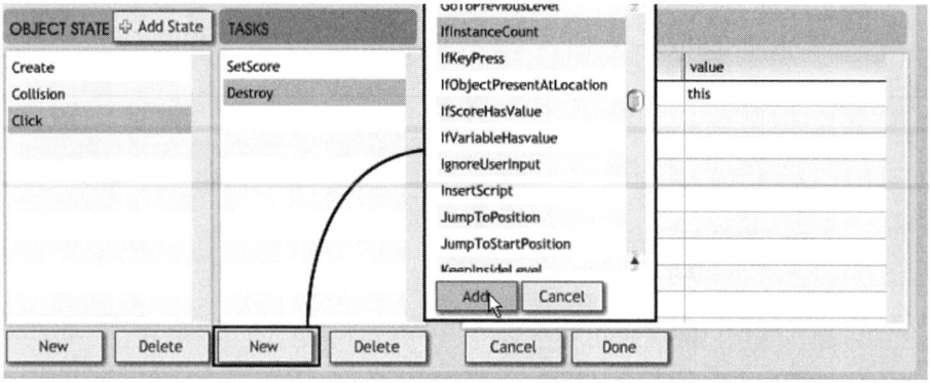

FIGURE 4.30
Adding the `IfInstanceCount` task.

`Operation` allows you to specify whether you want the `You Win!` message to be displayed when there are a number of instances left equal to a specific value. The commonly used `Operation` options are listed in Table 4.1.

You want the `You Win!` win message to display when the number of fish equals 0, so leave `Operation` as `==`.

To complete the game, you need to do a few more tasks. If there are no more `Fish1` objects, the player wins. A message has to be displayed to indicate that the player has won.

Table 4.2 lists the additional tasks you want to perform. To add the `StartBlock` task, click on the New Tasks button, select `StartBlock`, and then click Add.

TABLE 4.1 OPERATION OPTIONS

Symbol	Meaning
>	Greater than
<	Less than
>=	Greater than and equal to
<=	Less than and equal to
==	Equal to
!=	Not equal to

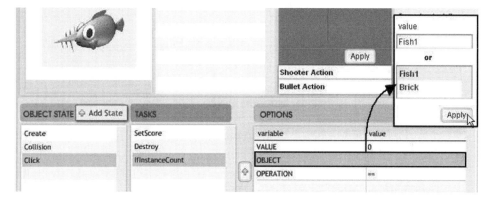

FIGURE 4.31
Configuring the IfInstanceCount task.

TABLE 4.2 OTHER TASKS TO ADD

Task	Options
StartBlock	None
DisplayMessage	You Win!
EndBlock	None

Next, click New Task, select `DisplayMessage`, and click Add. This allows you to add text to be displayed on the screen. The Options box now has a `Message` option. Click the blank box under the Value column next to the `Message` option, and, in the text box that pops up, enter a win message, such as `You Win!`, and click Apply, as shown in Figure 4.32.

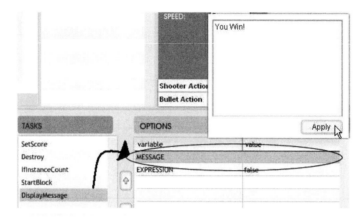

FIGURE 4.32
Configuring the `DisplayMessage` task.

To add the `EndGame` task, click New Task, select `EndGame`, and click Add, as shown in Figure 4.33.

Under Options, click Done. This closes the game after the `You Win!` message is displayed.

Finally, add one last task by clicking New under the Tasks list, selecting `EndBlock`, and clicking Add. This ends the block of tasks that began with the `StartBlock` task. See Figure 4.33 for a full listing of these tasks. Click Done in the bottom right of the screen, underneath the Options box.

With this series of tasks, when all the fish are destroyed, the player receives the winning message, and the game ends.

To see if this actually works, click the Done button and then click the Create Game tab. Click on Preview Game.

While the game is being built, you'll see a message displaying the progress.

After the game is built, it is launched, and you again see the bouncing creatures, just as you did in the first part of this tutorial.

But when you click on one of the fish, it disappears!

Also note that you have a score that increases by 10 each time you destroy a fish. When you destroy all the fish, you receive the `You Win!` message.

Well done! You have created your first game with the GameBrix Builder.

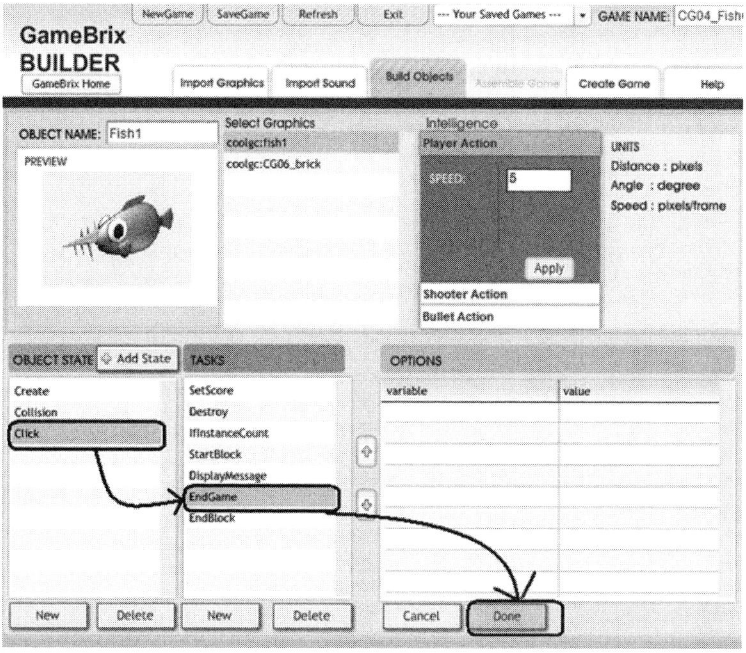

FIGURE 4.33
StartBlock, DisplayMessage, EndGame, and EndBlock Tasks.

Now you're ready to show your friends and to have some gameplay.

There are many ways that you can customize your game, so don't hesitate to explore the backgrounds or import sounds. Have fun!

SUMMARY

In this tutorial, you used GameBrix Builder to create a simple game. You also imported graphics into it and used them to create objects with intelligence. In addition, you learned how to perform various tasks with different object states. The next chapter takes an in-depth look at the Animator application to create graphics and animations, which can be used with both GameBrix Express and the GameBrix Builder.

5 Drawing with GameBrix Animator

In This Chapter

- Starting the Animator
- Drawing the Robot
- Animating the Robot
- Using the Robot in a Game

This chapter explores the features of the GameBrix Animator, a multifeatured tool that enables you to paint and animate images. You can then save each image into your GameBrix image library and use it to create Web-based games. You will be building a simple robot, animating it, and then incorporating it into your game.

STARTING THE ANIMATOR

To get started, navigate to Gamebrix.com and log in. Go to http://www.gamebrix.com, enter your username and password, and then click the Submit button.

If you are not a registered user, follow the "Getting Started" procedure outlined in Chapter 2, "Introduction to GameBrix," and then return here.

After logging into the system, click on the blue button labeled GameBrix Animator, which loads the Animator. After a few moments, you should see the Animator's default start screen, as shown in Figure 5.1. The GameBrix Animator is a simple-to-use Web application used to create simple pictures and animations. Hovering the mouse over the individual tools listed on the left indicates its type. The tools and their functionality are listed next:

- **Arrow.** Used to select graphics items on the drawing board
- **Anchor.** Used to select subelements of graphics items
- **Transform.** Used to scale the selected graphics element
- **Crop.** Used to crop a selected area
- **Pencil.** Used to draw lines
- **Brush.** Used to draw lines with different brush types
- **Erase.** Used to erase graphics
- **Bucket.** Used to fill enclosed areas
- **Oval.** Used to draw circle and oval shapes
- **Line.** Used to draw straight lines
- **Rectangle.** Used to draw rectangles and squares
- **Text.** Used to draw text
- **Bezier.** Used to draw curves using the three-point method
- **Modify Bezier Anchor.** Used to move Bézier anchor points
- **Delete Bezier Anchor.** Used to delete Bézier points
- **Camera.** Used to take pictures using a camera attached to your computer
- **Sprite Sheet.** Used to create animations from sprite sheets
- **Outline Color.** Used to define outline color
- **Fill Color.** Used to define fill color

All these tools have default options that come into effect when you choose them. For example, when you choose the Brush tool, the brush size is 7 and the brush color is black. These options are displayed in a properties window. You can modify them to suit your taste while you create your images and animations.

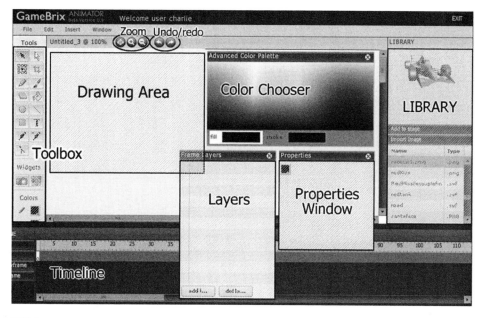

FIGURE 5.1
Animator start page.

First you'll arrange the default windows that are displayed to suit your convenience. Click the arrow tool, and use it to move the windows to the different locations shown in Figure 5.1. Click on the drawing area window and then on the properties window. Next, set the default width and height of the drawing area to 320×480 pixels in the properties window.

DRAWING THE ROBOT

It's time to draw and animate your robot. To make the drawing process easier, two tools will be used: the Oval tool and the Rectangle tool. Click the Oval tool, and in its Properties box, click on the Fill Color box. Then select a color, as shown in Figure 5.2.

Now, using the Oval tool, click and drag your mouse in the drawing area to create an oval robot head.

Next, click the Oval Properties box again, select yellow as the fill color, and create an eye for the robot, as shown in Figure 5.3.

You'll add a radio antenna using the Line tool.

Select the Line tool, and in its Properties, set Stroke Width to 3, as shown in Figure 5.4.

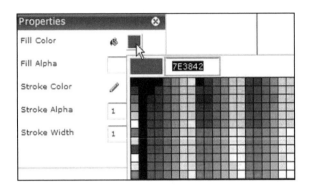

FIGURE 5.2
Oval tool, Fill Color for face.

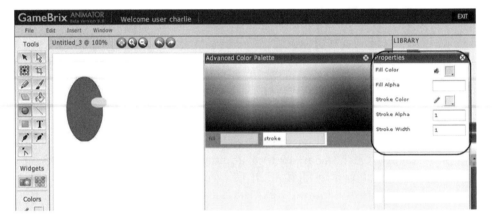

FIGURE 5.3
Oval tool, Fill Color for eye.

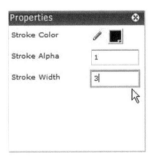

FIGURE 5.4
Line tool, Stroke, and Width.

Now draw an antenna. When you're finished, save the head. It's an important aspect of computing to always save your work; in this way, you minimize the possibility of losing your valuable efforts. From the main menu, click File, and then select Save Project, as shown in Figure 5.5.

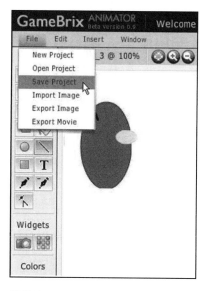

FIGURE 5.5
File, Save Project.

In the Save File dialog box, enter a file name, such as Robot, and click OK. Now, with your drawing saved, you'll continue with the robot's body. Click the Oval tool, set its Fill Color property, and draw a body. Then add a neck between the head and body using the Line tool (see Figure 5.6). When the outline is finished, select the Pour tool, choose a color, and fill the blank neck area with the chosen color.

Now you'll add a hip to your robot. Select the Oval tool and draw an oval-shaped hip, from left to right, as shown in Figure 5.7. Note that the color used in the Pour tool remains selected.

Save your robot again. The next step is adding legs and animating them.

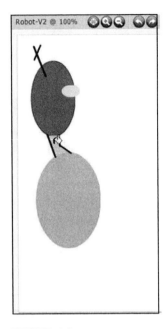

FIGURE 5.6
Neck, body addition.

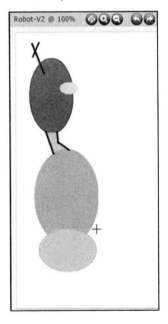

FIGURE 5.7
Hip addition.

ANIMATING THE ROBOT

You need to think about the flip book–based analogy to understand basic animation. In a flip book, images are drawn on different pages that, when flipped in sequence quickly enough, look like an animated movie. In the GameBrix Animator, you will be using the same technique, except that instead of drawing on different sheets of paper, you will be drawing on the digital equivalent of sheets of paper. Each sheet of paper used is termed a *frame*. Movies are made using several million frames, where each frame is slightly different from the previous one. The eye sees one picture and then sees the next picture. If there is some difference between the two, the brain handles these as if the difference between them were a smooth transition.

Animator frames are similar to movie frames. To create robot legs that move, place the legs on different layers in one frame, and then in the next frame, slightly change the position of the legs. Here's how the whole sequence is done.

In the Frame Layers option window, click Add Layer, as shown in Figure 5.8. Note that the layer has a unique name. Animator automatically gives layers unique names.

FIGURE 5.8
Frame Layers window.

Looking closely at the result in Figure 5.9, you'll see that the original layer is moved to the bottom, and the new layer is highlighted and added to the top. Each layer also has a dark eye icon on the left.

Click the eye icon. You'll notice that the "eye" disappears, as shown in Figure 5.10, as does your robot. Click the icon again, and you'll see the robot and the eye icon return.

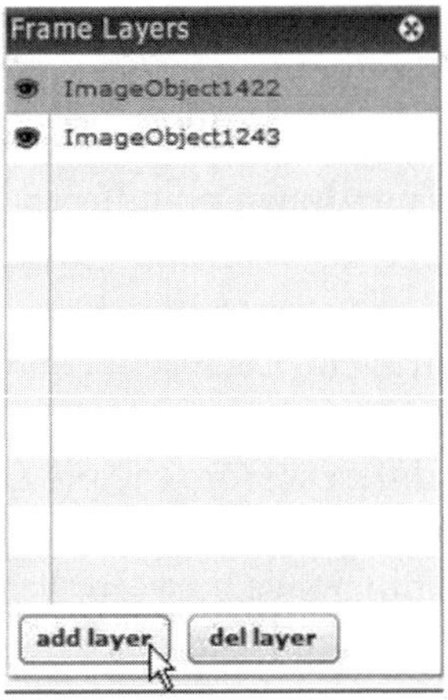

FIGURE 5.9
Multiple frames.

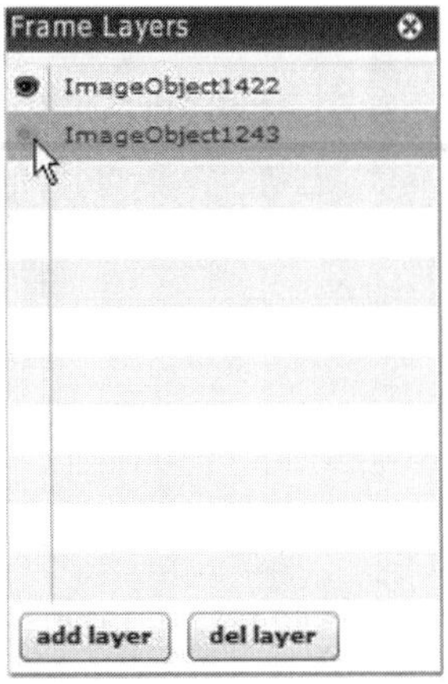

FIGURE 5.10
Hidden layer.

Clicking this icon simply makes the layer visible or invisible. When a layer is invisible, or "hidden," you can't alter or edit it. Click the eye icon beside the bottom layer once more to hide the layer. Then select the new, top layer.

The Frame Layers window should look like that shown in Figure 5.11. You can now work on this layer without affecting the other layer. Add a leg on this layer. Think of each Animator layer as a single transparent sheet of paper on which you can draw whatever you want. Multiple layers amount to multiple sheets of paper stacked on top of each other.

FIGURE 5.11
Select the upper layer.

Next, draw a leg on this new layer. Click on the Oval tool and draw an oval leg, as shown in Figure 5.12. Then select the Transform tool, click next to an outside corner of the outline drawn, and rotate the leg, as shown in Figure 5.13.

FIGURE 5.12
Oval leg on upper layer.

FIGURE 5.13
Rotated leg on upper layer.

Make the bottom layer visible again so you can position the leg correctly with the robot's body. Make sure you have the top layer selected; then, with the Transform tool, correctly position the leg with the hips, as shown in Figure 5.14.

Next, create the other leg. This time use the copy and paste mechanism available with the Animator. Now, using the Edit menu, select the leg and copy it using Copy, under the Edit menu, as shown in Figure 5.15.

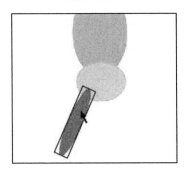

FIGURE 5.14
Rotated leg positioned correctly.

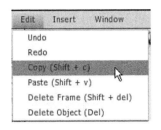

FIGURE 5.15
Edit, Copy menu.

Using Frame Layers, add another layer, select the top layer, and paste the robot's other leg onto the new layer by clicking the Edit menu and selecting Paste, as shown in Figure 5.16.

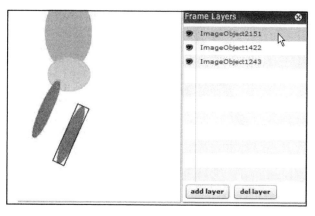

FIGURE 5.16
Paste operation.

Now, using the Transform and Arrow tools, reposition the leg so that it looks as if it is walking or running, as shown in Figure 5.17. Click the layer icons, turning them on and off to get a feel for how they work.

FIGURE 5.17
Reposition the leg.

You may have noticed that both legs are on the same side of the body. You'll move one of the legs to a layer behind the body using the Frame Layers window. Layers within this window can be moved forward or behind by clicking and dragging the layer appropriately. You'll drag and drop the layer with the new leg so that it aligns behind the robot's hips—as if it were on the other side of the robot's body.

Select the top layer—with the new leg—and drag it to the bottom of the layer stack, as shown in Figure 5.18. Notice that it appears to go behind the hips. Save your project. Next, you'll animate this robot to make it look as though it's walking!

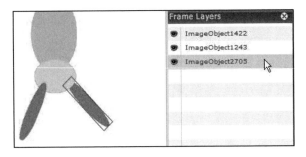

FIGURE 5.18
Changing layers.

As mentioned earlier, to create an animation, you need multiple pictures that are displayed sequentially at any pace, but in this case, rapid. It's time to start creating these pictures. Unlike traditional drawing on paper, you can create copies of the picture quickly and easily.

Look at the bottom-left corner of the Animator. Here, you will see what is called a *timeline*, with the options to create three types of frames:

- New frames (regular frames)
- Keyframes
- Blank keyframes

Remember, each new frame (*regular frame*) or *keyframe* is like a new page in a flipbook. Notice that the timeline currently contains one keyframe. This keyframe has your entire robot drawn on it. Regular frames contain the image as it appears in the previous frame, so if you create a new frame and adjust the robot in that frame, the robot will also be adjusted in the first keyframe. When a new keyframe is created, an exact copy of whatever images appeared on the previous frame is placed in the new keyframe. Keyframes contain changes to the image, so if you create a new keyframe and adjust the robot in that keyframe, it will change in the new keyframe but not in any of the previous frames. *Blank keyframes* are keyframes with no images on them, so if you create a blank keyframe, the robot will not appear on that frame.

Clicking on the Keyframe button found on the lower-left corner of the Animator creates a new copy of the image. Go ahead and click on the Keyframe button shown in Figure 5.19 to add another keyframe to the timeline. Each keyframe is displayed with a blue bar above and a gray box with a blue circle below the timeline, as shown in Figure 5.19.

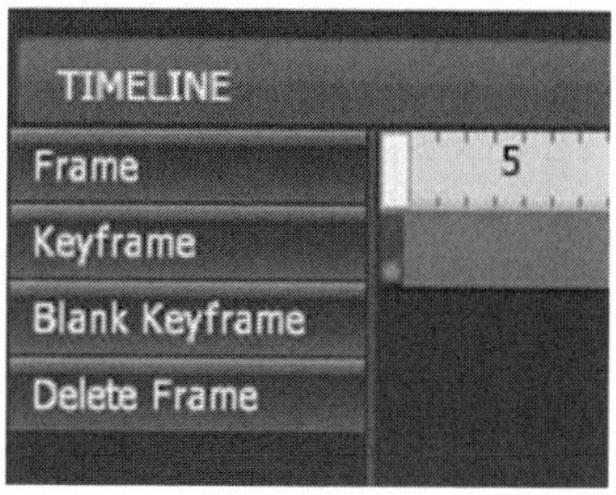

FIGURE 5.19
Adding keyframes.

Repeat this step six more times. You should see several blue boxes with blue circles. Then click on the blue bar of the first new keyframe.

This takes you to that frame that has your robot image, with the three frame layers: one for the body and two for each leg. In fact, each of the new keyframes you created has a copy of your robot—including all its layers. You can move the legs using the Transform tool.

Now you'll edit each keyframe, using the Transform tool to move the legs—repositioning them as in Figure 5.20.

Once you have completed this editing task, click Export Movie from the File menu, as shown in Figure 5.20. The Animator will start rendering your frames.

Once the frames are rendered, you will see a preview that shows your robot walking (see Figure 5.21).

You may discover that the legs move too fast. If so, click on each keyframe (blue box), and then click the Frame button, as shown in Figure 5.22. This adds a frame (a gray box) after your first keyframe. Repeat this process—keyframe, frame, keyframe, frame—until you have added one frame after each keyframe. This will slow down your animation by displaying each leg movement for a little bit longer than before.

Click Export Movie under the File menu.

Congratulations! Your robot can walk now! The next section discusses how to use this robot in a game.

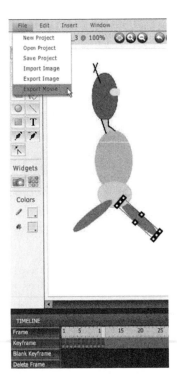

FIGURE 5.20
Moving the legs and exporting the movie.

FIGURE 5.21
Animated robot preview.

FIGURE 5.22
Slowed down animation.

USING THE ROBOT IN A GAME

Bringing images and animated graphics into your game is easy. Once you have saved your work done with the Animator, it is instantly added to your GameBrix image library.

It's time to test whether you can see your creation inside GameBrix Game-Builder. Click on the green GameBrix GameBuilder button. The GameBrix engine and your profile load, as shown in Figure 5.23. The GameBuilder Import Graphics screen loads next, as shown in Figure 5.24.

FIGURE 5.23
GameBuilder profile loader.

In the Graphics list, scroll to the name you gave your robot, and click its name. The Add Sprite button shown in Figure 5.25 should be enabled. Click it. This adds your robot to your Sprites list and enables you to use your robot inside the games you build. Well done! You've created your first animation using the GameBrix Animator.

GameBrix
BUILDER

NewGame | SaveGame | Refresh | Exit | --- Your Saved Games --- ▾ | GAME NAME:

Import Graphics | Import Sound | Build Objects | Assemble Game | Create Game | Help

GRAPHICS

GRAPHICS

charlie:DownFish
charlie:Face
charlie:Face-Mouth
charlie:Face-Mouth
charlie:Face-Mouth-Down
charlie:LeftFish
charlie:LittleGuy
charlie:Logo-72-48pixels
charlie:Missilecouplefinal
charlie:PlainGreenBackground
charlie:RedMissilecouplefinal
charlie:RightFish
charlie:Untitled_2
charlie:UpFish
charlie:bear
charlie:beePlayer
charlie:bird1
charlie:birdfly
charlie:blueKiss

Delete | Upload

SPRITES

PREVIEW

loading

◀ ▶ FRAME NO: ■ ▶

BACKGROUNDS

FIGURE 5.24
GameBuilder Import Graphics screen.

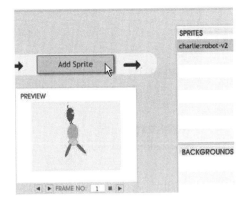

FIGURE 5.25
Add Sprite button.

SUMMARY

This chapter looked at how to draw images using the Animator tool. It then looked at how to create animations and export the images and animations to GameBrix GameBuilder.

You learned how to draw images using the Animator tool. You also learned how to create animations and export the images and animations to GameBrix GameBuilder. You can now use this knowledge to create and use assets within the GameBrix GameBuilder and GameBrix Express Web applications. In the next chapter, you start to build a platform game.

6 Building a Platform Game

This chapter describes the process involved in building a platform game. This could be a 2-D sidescroller (*Mario*) or a 3-D game (*Super Mario 64*), in which the player moves along or jumps across platforms and ledges. Along the way, enemies need to be destroyed, and collectible objects need to be picked up. *Super Mario Bros.* from Nintendo is a typical platform game that has revolutionized the video game industry. Platform games have entertained people for the past 30 years and have evolved significantly. Having gained an insight into how game objects are created and what purpose they serve in the GameBrix portal, it's time to start creating different types of games.

GAME DESCRIPTION

The game to be built in this chapter is a 2-D sidescroller. The story behind the game is that MomoNinja, a courageous ninja whose clan recently lost a fierce battle to the Shamano clan, wants to reclaim the honor of his clan by going to a remote temple to receive advice. He starts his journey at one corner of a large underground cave, with a goal to reach the shrine on the other end. He starts his valiant quest by traversing through a mountain range. While on his adventure, he encounters a stray group of Shamano enemies who have been trapped near the temple. Their appearance has changed after spending ages in the dark caves that line the mountain. MomoNinja finds a magical concealed weapon known as a shuriken that helps him defeat the Shamanos, in addition to many gold coins that miners have lost over the years. He needs help collecting these coins to take to the shrines. He needs the powers endowed by the magical shuriken to destroy the enemies that hinder his progress along the way.

GameBrix technology facilitates the creation of virtually any kind of Flash game. There are distinct mechanisms to create games catered to three groups of users:

- Game programmers
- Game artists
- Game publishers

Remember, game programmers and game designers are different. Game programmers actually code the game, whereas designers build the world and characters. Sometimes one person does both jobs. Game programmers are mostly left-brained thinkers who can build their own objects from first principles. They can use Adobe ActionScript 2.0 with a mix of GameBrix tasks and states to create custom game objects. Game programmers are creators of game objects designed to specifications of the game designer.

Game artists are mostly right-brained thinkers who make important decisions related to visual elements of the game. In the GameBrix portal, game artists can see their creative game ideas in action by leveraging the availability of intelligent game objects. They can assemble and build the game quickly using basic building blocks available in the form of game objects.

Game publishers look at game creation from a higher level. They can build and publish games in a few minutes and provide input for enhancements. Publishers leverage the availability of Game Definition Format (GDF) files inside the GameBrix portal. GDF files, which are an assembly of premade game objects that describe a game, have instructions for assembling a game from ready-made objects. You can share them within a group or buy them from the GameBrix store.

The artist and publisher methods for game creation are described in this chapter. The artist's method revolves around the use of ready-made components, and the publisher's method revolves around the use of ready-made GDF files. The programmer's method involves the use of Adobe ActionScript programming—a complete description of which is beyond the scope of this book. Introductory ActionScript concepts are covered in Chapter 8, "Scripting with ActionScript 2.0," and more detailed concepts are covered in Chapter 13, "Going Green—Build a Recycling Game."

Building the Game Using the Artist's Approach

The first step is to log in to Gamebrix.com if you are not already logged in. The next sequence of steps involves obtaining all the images, animations, and intelligence required for building the game. Images and animations are the basic raw materials required for building games. Images can be in the PNG or JPG format. Animations can only be in the Flash SWF format.

The GameBrix portal facilitates the purchase of game assets such as pictures, animations, backgrounds, GDF files, and game objects using a virtual currency known as Brix. Accounts created on GameBrix have 500 Brix of virtual currency by default. To build this game, a budget of 46 Brix is required to get all the required assets from the online GameBrix store.

In a distributed game development team, it is easy to share creative assets such as images and animations, but when it comes to game mechanics, it becomes a little complicated. A game could have hundreds of objects that all behave differently. In GameBrix, each set of encapsulated behaviors for an object is called *object intelligence*, or *intelligence* for short. You can save and share intelligence with other members of the team.

GameBrix intelligence is an asset type that contains an object's complete behavior. For example, there can be a shooter intelligence that has all the complex logic for making an object shoot certain projectiles. When you apply shooter intelligence to the object, the object shoots projectiles. No further programming is required. The ease of use of objects encapsulated with complex intelligence enables creative right-brained people to build game objects with little or no programming experience.

Images Required

Now it's time to get the images required for the *MomoNinja* game from the online GameBrix store. Go to the online store by clicking on the link labeled Store. In the Search by Name text box, type in CG06, and select Images as the content type you are interested in, as shown in Figure 6.1. The owner of these items is coolgc.

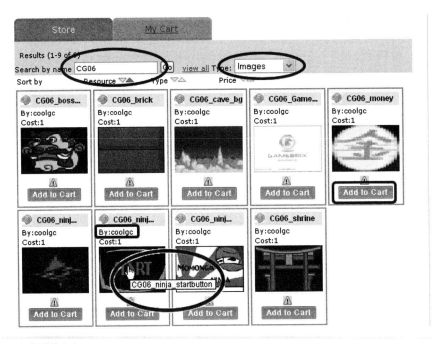

FIGURE 6.1
The required images from the store.

The images required are described in Table 6.1. The name of the item may not be displayed completely, as shown in Figure 6.1, if it is longer than 10 characters. Hovering your mouse over the thumbnail of the image should display the full name.

Buy all the items listed by clicking on the Add to Cart button. After all the items are in your shopping cart, click on the My Cart tab. It may take a few seconds for the system to process items in your cart. The next screen displays all the items in your cart by file name and item name. If you already have an item in your inventory by the same file name or item name, that item is displayed in red text. You need to change the name of that item on this screen to avoid name conflicts and overwriting your file. If you have already purchased an item that shows up in red text, you can remove the item from your shopping cart using the Remove button on the same row. Figure 6.2 shows all the items in the shopping cart.

TABLE 6.1 IMAGES REQUIRED

Item Name	Description
CG06_boss_head	The enemies
CG06_cave_bg	The background image
CG06_brick	The platform
CG06_Gamebrix_Splash	The splash screen
CG06_money	The gold coins
CG06_ninja_star	The power-up
CG06_ninja_startbutton	The Start button
CG06_Ninja_title	The title screen
CG06_shrine	The shrine

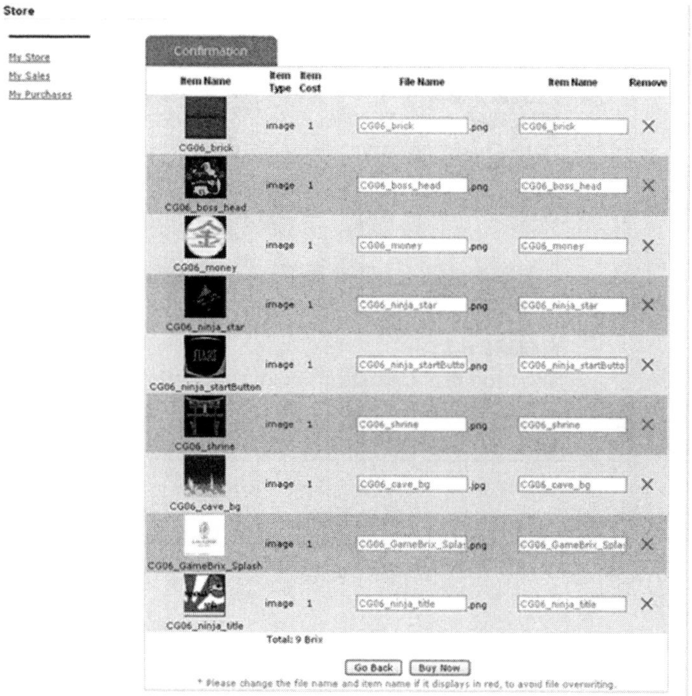

FIGURE 6.2
Items in the shopping cart.

Click the Buy Now button at the bottom of the screen. The system may take a few moments to process your order. On completion of the transaction, the items are added to your inventory, and the store screen displays. That completes the process of assembling the images required for this game.

ANIMATIONS REQUIRED

The next step is to get all the animations required from the online store by using a process similar to the one you used to get the images. In the Search by Name text box, type in CG06 and select Animation as the content type you are interested in (see Figure 6.3). Again, the owner of these assets is coolgc. The icons displayed for all animations resemble a snippet of camera film. If you are interested in seeing the animation, click on the icon, which displays the animation in a new window. Table 6.2 lists the animations that you need. Buy these items from the store, and complete the purchase just as you did in the earlier section.

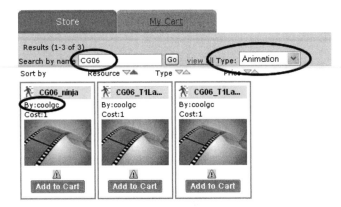

FIGURE 6.3
The required animations from the store.

TABLE 6.2 ANIMATIONS REQUIRED

Item Name	Description
CG06_ninja	The player
CG06_T1LabelcompSL	A small label used for displaying text
CG06_T1LabelcompML	A medium-sized label used for displaying text

INTELLIGENCE REQUIRED

The next step is to get all the intelligence required from the online store. In the Search by Name text box, type in CG06 and select Intelligence as the content type, as shown in Figure 6.4. coolgc owns all the intelligence. The icons displayed for all object intelligence assets resemble a single gear. You cannot view or preview object intelligence directly. You can view it only when you use it inside GameBrix Game-Builder. Table 6.3 lists the intelligence that you need. Buy these items from the store, and complete the purchase just as you did in the earlier section.

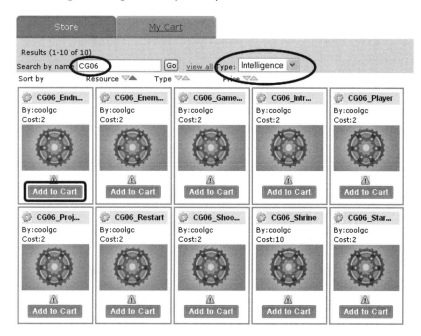

FIGURE 6.4
The required object intelligence assets from the store.

TABLE 6.3 INTELLIGENCE REQUIRED

Item Name	Description
CG06_EndNinja	The player
CG06_EnemyObject	A small label used for displaying text
CG06_GameoverLabel	A medium label used for displaying text
CG06_IntroNinja	The player
CG06_Player	A small label used for displaying text
CG06_Projectile	A medium sized label used for displaying text
CG06_Restart	The player
CG06_ShooterPower	A small label used for displaying text
CG06_Shrine	A medium label used for displaying text
CG06_StartButton	A medium label used for displaying text

BUILDING THE OBJECTS

With all the raw materials in place, it's time to start building the game objects. Open the GameBrix GameBuilder by clicking on the large tab labeled Game Builder. When the application loads, you are, by default, at the Import Graphics screen.

On the left side of the screen is a set of images and animations in your library. Select the following images, and add them to the Sprites section on the right, as shown in Figure 6.5.

- CG06_boss_head
- CG06_brick
- CG06_money
- CG06_ninja_star
- CG06_ninja_startButton
- CG06_shrine
- CG06_ninja
- CG06_T1LabelcompSL
- CG06_T1LabelcompML

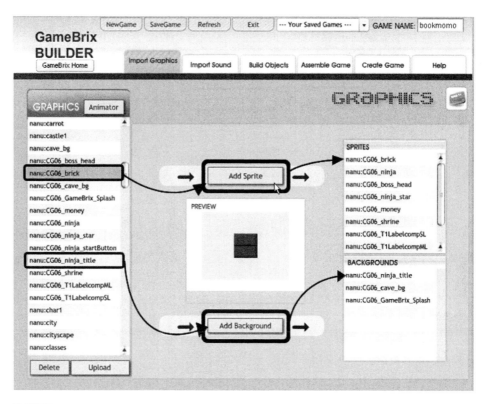

FIGURE 6.5
Assembling the sprites.

Select the following images, and move them to the Backgrounds section on the right:

- CG06_cave_bg
- CG06_Gamebrix_Splash
- CG06_Ninja_title

It's time to build game objects. Click on the Build Objects tab and select the New Object button to proceed.

Choose the brick image from the list of images displayed in Figure 6.6. Name the object BrickObject by typing it in the Object Name text box. Then click the Done button to complete the object creation process.

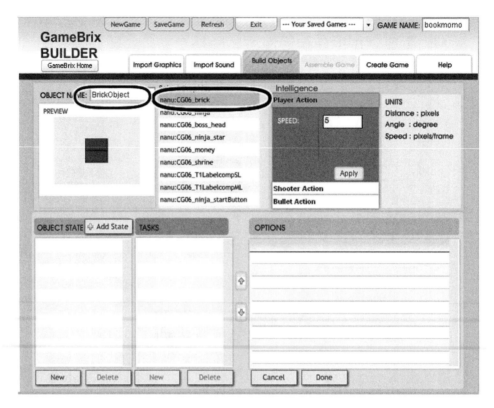

FIGURE 6.6
Object creation process.

Repeat this step and create the 11 other objects that are listed in Table 6.4. The table lists their object names and the images or animations that are attached to them.

After creating all the objects, click the SaveGame button shown in Figure 6.7. Provide a title and description when you save. The file name you specify should not contain spaces or special symbols.

TABLE 6.4 OBJECTS REQUIRED

Object Name	Image/Animation Required
BrickObject	CG06_brick
CollectObject	CG06_money
EndNinja	CG06_ninja
EnemyObject	CG06_boss_head
Gameoverobj	CG06_T1LabelcompML
IntroNinja	CG06_ninja
LevelEndObject	CG06_shrine
PlayerObject	CG06_ninja
ProjectileObject	CG06_ninja_star
Restart	CG06_T1LabelcompSL
ShooterPowerup	CG06_ninja_star
StartButton	CG06_ninja_startbutton

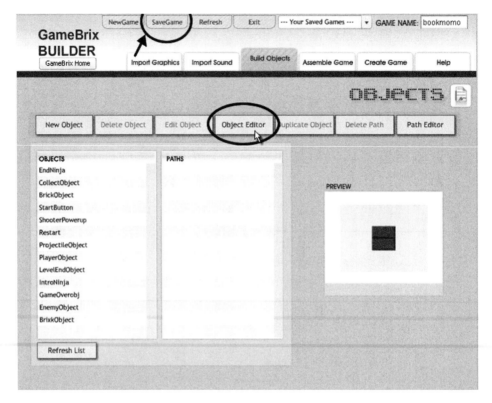

FIGURE 6.7
Object creation process.

The objects that have been created up to this point have not had assigned behaviors. In other words, you have not created states and tasks to be executed in these objects. The normal approach is to individually add each of the states and tasks to each object. An alternative solution would be to use the predefined object intelligence that you bought from the store. This is a much quicker approach for building games, and it provides the opportunity to look at the intelligence and see how it was created.

It's time to add behavioral intelligence to your objects. Click on the Object Editor button shown in Figure 6.7. This opens a new window with several sections, as shown in Figure 6.8.

FIGURE 6.8
Object Editor screen.

The section labeled States lists all the valid states the object can be in. The Tasks section lists all the tasks that can be performed, and Intelligence lists all the encapsulated behaviors that you have at your disposal. The section in the middle, labeled Variable Definitions, lists all the variables that apply to this object. The area beneath this is the Object Behaviors section; it is usually empty when you start building a fresh object. The section on the right labeled Object Info displays the image or animation attached to the object. The section below that labeled Game Objects lists all the game objects that have been created. World Vars lists all the variables that have global scope.

The things of importance to note are the list of objects present in the Game Objects section and the list of object intelligence found in the Intelligence section. BrickObject and CollectObject do not have behaviors. They do not do anything other than stay in one place.

Select the object named EndNinja by clicking on it in the Game Objects section. Clicking and choosing different objects within this section displays the selected object's behavior in the center of the screen. Double-click on CG06_Endninja in the Intelligence section. You are prompted with a dialog box asking you if you want to overwrite your object's behavior, as shown in Figure 6.9. Click Yes. That should populate the object with one or more states and tasks, as shown in Figure 6.10. This object now has one or more tasks assigned to two states. In the Create state, the tasks performed are GoToFrame and StartMoving. In the Outside Room state, the Display Message task is performed.

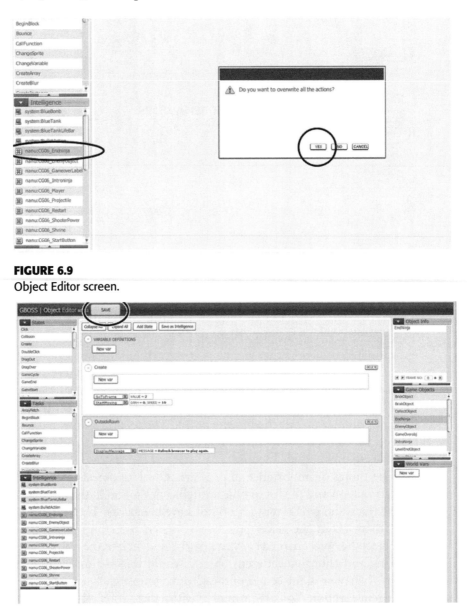

FIGURE 6.9
Object Editor screen.

FIGURE 6.10
Populated Object Editor screen.

That completes the creation of the `EndNinja` object. Using prebaked intelligence to define an object's behavior makes the task so much easier.

The same sequence of steps is required to create all the other objects. Note that objects require different intelligence. Table 6.5 lists all the objects and the appropriate intelligence they require.

TABLE 6.5 INTELLIGENCE ASSIGNMENT

Object Name	Intelligence Required
BrickObject	No intelligence required
CollectObject	No intelligence required
EndNinja	CG06_Endninja
EnemyObject	CG06_EnemyObject
Gameoverobj	CG06_GameoverLabel
IntroNinja	CG06_Introninja
LevelEndObject	CG06_Shrine
PlayerObject	CG06_Player
ProjectileObject	CG06_Projectile
Restart	CG06_Restart
ShooterPowerup	CG06_ShooterPower
StartButton	CG06_StartButton

After you have assigned these objects the appropriate intelligence, click the Save button found at the top of the Object Editor screen. This is an important step, so don't skip it. A message box displays the message `Save complete`. Close it by clicking the OK button. You can then minimize the Object Editor window, which brings you back to the Build Objects screen that displays the message `Game ready to build`, as shown in Figure 6.11. Click the OK button to continue the game creation process.

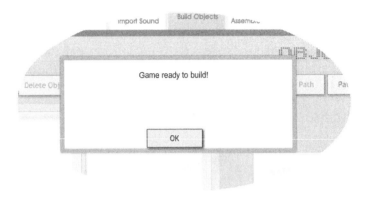

FIGURE 6.11
Game ready to build **screen**.

ASSEMBLING THE GAME

Now that all your objects are ready, it's time for the fun part of assembling the game and testing it. Click the Assemble Game tab. This screen has several buttons and fields. The area on the left labeled Levels lists all the levels that you have created. Level1 is always created by default.

LEVEL DESCRIPTION

The area labeled Objects lists all the objects that you have created. These are the toys you get to play with in the Assemble Game tab. The area in the center, Game Assembly Area, is where you place game objects (see Figure 6.12).

There are several configurable items in the Assemble Game tab. View defines the size and color of the visible area of the game when it is built. Level Size defines the virtual size of the level, which can be many times larger than the view size. For example, in the *MomoNinja* game, the level size is three times the view size.

The name of the level is specified in the text box above the Game Assembly Area. You can change the name.

The currently selected object's instance name is displayed in the Instance Name text box. *Instances*, in simple terms, are clones of objects they are derived from.

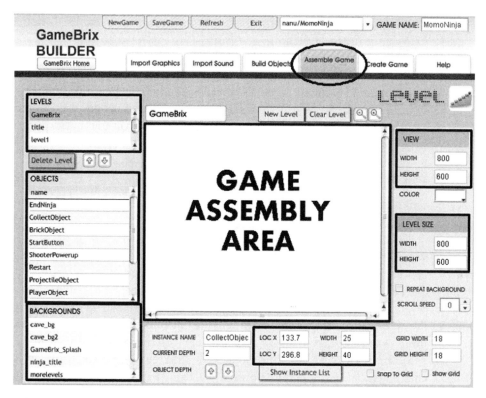

FIGURE 6.12
Game Assembly Area.

The Current Depth text box displays the object's depth. *Depth* of an object defines its position relative to other objects. The easiest way to understand depth is to take a printed book and lay it on a table with the cover face down and the back cover facing the ceiling. Page 10 is found deeper in the book than page 20. Since page 20 is above page 10, the contents on page 10 will not be visible because they are beneath page 20. Adobe Flash uses the same concept. Objects placed at a depth of 12 can be hidden under an object of depth 14. The lower an object's depth, the deeper it is. This is just the opposite of the real-world concept of ocean depth, for example, where the higher the object's depth, the deeper it is. You can change the object's depth by using the Object Depth button, found under the Game Assembly Area. The Up arrow button moves the object higher and increases its depth. The Down arrow button moves the object lower and decreases its depth. While using Adobe Flash technology, you need to switch your thought process and think of depth as the height from the bottom of the ocean.

The LocX, LocY, Width, and Height boxes found under the Game Assembly Area define the location and dimensions of the selected object.

You can display a grid by clicking the Show Grid check box found in the bottom-right corner. You can make objects snap to the grid by using the Snap to Grid check box. The Grid Width and Grid Height boxes define the dimensions of the grid.

Clicking the Show Instance List displays the list of instances on this level.

The Repeat Background check box lays the background images over a relatively large area using the tiling concept.

ASSEMBLING LEVEL 1

This game has four levels: a splash screen, the title screen, the real game, and the end of game screen.

The first screen, as a splash screen, appears for just a few seconds. MomoNinja starts moving from the left corner of the screen toward the right. The game advances to the next level when he reaches the other end of the screen.

Level 1 is the first level created by default for every game. You need to configure several things for it. Set the View and Level Size to 800×600, as shown in Figure 6.13. From the list of backgrounds found on the bottom-left corner of the screen, click on the GameBrix_Splash background. This places the background onto the Game Assembly Area. Next, from the Objects list, find the object named IntroNinja. Click, and drag the IntroNinja object onto the bottom-left corner, as shown in Figure 6.13. That completes the Level 1 assembly process. You can change the name of the level if you want by typing in the new name in the Level Name box. Save your work once again by clicking the SaveGame button.

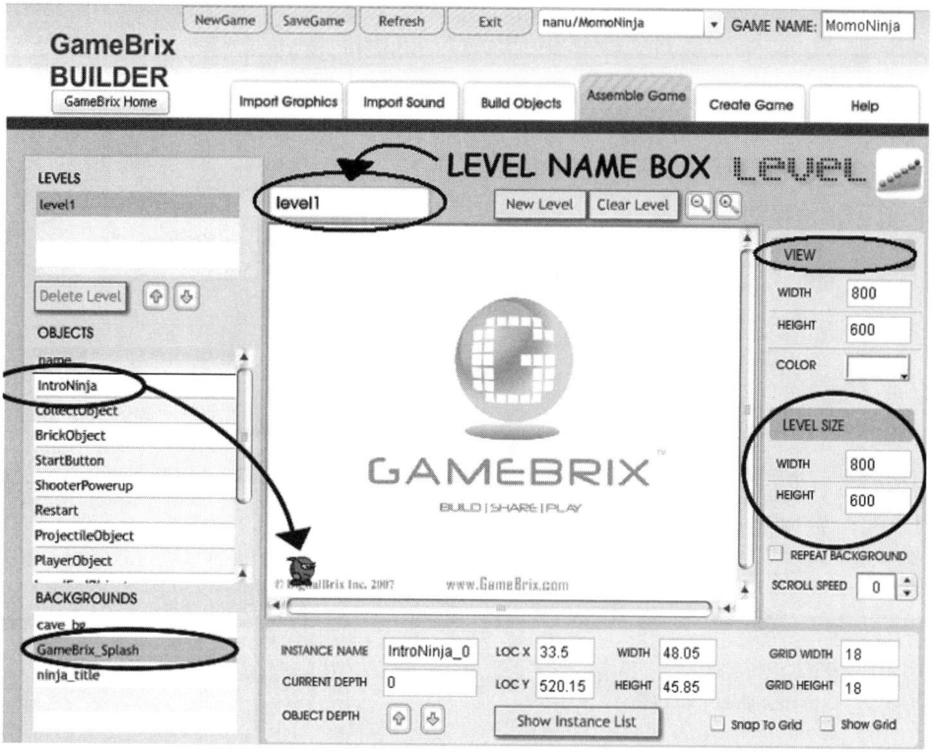

FIGURE 6.13

Level1 assembled.

ASSEMBLING LEVEL 2

The second level is the title screen. It introduces the game and includes the Start button. To create this new level, click the button labeled New Level. Change the name of the level to title. Change the width and height of both the Level and View Size areas to 800×600. Select Ninja_title as the background by clicking on it from the Backgrounds list. Click and drag a StartButton object from the Objects list onto the bottom-left corner of the Game Assembly Area, as shown in Figure 6.14.

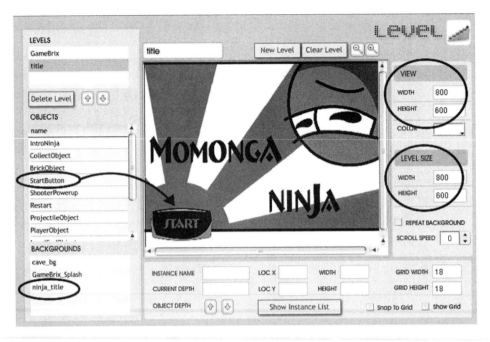

FIGURE 6.14
Level 2 assembled.

ASSEMBLING LEVEL 3

Create a third level, which houses the actual game. Name it gamelevel, and set Level Size to 2400×600. Leave View Size at 800×600.

Select cave_bg as the background by clicking on it from the Backgrounds list. Create platforms in this level using the BrickObject. If you want a long platform, place a BrickObject at the required spot, and transform it to the right size. Clicking on any object placed in the Game Assembly Area displays handles (manipulators) for that object. Using these handles, as shown in Figure 6.15, you can resize and rotate the object. Moving the mouse cursor close to the corner handles of the selected object displays the object's rotation handle.

Using the scroll bar, you can view different areas of the game room. Create more platforms throughout the whole level using BrickObjects. Figure 6.16 shows a complete visual overview of the game with all the platforms in place.

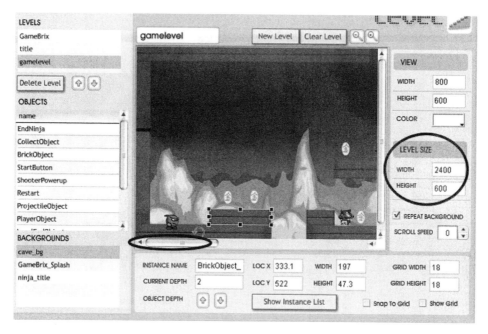

FIGURE 6.15
Object manipulators.

FIGURE 6.16
The complete game room assembled.

Add one `PlayerObject` a few pixels above the `BrickObject` on the lower-left corner, as shown in Figure 6.15. Next, place several instances of the `Enemyobject`, `CollectObject`, and `ShooterPowerup` objects at different locations. Drag the horizontal scroll bar in the Game Assembly Area to the extreme right to view the rightmost end of the level, as shown in Figure 6.17. Place the shrine in the upper-right corner of the game room by dragging and dropping the `LevelEndObject` to the desired location shown in Figure 6.17.

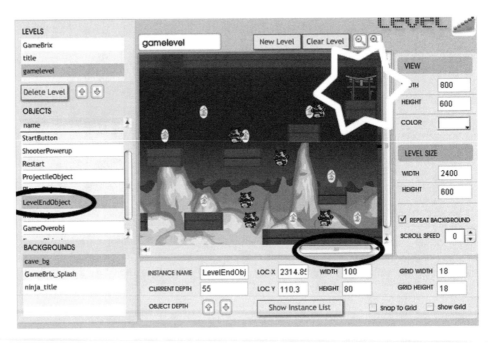

FIGURE 6.17
Placing the shrine.

This completes assembly of the `gamelevel`. You can make the game more difficult by adding more enemies or by making the platforms wider.

ASSEMBLING LEVEL 4

Add another level to the game by clicking on the New Level button. Change the name of this level to `Gameover`, and choose `ninja_title` as the background image. Add a Restart object to the bottom-left corner of this level. Figure 6.18 shows the completely assembled level.

FIGURE 6.18
The Gameover screen.

CREATING THE GAME

Click the Create Game tab, and then click the Preview button.

The game opens in a new window. Make sure your pop-up blocker is turned off so you can see the game.

Congratulations! You have just built your first platform game.

BUILDING THE GAME USING THE PUBLISHER'S APPROACH

The second method to build this platform game is to use a black-box approach and buy the complete source for the game. The game source is kept in the GameBrix system as a GDF file. Click on Store, and search for MomoNinja. Then change the asset type to GDF Files. In the search results, look for the file owned by coolgc, and add this asset to your shopping cart. Then click on the My Cart tab. After you have loaded the shopping cart, scroll down and click the button labeled Buy Now. When the transaction is complete, this GDF file is added to your inventory. The GDF file appears in the section Your Saved Games when you load GameBrix GameBuilder. Open this file and build it directly from the Create Game tab. The game builds with all its glory in one step. You can customize it by clicking the Build Objects tab and modifying each object.

SUMMARY

In this tutorial, you used two methods to create a platform game. The first method involved using raw materials you purchased from the store. The second method involved using the GDF file to build the platform game in a matter of minutes. A third method to build a game involves understanding all the states and tasks to create each of these objects from scratch with or without the use of ActionScript. The next chapter explores creating a banner game.

7 Building a Banner Game

In This Chapter

- Game Description
- Building the Game Using the Designer's Approach
- Building the Objects
- Assembling the Game
- Creating the Game
- Building the Game Using the Publisher's Approach

This chapter describes the process involved in building a banner game that can be used as an adver game. A typical banner game is short, fun, and hosted on Web pages either in horizontal banners or vertical banners. The header, footer, and margin areas of Web sites are typical locations for banner games. They engage the user and build brand awareness of a particular product or service. The Interactive Advertising Bureau (IAB) has guidelines for dimensions of various types of banners. It defines *rich media* as interactive advertisements that users can interact with, as opposed to passive animation. GameBrix.com enables users to generate rich media advertisements in the form of banner games. You can create these games in combination with various technologies including sound and video using Flash ActionScript. A full horizontal banner is 468 pixels wide and 60 pixels high. A vertical skyscraper banner is 160 pixels wide and 600 pixels high.

GAME DESCRIPTION

In the *Antz* banner game, you play an ant whose high tree nest has been invaded by a family of woodpeckers. The attack was swift and unexpected, and all your fellow colony members are now rapidly falling toward the ground. You must save your friends and family by throwing them a leaf. You instruct them to grab hold of the leaf and float safely to the ground.

BUILDING THE GAME USING THE DESIGNER'S APPROACH

Game designers start with a concept document for the storyline in a game; they specify the game sprites required and the game mechanics for intelligence in the game. In building a game using the designer's approach, the first step is to log in to Gamebrix.com if you have not already done so. The next sequence of steps involves obtaining all the images, animations, and intelligence required to build the game. A budget of 36 Brix is required to buy all these items from the online GameBrix store.

IMAGES REQUIRED

Now it's time to get the images required for the banner game from the online GameBrix store. Go to the online store by clicking on the Store link. In the Search by Name text box, type in CG07, and select Images as the content type, as shown in Figure 7.1. The owner of these items is coolgc.

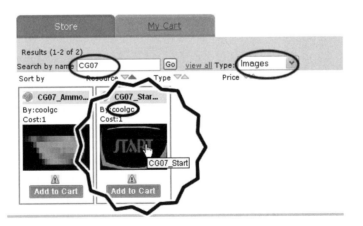

FIGURE 7.1
The required images from the store.

The images required are described in Table 7.1. The name of the item may not be displayed completely as shown in Figure 7.1 if it is longer than 10 characters. Hovering your mouse over the thumbnail of the image should display the full name.

TABLE 7.1 IMAGES REQUIRED

Item Name	Description
CG07_Ammo	The projectile that the player shoots
CG07_Start	The Start button

Buy all the items listed by clicking on the Add to Cart button. After all the items are in your shopping cart, click on the My Cart tab. It may take a few seconds for the system to process items in your cart. The next screen displays your cart contents. The list shows a file name and an item name. If you already have an item in your inventory by the same name, it is displayed in red text. You need to change the name of that item on this screen to avoid name conflicts and overwriting your file. If you have already purchased an item that shows up in red, you can remove it from your shopping cart using the Remove button on the same row. Figure 7.2 shows all the items in the shopping cart.

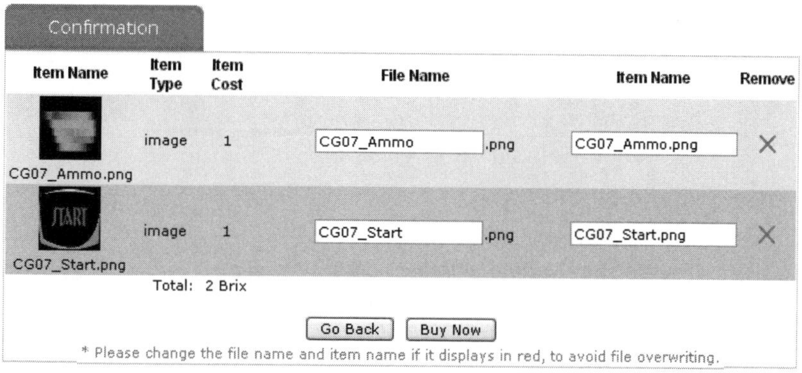

FIGURE 7.2
Items in the shopping cart.

Please change the file name and item name if it displays in red to avoid file overwriting. Click the Buy Now button at the bottom of the screen. The system may take a few moments to process your order. On completion of the transaction, the items are added to your inventory, and the store screen displays. That completes the process of assembling the images required for this game.

ANIMATIONS REQUIRED

The next step is to get all the animations required from the online store by using a process similar to the one you used to get the images. In the Search by Name text box, type in CG07 and select Animation as the content type you are interested in, as shown in Figure 7.3. Again, the owner of these assets is coolgc. The icons displayed for all animations resemble a snippet of camera film. If you are interested in seeing the animation, click on the icon, which displays the animation in a new window. Table 7.2 lists the animations that you need. Buy these items from the store, and complete the purchase just as you did in the earlier section.

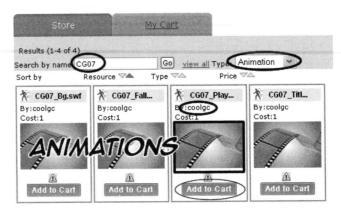

FIGURE 7.3
The required animations from the store.

CG07_Falling is a two-frame animation of the falling ant. Frame 1 is an animation of the ant falling. Frame 2 is an animation of the ant after it touches a leaf that the player shoots to it.

TABLE 7.2 ANIMATIONS REQUIRED

Item Name	Description
CG07_Player	The player
CG07_Falling	The ants that need to be saved
CG07_Bg	The background of the game
CG07_Title	The title screen

INTELLIGENCE REQUIRED

The next step is to get all the intelligence required from the online store. In the Search by Name text box, type in CG07 and select Intelligence as the content type, as shown in Figure 7.4. coolgc owns all the intelligence. The icons displayed for all object intelligence assets resemble a single gear. You cannot view or preview object intelligence directly. You can view it only when you use it inside GameBrix Game-Builder. Table 7.3 lists the intelligence that you need. Buy these items from the store, and complete the purchase just as you did in the earlier section.

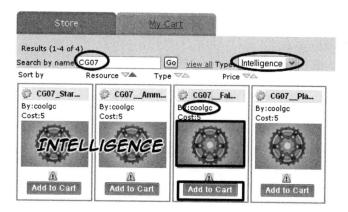

FIGURE 7.4
The required object intelligence assets from the store.

TABLE 7.3 INTELLIGENCE REQUIRED

Item Name	Description
CG07_AmmoIntl	Bullet/projectile intelligence
CG07_FallingIntl	Behavior for ants that are falling
CG07_PlayerIntl	Player (arrow keys and spacebar)
CG07_StartIntl	Start button

BUILDING THE OBJECTS

With all the raw materials in place, it's time to start building the game objects. Open the GameBrix Builder by clicking on the large tab labeled Builder. When the application loads, you are, by default, at the Import Graphics screen.

On the left side of the screen is a set of images and animations in your library. Select the following images, and add them to the Sprites section on the right, as shown in Figure 7.5.

- CG07_Ammo
- CG07_Falling
- CG07_Player
- CG07_Start

Select the following images, and move them to the Backgrounds section on the right:

- CG07_Bg
- CG07_Title

It's time to build game objects. Click on the Build Objects tab and then on the New Object button. That takes you to the screen shown in Figure 7.6. Choose the image named CG07_Ammo from the list of images displayed under the Select Graphics label. Name the object AmmoObj by typing it in the Object Name text box. Then click the Done button to complete creation of the AmmoObj object.

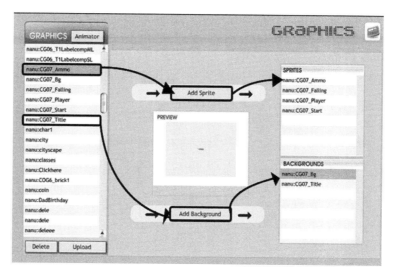

FIGURE 7.5
Assembling the sprites.

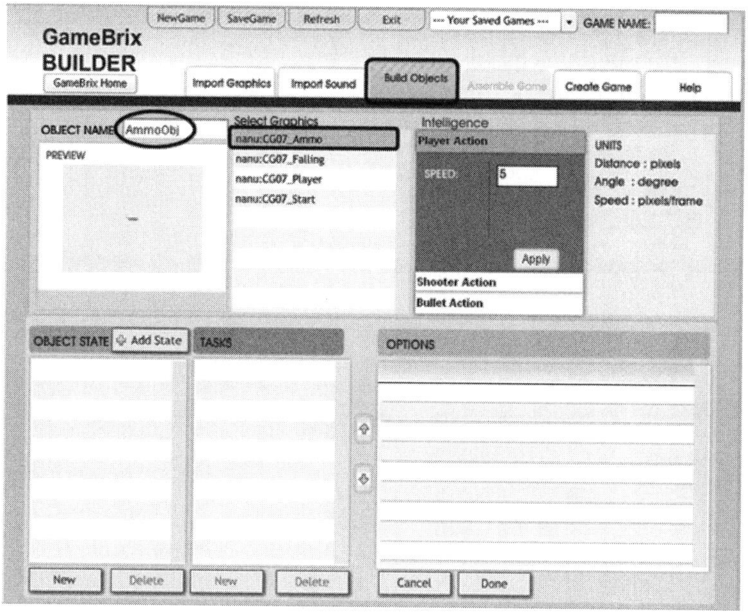

FIGURE 7.6
Object creation process.

Repeat this step and create the other objects listed in Table 7.4. The table lists their object names and the images or animations that are attached to them. Please note that the object names you type are case sensitive and have to match the ones provided in Table 7.4. Your game might not function with incorrect object names.

TABLE 7.4 OBJECTS REQUIRED

Object Name	Image/Animation Required
AmmoObj	CG07_Ammo
FallingObj	CG07_Falling
PlayerObj	CG07_Player
StartObj	CG07_Start

After creating all the objects, click the SaveGame button shown in Figure 7.7. Provide a title and description when you save. The file name should not contain spaces or special symbols. A dialog box signals the completion of the SaveGame process. Click the OK button to proceed.

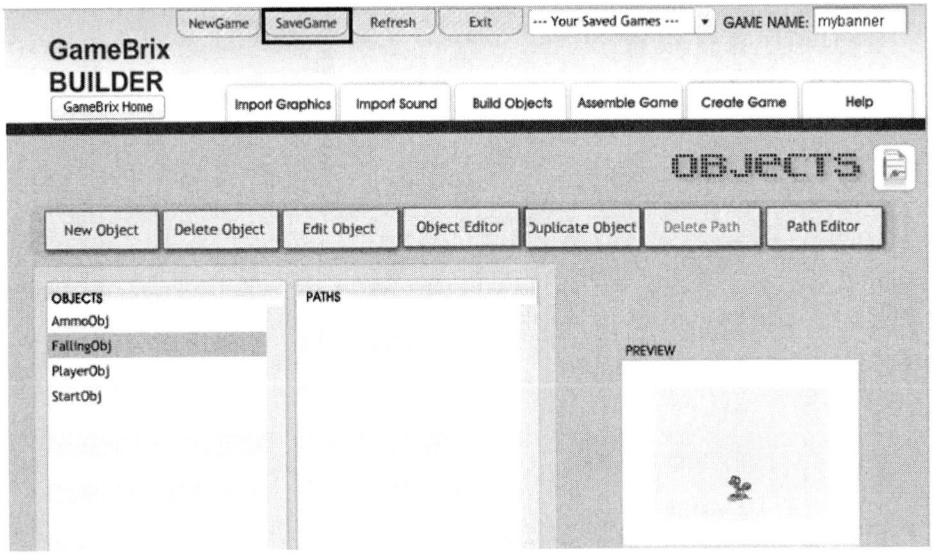

FIGURE 7.7
Object creation process.

It's time to use the Object Editor to add behavioral intelligence to your objects. Click on the button labeled Object Editor shown in Figure 7.7, which opens the Object Editor window. Descriptions of all areas of the Object Editor were provided in Chapter 6, "Building a Platform Game." See Figure 6.8 to refresh your memory.

Here are the things of importance to note:

- The list of objects present in the Game Objects section
- The contents of the Intelligence section
- The empty section labeled World Vars

Select the object named FallingObj by clicking on it in the Game Objects section. Then double-click on CG07_FallingIntl in the Intelligence section. You are prompted with a dialog box asking you if you want to overwrite your object's behavior. Click Yes. That should populate the object with one or more states and tasks, as shown in Figure 7.8.

That completes the creation of the CG07_FallingObj object.

Perform the same sequence of steps to create all the other objects listed in Table 7.5. Keep in mind that different objects require different intelligence assigned to them. Table 7.5 lists all the objects and the appropriate intelligence they require.

TABLE 7.5 INTELLIGENCE ASSIGNMENT

Object Name	Intelligence Required
FallingObj	CG07_FallingIntl
AmmoObj	CG07_AmmoIntl
PlayerObj	CG07_PlayerIntl
StartObj	CG07_StartIntl

All the required objects have been created. This game requires two world variables. *World variables* are pieces of information that are shared across all objects in the game. Normally, each game object has access only to the information that belongs to it. But sometimes information needs to be shared across all objects in a game. That's when world variables are used. This game requires two world variables: one to keep track of the score and the other the speed with which the objects come down.

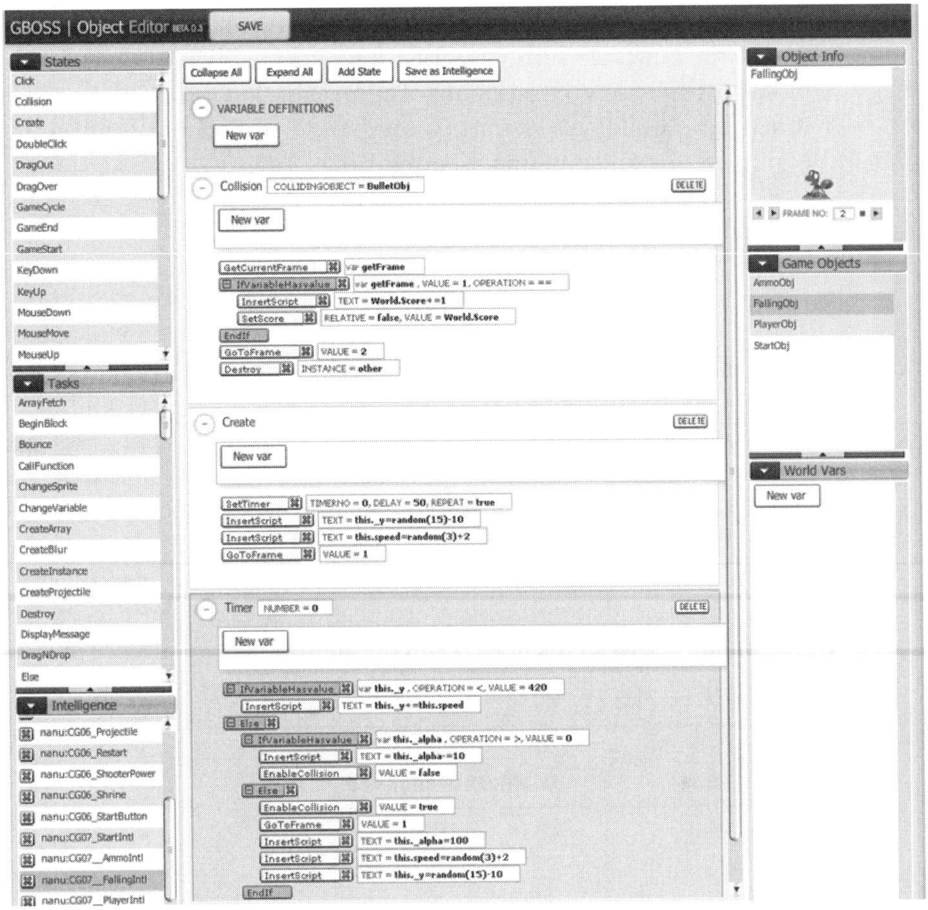

FIGURE 7.8
Populated Object Editor screen.

Click the New Var button in the Object Editor, as shown in Figure 7.9. The Variable Editor dialog box is displayed. Carefully enter data into this dialog box using information provided in Table 7.6 to create the score variable. Again, variable names are case sensitive, and the game may not work with incorrect variables names.

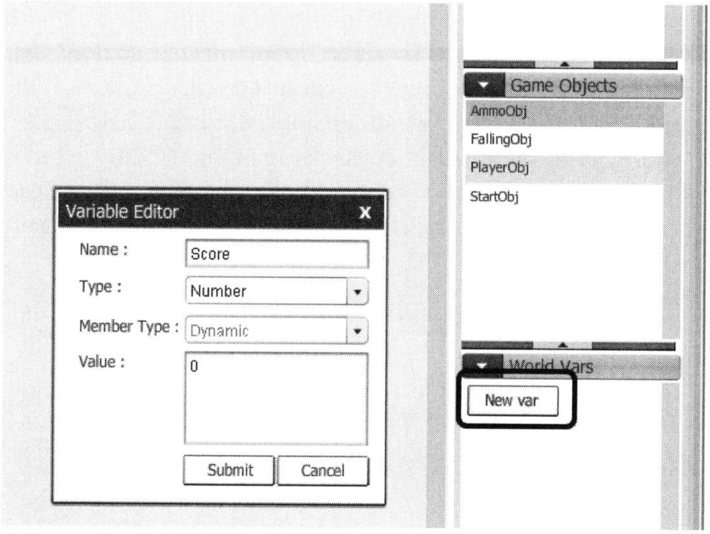

FIGURE 7.9
Creating world variables.

TABLE 7.6 WORLD VARIABLES

Variable Name	Variable Type	Member Type	Value
Score	Number	Dynamic	0
FallingSpeed	Number	Dynamic	3

Next, create the variable named `FallingSpeed` using information provided in Table 7.6. The two variables are visible under the World Vars section shown in Figure 7.10.

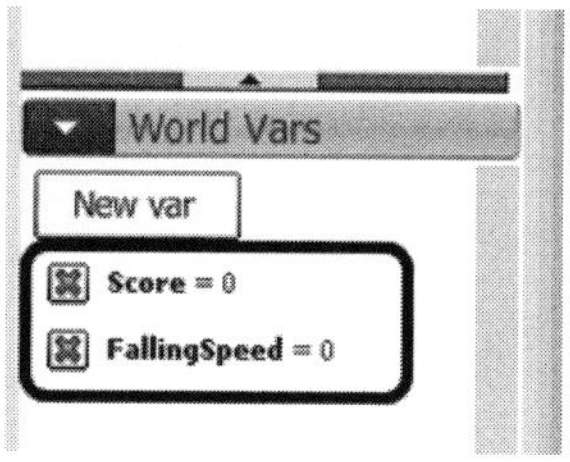

FIGURE 7.10
World variables initialized.

After you've created the two world variables, click the Save button found at the top of the Object Editor screen. This is an important step, so don't skip it. A message box displays the message `Save complete`. Close it by clicking the OK button. You can then minimize the Object Editor window using the standard Microsoft Windows Minimize button found in the top-right corner of the Object Editor window. That brings you back to the Build Objects screen that also displays the message `Game ready to build`, as shown in Figure 7.11. Click the OK button to continue the game creation process.

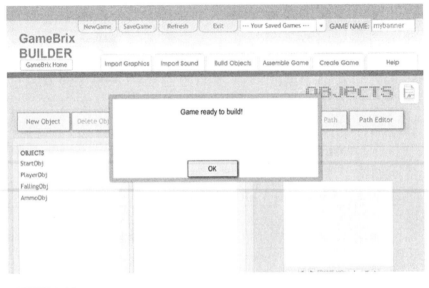

FIGURE 7.11
`Game ready to build` screen.

ASSEMBLING THE GAME

Now that all your objects are ready, it's time for the fun part of assembling the game and testing it. Click the Assemble Game tab. This screen has several buttons and fields. The area on the left labeled Levels lists all the levels that you have created. Level 1 is always created by default.

LEVEL DESCRIPTION

The Objects area lists all the objects that you have created. These are the toys you get to play with in the Assemble Game tab. In the center is the Game Assembly Area. Figure 6.12 in Chapter 6 describes all areas of the Assemble Game tab.

This game has two levels: a title screen and the game screen.

ASSEMBLING LEVEL 1

Assembling the title screen with a Start button is simple. First change the name of the level to title. Then change the width and height of both the Level and View Size areas to 160×500. Select CG07_Title as the background by clicking on it from the Backgrounds list. Click and drag the object named StartObj onto the area displaying the Play message from the title graphic. Click on StartObj, and resize it to completely overlap the Play message displayed in the title graphic. The Play message will be hidden by the StartObj. The Start button for the game, title, room size, and background used are shown in Figure 7.12. That completes the Level 1 assembly process.

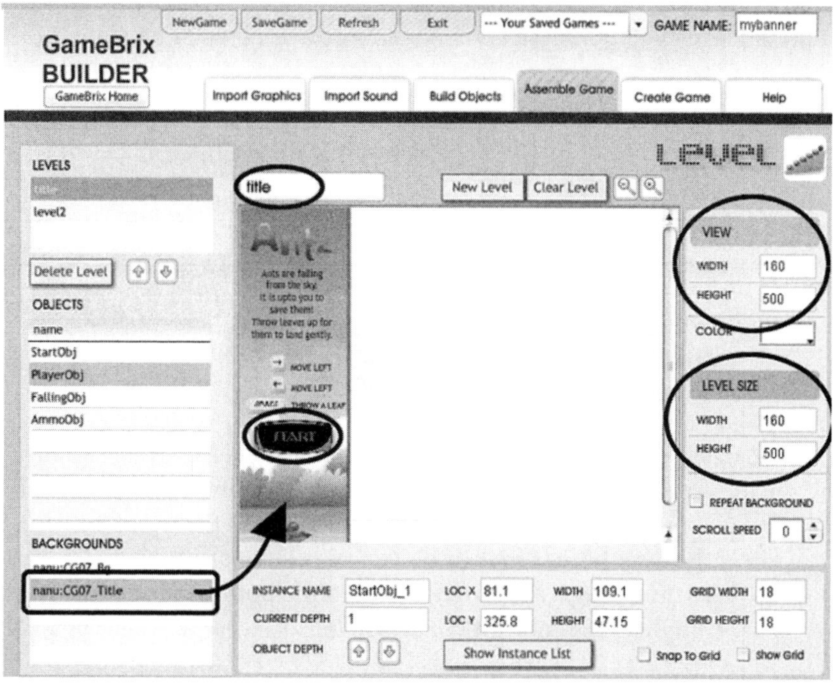

FIGURE 7.12
Level 1 assembled.

ASSEMBLING LEVEL 2

Create a second level by clicking the New Level button. This level houses the actual game. Name the level gamelevel, and set both the Level and View Size areas to be 160×500.

Click the background labeled CG07_Bg, and place it in the Game Assembly Area, as shown in Figure 7.13.

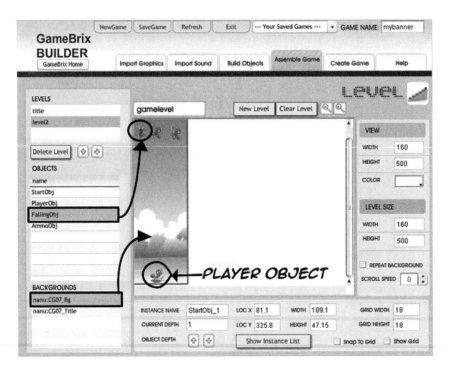

FIGURE 7.13
The complete game room assembled.

Click and drag an instance of the object named FallingObj to the top-left corner of the vertical banner. Place one more instance on the top-right corner of the banner, and place a third instance between the two others at the top of the banner. Figure 7.13 shows the three objects in their respective positions.

Click and drag a PlayerObj object to the bottom of the Game Assembly Area. That completes assembly of the gamelevel.

CREATING THE GAME

Next, click the Create Game tab, and then click the Preview button. The game opens in a new window. Make sure your pop-up blocker is turned off so you can see the game.

Congratulations! You have just built your first banner game!

BUILDING THE GAME USING THE PUBLISHER'S APPROACH

The second method to build this banner game is to use a black-box approach and buy the complete source for the game. The game source is kept in the GameBrix system as a GDF file. Click on Store, and search for CG07_Banner. Then change the asset type to GDF Files. In the search results, look for the file owned by coolgc, and add this asset to your shopping cart. Then click on the My Cart tab. After you have loaded the shopping cart, scroll down and click the Buy Now button. When the transaction is complete, this GDF file is added to your inventory. The GDF file appears in the section Your Saved Games when you load GameBrix GameBuilder. Open this file and build it directly from the Create Game tab. The game builds with all its glory in one step. You can customize it by clicking the Build Objects tab and modifying each object. To ensure good visual performance, the IAB Ad Sizes Working Group recommends a maximum of 18 frames per second when you're creating animated sprites in a banner game.

SUMMARY

In this tutorial, you used the GameBrix Builder to create a vertical banner game. With this knowledge, you can create and publish any kind of banner for a Web site. The next chapter looks at the basics of how to use ActionScript 2.0 inside games and how to debug games.

8 Scripting with ActionScript 2.0

In This Chapter

- Understanding Objects
- ActionScript 2.0 Basics
- Experimenting with GameBrix Objects
- Rotating the Object
- Using Math Functions
- Debugging in GameBrix
- Using Variables
- Masking Example

Creating interactive animation and games involves a lot of behind-the-scenes computation, most of which the user never sees. For example, to realistically simulate a ball falling under gravitational force, you need to apply Newton's laws of physics. The application of Newton's laws of motion in this scenario may be easy from a programmer's perspective but may seem quite esoteric from a creative designer's perspective.

Although GameBrix hides such complex algorithms, it sometimes becomes necessary to use the power of Adobe's scripting language, ActionScript 2.0, to take a project the extra mile. Used in conjunction with the GameBrix applications, ActionScript is similar to a Swiss Army knife; it is a versatile tool that you can use to complete virtually any task within a Flash application. You can build complete games using only ActionScript. This chapter covers the basics of version 2.0.

UNDERSTANDING OBJECTS

Before this chapter delves into scripting, you need to understand the concept of a Flash MovieClip. In GameBrix, every GameBrix game object is an extended version of a Flash MovieClip. So the terms *Flash MovieClip* and *GameBrix object* are synonymous and interchangeable in this book.

Games are essentially interactive simulations. For realistic simulations, you need a variety of game objects that can take on different roles. You can view it as a play acted onstage, with different objects taking the roles of various characters. Each object has a costume that is appropriate for it, as well as a programmed behavior to emulate the fictional character it represents. Building an object is similar to getting an actor ready for a theatrical performance. The game object has to be given instructions, or programmed, and it must be dressed appropriately for the role.

Assembling all these objects onstage and having them perform their parts results in the creation of a game. In a stage play, the audience does not control the behavior and sequence of events about to unfold on the stage; it is predefined. However, in a game, the audience, or the player, controls the sequence. This may be likened to an improvisational play, in which the audience can give the actors a cue card or list of topics.

For example, one player may instruct the hunter to pick up food and then instruct the boy to catch the butterfly, whereas the other may start the game or play in a different way.

The hunter knows to pick up food, and the boy knows to catch the butterfly. They are intelligent objects that know to perform certain tasks when events occur. In GameBrix game objects, the occurrence of various external events transfers an object to a corresponding object state.

For human beings, common states include the sleepy state, the awakened state, the hungry state, the happy state, and more. In simple terms, if the body triggers a tired event, the body moves into the sleepy state. Different external and internal events move a game object from one state to another. Defining a set of unique tasks to be performed when objects move from one state to another creates a compelling game. The interaction of these various objects results in an interesting game.

Game objects can be in one of several states at any moment in time. See the Appendix, "Object States and Tasks." Four commonly used states in this chapter are listed in Table 8.1.

TABLE 8.1 COMMON OBJECT STATES

Item Name	Description
Click state	The object goes into this state when it is clicked on and receives a click event.
Create state	The object goes into this state as soon as it is "born," or created in the game.
KeyDown state	The object goes into this state when a certain key is pressed.
KeyUp state	The object goes into this state when a certain key is released.

ACTIONSCRIPT 2.0 BASICS

ActionScript 2.0 (AS2) forms the core component of all the GameBrix games. Although ActionScript 1.0 (AS1) is also supported in GameBrix, it is not object oriented and is not recommended for use. AS2 is an object-oriented programming language used to control the behavior of Flash objects and GameBrix objects. Flash objects encompass all SWF content created using the Adobe Flash Integrated Development Environment (IDE). GameBrix objects include all the objects created within the GameBrix Builder application.

GameBrix game objects have properties just as real-world objects do. For example, some of the properties of a real-world car are listed in Table 8.2. You can change properties of game objects quite easily, unlike those of real-world objects. Changing the color of a game object can be done in a matter of minutes, but changing the color of a car may take a few days in a workshop. Table 8.3 lists some of the commonly used customizable properties of a game object.

TABLE 8.2 CAR OBJECT PROPERTIES

Property Name	Property Value	Property Description
Weight	4800	The car weighs 4,800 pounds.
Color	Red	The car is red.
Current Speed	25	The car is traveling at 25mph.
Maximum Speed	100	The car's maximum speed is 100mph.
Wheel Count	4	The car has four wheels.

TABLE 8.3 IMPORTANT GAMEBRIX GAME OBJECT PROPERTIES

Property Name	Property Value	Property Description
_x	120	Object's horizontal offset from the top-left corner
_y	100	Object's vertical offset from the top-left corner
_name	car	Object's name
_target	/level1/car	Complete "name" of the object (path included)
_alpha	100	Object's opacity value
_xscale	100	Horizontal scale of the object
_yscale	100	Vertical scale of the object
_rotation	120	Angle of the object's rotation
_visible	true	Visibility of the object
_width	24	Width of the object in pixels
_height	45	Height of the object in pixels

Apart from properties, GameBrix objects have several tasks they can perform by default. Being built on top of Adobe Flash technology, GameBrix game objects inherit a set of common tasks from the Flash MovieClip object that they can perform. Some of the more common tasks are listed in Table 8.4. Please see the Adobe Flash documentation for more details on these tasks.

TABLE 8.4 TASKS DIRECTLY MAPPED TO ACTIONSCRIPT 2.0

Task Name	Task Description
lineTo	Draws a line to a specified location
getURL	Loads a specified Web page
getDepth	Gets the object's depth
createTextField	Creates a text field
curveTo	Draws a curve to a selected location
duplicate	Makes a clone of this object
unloadMovie	Removes the object
attachMovie	Attaches a new object

EXPERIMENTING WITH GAMEBRIX OBJECTS

This section investigates the inner details of GameBrix objects with a couple of ex-amples. Referring to a property directly and assigning it a name can change it. For example, to rotate an object by 45 degrees, you can use the following command:

```
_rotation = 45;
```

Objects have tasks they can perform, as seen in Table 8.4. You can embed a set of tasks inside an entity within the object, called a *method*. You can call object methods directly to perform a set of commands. By default, every GameBrix object has a set of methods for performing high-level tasks. For example, to navigate to a Web page, you can invoke the following method available within every object:

```
getURL("http://www.gamebrix.com");
```

Apart from changing an object's own properties, it is also possible to use that object to change properties of other objects using the object's full name and prop-erty name. The following experiments require a test object. Build a brickObject as shown in Figure 8.1, and add the Click state. You will add various tasks to this object to perform different diagnostic tests.

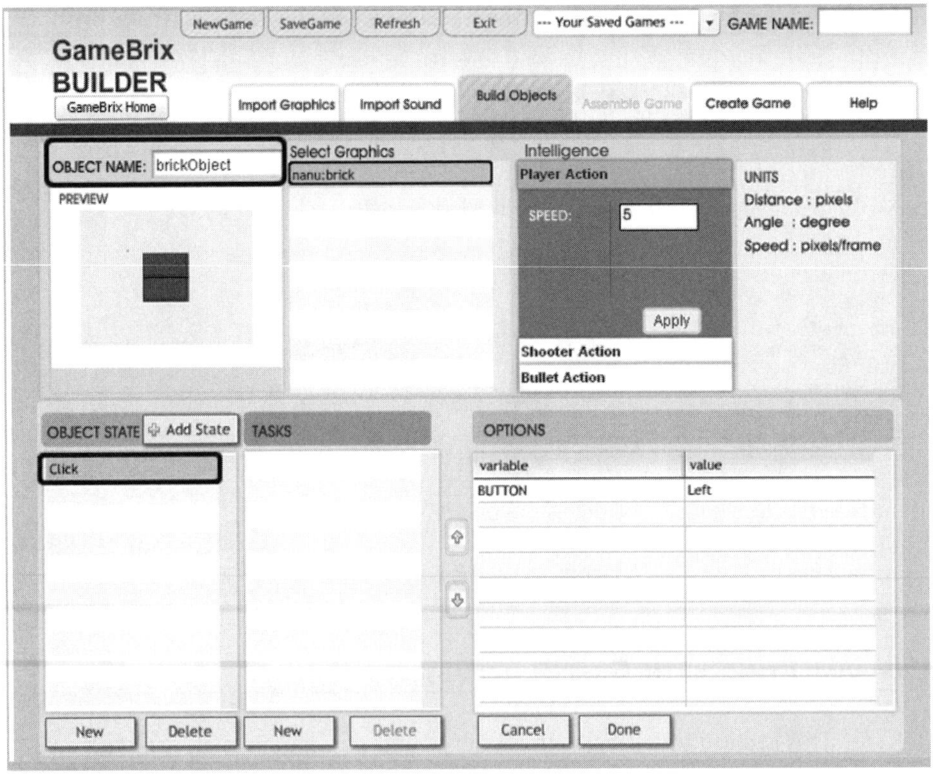

FIGURE 8.1
The default test object.

USING THE TRACE FACILITY

It's time to look at mechanisms to display properties of GameBrix objects. This will be useful for investigation purposes when objects do not work as planned. The Trace task displays all the inner details of game objects. A buggy game object is like a sick patient in a hospital. Just as doctors use a stethoscope to read the vital signs of a sick patient, the game developer uses the Trace command to read and display information from GameBrix game objects.

Starting with the default test object shown in Figure 8.1, add a Trace task to the Click state. Click on the Message option, and type in Hello World! as shown in Figure 8.2. Then click the Apply button, leaving the Expression value at its default option value of false.

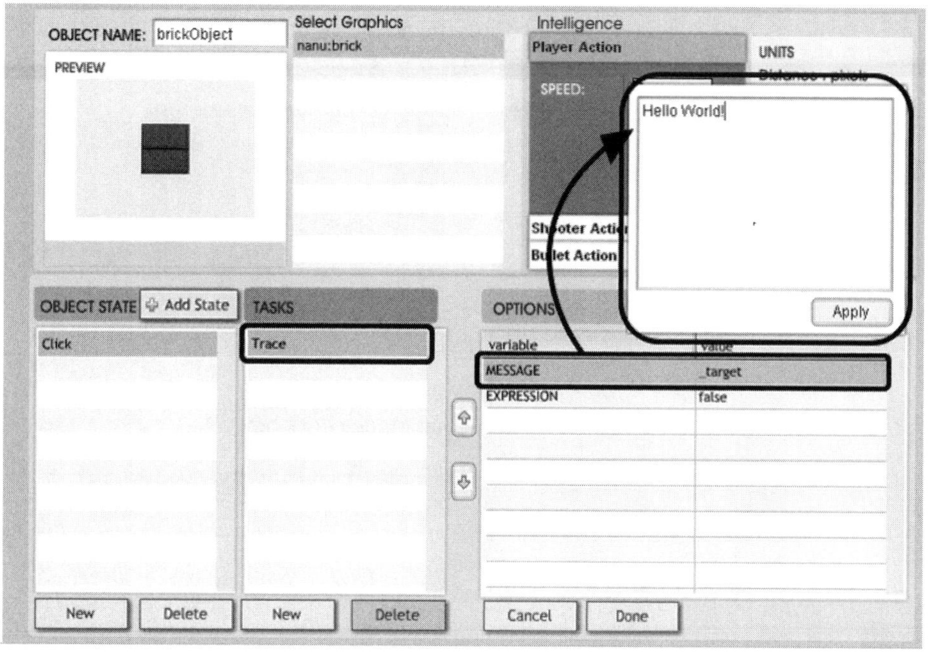

FIGURE 8.2
The `Trace` command.

Click the Done button to complete creation of the test object. Then go to the Assemble Game tab and drag and drop a single instance of `brickObject`, the test object, onto the Game Assembly Area. Click the Create Game Tab, noting the presence of the Debug Mode check box. This check box is used in conjunction with the `Trace` command. Enabling the Debug Mode check box opens a debug window when the game is running. All output from the `Trace` command is displayed in this Debug window.

Enable the Debug Mode check box as shown on Figure 8.3, and then click on the Preview Game button. Click on the Play Game button. Then click on the `brickObject`. Every click displays the message `Hello World!` in the Debug window, as shown in Figure 8.4.

FIGURE 8.3
The Debug Mode check box.

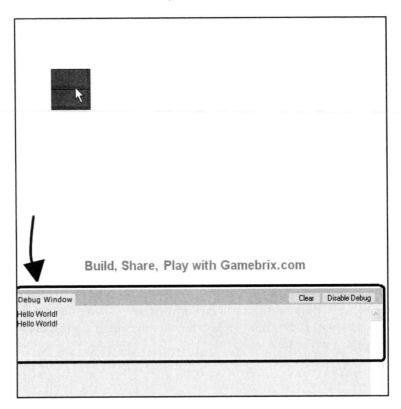

FIGURE 8.4
Messages in the Debug window.

Now it's time to display some properties of brickObject. Replace the string Hello World! by typing in the following string for the Trace command shown in Figure 8.5. This time, set the expression option set to true.

```
"My full name is " + _target + " and my short name is " + _name
```

In the previous expression, four pieces of information are combined, or *concatenated*, using the plus operator and then displayed. The first part consists of the following string:

```
"My full name is "
```

Strings are always enclosed in double quotes. The second part of the string is the concatenation operator (+) followed by the name of the property (_target) to be displayed, as shown here:

```
+ _target
```

The third part is the concatenation operator followed by another string, as follows:

```
" and my short name is "
```

The fourth part is the concatenation operator followed by the property name (_name), as shown here:

```
+ _name
```

Now when you click on the brickObject in the game, you see the following message:

```
My full name is _level1/myGameController/level1/brickObject_1 and my
short name is brickObject_1
```

The short name displayed as brickObject_1 is actually the instance name. The property _target defines the complete path to the object. It serves as a resource locator that defines the complete path to the object.

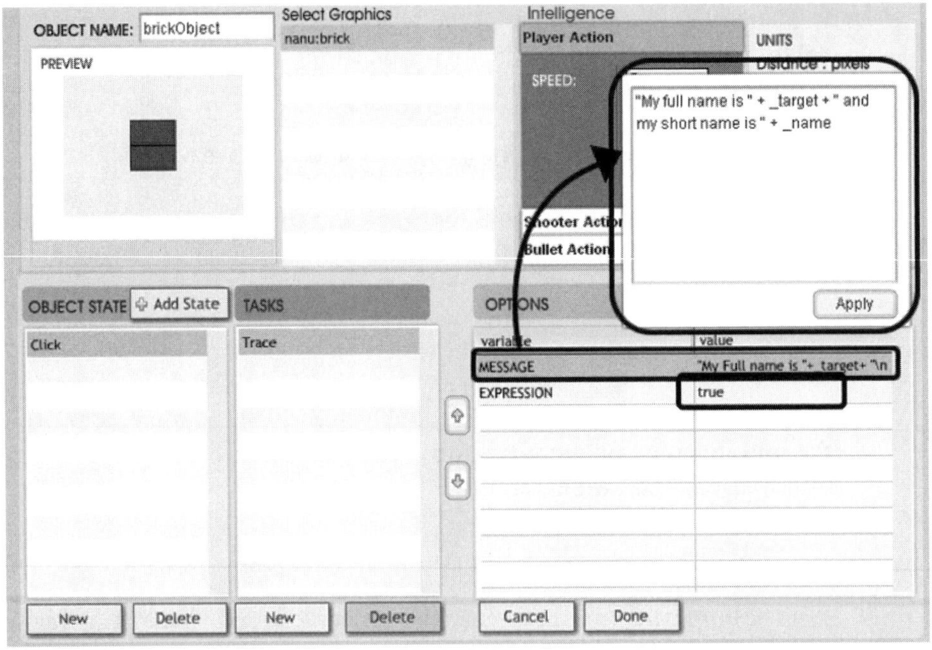

FIGURE 8.5
The Trace command.

Go back to the Assemble Game tab and place a few more instances of the brick-Object. Then build the game. Clicking on each of the brickObjects displays the complete name of the instance. Note that instance names are unique, as shown here:

```
My full name is _level1/myGameController/level1/brickObject_1 and my
short name is brickObject_1
My full name is _level1/myGameController/level1/brickObject_2 and my
short name is brickObject_2
My full name is _level1/myGameController/level1/brickObject_3 and my
short name is brickObject_3
```

Instance names have an underscore appended to the object name followed by a number that is incremented for each instance that is created. brickObject_2 is the second instance, and brickObject_3 is the third instance created.

Use the Trace command to display all properties of the object. Table 8.5 shows a few more examples of the Trace command that you can use.

TABLE 8.5 TRACE COMMAND EXAMPLES

Trace Command	Description
`"Objects X location = " + _x`	Shows the object's X coordinate
`"Objects Y location = " + _y`	Shows the object's Y coordinate
`"Object width = " + _width`	Displays the object's width
`"Object height = " + _height`	Displays the object's height

MOVING THE OBJECT

Every GameBrix game object has properties that define its X and Y coordinates. You can move game objects by incrementally changing their X and Y coordinates. You can set properties of objects directly by using the `InsertScript` command. The `InsertScript` command requires the use of AS2.

You can access or set properties of objects using the dot notation syntax. The typical syntax for setting an object's property is shown here:

```
Objectname.propertyname = value;
```

Objectname refers to the object's name. You can either use its full name or, if the object is accessing its own properties (rather than accessing the properties of another object), you can use the keyword `this` as the object name. The *property name* can be any of those listed in Table 8.3. The value assigned to the property is provided after the equal sign. The semicolon at the end signifies the end of any AS2 command.

Table 8.6 shows a few examples of using the `this` keyword to set an object's own properties.

If properties of an object are to be displayed from within the object, you can omit the `this` keyword. So the following two statements are identical:

```
this._x = 20;
_x = 20;
```

You can set properties of other objects only by using the complete name of the object. The format follows:

```
CompleteObjectName.property = value;
```

TABLE 8.6 COMMANDS USING THE THIS KEYWORD

Command	Description
`this._x = 20;`	Sets the current object's X location
`this._x = this._x + 20;`	Adds 20 pixels to the current object's X location
`this._x += 20;`	Adds 20 pixels to the current object's X location
`this._y = 40;`	Sets the current object's Y location
`this._width = 48;`	Sets the current object's width to 48

From the previous section, the full names of objects were of the form

```
_level1/myGameController/level1/brickObject_1
```

To set properties of this object, you need to use dot notation to define the object. Replacing every front slash (/) with a period (.) converts the name to the dot notation format shown here:

```
_level1.myGameController.level1.brickObject_1
```

To set this object's X location to 20, use the following command:

```
_level1.myGameController.level1.brickObject_1._x = 20;
```

To add 20 to this object's X location, use the following AS2 command:

```
_level1.myGameController.level1.brickObject_1._x += 20;
```

Using the same `brickObject` that you used earlier, delete all the tasks in the `Click` state. Add an `InsertScript` task instead, as shown in Figure 8.6. In the Text Field Value option box, type in the command

```
_level1.myGameController.level1.brickObject_1._x += 20;
```

This command moves the `brickObject_1` instance 20 pixels to the right on every click. Build the game and run it. Then click on any brick in the game. The brick instance named `brickObject_1` should move to the right on every click. If nothing moved, either you typed the command incorrectly or the instance named `brickObject_1` does not exist in the game. To view the Instance Name of the `brickObject`, go to the Assemble Game room and click on the instance of the object. The name is displayed in the Instance Name text box found at the lower left. When placing and deleting objects from the room, the Instance Number of the object changes. Table 8.7 lists the state and tasks required for this example.

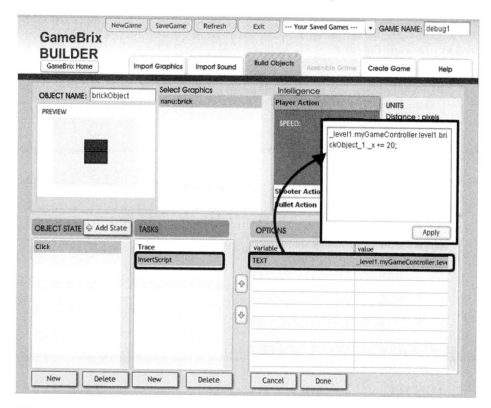

FIGURE 8.6
The InsertScript task.

TABLE 8.7 BRICKOBJECT STATE AND TASK FOR MOVEMENT

State	Task	Text Option
Click	InsertScript	_level1.myGameController.level1.brickObject_1._x += 20;

When you click and select instances in the Assemble Game tab, short names of instances are displayed next to the Instance Name text box, found under the Game Assembly Area. If the full name is required, use the Trace command to display it.

ROTATING THE OBJECT

Modifying the _rotation property can rotate an instance of an object. Using the same brickObject, change the InsertScript task as shown in Figure 8.7 to execute the command:

```
this._rotation += 20;
```

Build the game and run it. When any of the brick instances are clicked, only the brickObject_2 instance rotates by 20 degrees.

If you only need to rotate the instance named brickObject_2, use the command:

```
_level1.myGameController.level1.brickObject_2._rotation += 20;
```

Try this command using the InsertScript task. Clicking on any brickObject instance rotates the instance named brickObject_2 by 20 degrees. Table 8.8 lists the state and tasks required for this example.

TABLE 8.8 BRICKOBJECT STATE AND TASKS FOR ROTATION

State	Task	Text Option
Click	InsertScript	_level1.myGameController.level1.brickObject_2._rotation += 20;

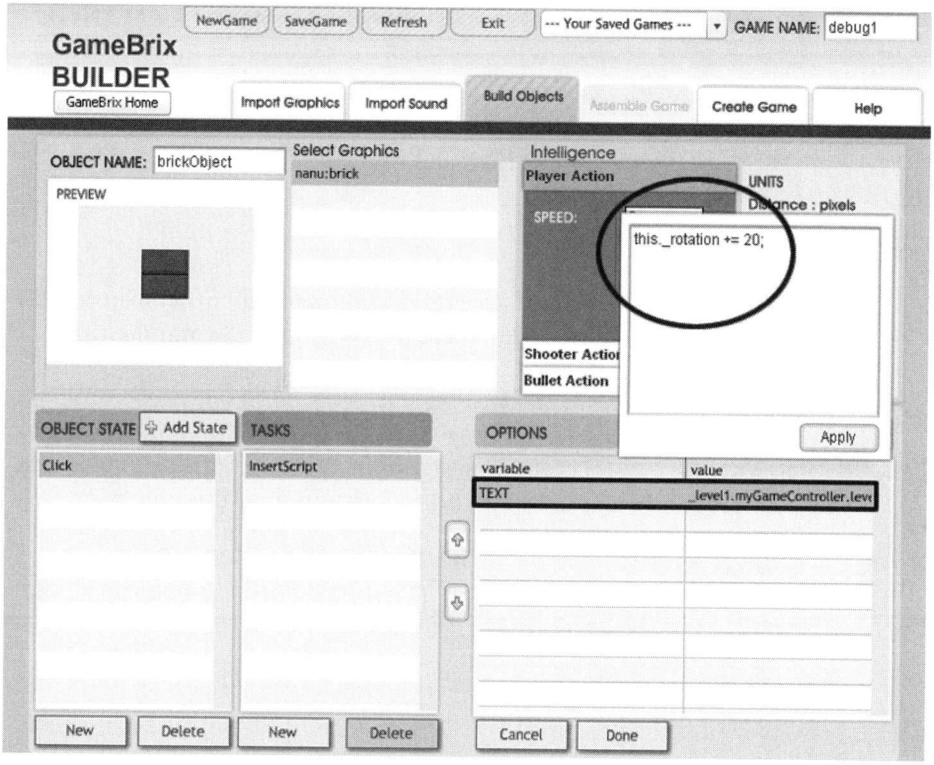

FIGURE 8.7
The rotation command.

MAKING AN OBJECT TRANSPARENT

Modifying the _alpha property can change the transparency of an object. The lower an object's _alpha property, the more transparent the object will be. Using the same test object, change the InsertScript task to execute the following command:

```
this._alpha -= 5;
```

This command reduces the _alpha of the instance by 5 percent. Since this command is executed on every mouse click, the instance clicked on becomes more transparent with every click.

If the following command is used in the Click state, only the instance named brickObject_2 becomes transparent on every click. Table 8.9 lists the states and tasks required for this example.

```
_level1.myGameController.level1.brickObject_2._alpha -= 5;
```

TABLE 8.9 BRICKOBJECT STATE AND TASK FOR ALPHA CHANGE

State	Task	Text Option
Click	InsertScript	_level1.myGameController.level1.brickObject_2._alpha -= 5;

JUMPING TO A WEB SITE

GameBrix game objects can have embedded intelligence that instructs the browser to load a specific Web page. This is done using the AS2 command:

```
getURL("http://www.gamebrix.com");
```

Modify the InsertScript task to run the previous command when the object is clicked. Table 8.10 lists the state and task required for this example.

TABLE 8.10 BRICKOBJECT STATE AND TASK FOR GETURL

State	Task	Text Option
Click	InsertScript	getURL("http://www.gamebrix.com");

USING MATH FUNCTIONS

AS2 has several built-in functions that you can use while building GameBrix game objects. One of them is a set of math functions. Using the InsertScript command, you can invoke all the built-in Flash functions. Here are a few examples.

To set the X coordinate of an object to a random number between 0 and 10, use the following math function:

```
this._x = Math.random()*10;
```

The ActionScript function Math.random() randomly generates a value that is greater than or equal to 0 and less than 1. Multiply this value by 10 to get a number between 0 and 10. To test this command, use the brickObject. Set the object to execute the InsertScript task in the Click state, as shown in Table 8.11, instead of the earlier AS2 command. Create the game and click on any brickObject. The brickObject will move to a random position that is a distance between 0 and 10 pixels horizontally from the origin.

TABLE 8.11 BRICKOBJECT STATE AND TASK FOR MATH.RANDOM

State	Task	Text Option
Click	InsertScript	this._x = Math.random()*10;

To generate a number between 20 and 25, you need a combination of two Math functions.

```
this._x = 20 + Math.floor(Math.random()*5);
```

Math.random()*5 generates values between 0 and 5. The floor function removes the fractional part of the number. Applying the Math.floor function results in a number that is greater than 0 and less than or equal to 5. Adding 20 to this result gives an integer in the range between 20 and 25.

Another Math function of interest is max, which returns the larger of two numbers that it has passed. In the following example, _x is assigned the value 200:

```
this._x = Math.max(100,200);
```

Similarly, there is a min function that can be used the following way:

```
this._x = Math.min(100,200);
```

DEBUGGING IN GAMEBRIX

You debug objects in GameBrix using the Trace command. The Trace command can display all kinds of data but is especially useful in displaying information about values held in variables. The Trace command displays results only when the Debug flag is checked in the Create Game tab. Here are some examples of Trace commands to display the contents of different variables.

To display the contents of a variable called myHealth, you can use the following Trace command:

```
Trace ("myhealth = "+ myHealth);
```

To display the contents of a world variable called enemyCount, you can use this Trace command:

```
Trace ("enemyCount = " + World.enemyCount);
```

To display the X and Y coordinates of the mouse, use this:

```
Trace ("Mouse X = " + root_xmouse + " Mouse Y position = " +
root._ymouse);
```

GameBrix provides two `ActionScript` commands for tracing: the `InsertScript` and the `Trace` task. Static information to be displayed in a `Trace` task is enclosed inside parentheses. Variables to be displayed are not parenthesized. For example, the `Trace` command shown next uses static content in parentheses and variables:

```
Trace ("myhealth =   + myHealth);
```

becomes the `Trace` task in GameBrix Builder, as shown in Table 8.12.

TABLE 8.12 EXAMPLE TRACE TASK

State	Task	Text Option	Expression
Click	Trace	"myhealth = " + myHealth	true

The `Trace` task is built on principles similar to the AS2 `Trace` command. All tracing functionality available within the AS2 `Trace` command is available with the GameBrix `Trace` task.

USING VARIABLES

Variables are storage areas to hold numbers, text, arrays, and other types of data. GameBrix supports three types of variables with different access scopes. *World variables* in GameBrix are variables that you can access from anywhere. *Class variables* are accessible from within the instance of the object. *Local variables* are accessible within the function where they are defined. Figure 8.8 shows the three buttons used to create these types of variables.

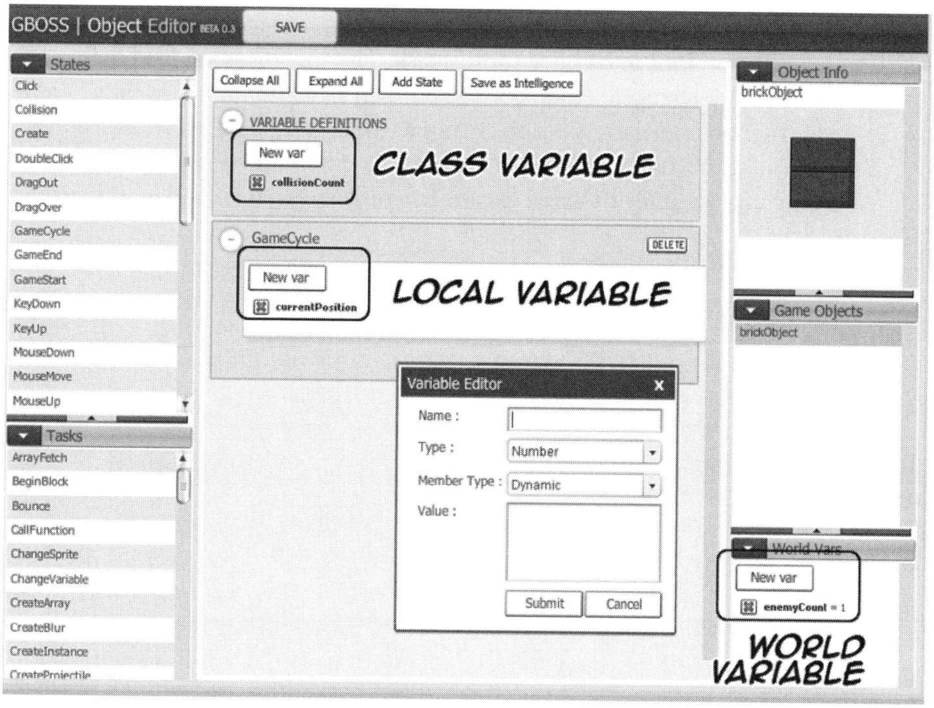

FIGURE 8.8
Creating variables.

You can create all three kinds of variables from the Object Editor screen. Clicking the New Var button in the bottom right of the screen creates world variables. Existing world variables are displayed in the box at the bottom-right corner of the Object Editor screen. Class variables are created by clicking the New Var button at the top of the object definition area in Figure 8.8. All existing class variables are listed beneath this button. You can create class variables as static variables or dynamic variables. If you choose the static option, all instances of the class have only one unique copy of the variable that they share. If one instance modifies the variable, the others can see the change. Dynamic variables are different; every instance has its own copy of the variable. So if one instance modifies the variable, the change is not visible to other instances.

Clicking the New Var button found under every state that has been added to the object can create local variables. Figure 8.8 shows the New Var button used to create local variables for the GameCycle event. All local variables that have already been created are listed under this button.

You can modify all types of variables using the ChangeVariable task. Figure 8.9 shows the options to be filled for this task. The VariableName field defines which variable is being changed. Adding a prefix, such as World, to the variable name changes world variables. For example, to change a world variable called enemyCount, the variable name used in the ChangeVariable option box should be World.enemyCount. Directly typing in the name of a variable can change class variables and local variables.

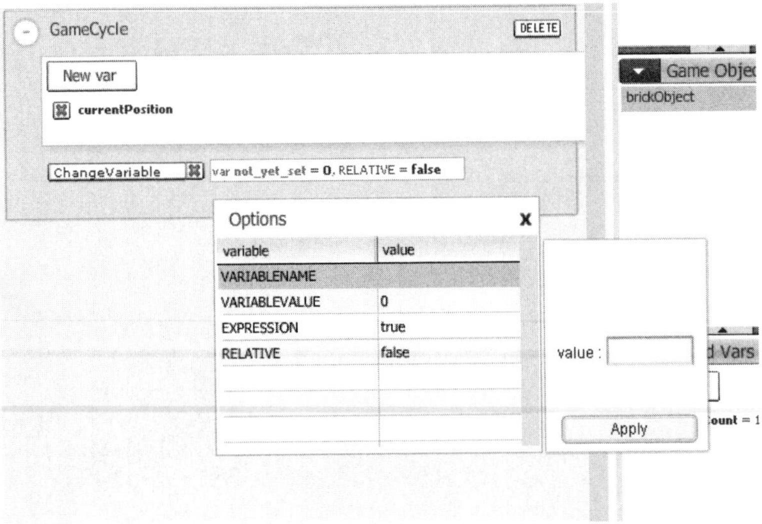

FIGURE 8.9
Modifying values of variables.

An *array* is a special type of variable that can hold a list of items that can be accessed using an index. The list of items usually is the same type—numbers, strings, or any other data type. Arrays are created with World, Class, or Local scope by clicking the appropriate New Var button.

Clicking the New Var button displays the Variable Editor dialog box shown in Figure 8.10. Type book_array as the name of the array. From the option in the drop-down box next to the label, choose the Array option. Then click the Submit button to create the book_array. At the moment, this book array is empty. You can use AS2 commands to populate it with items. The following command adds three items to the array:

```
book_array.push("book1", "book2", "book3");
```

You can remove the last item inserted using the pop method, as shown here:

```
var currBook = book_array.pop();
```

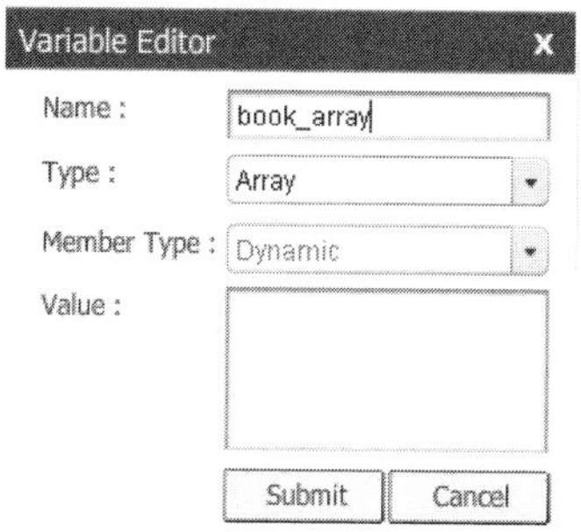

FIGURE 8.10
The Create Array options.

Several other AS2 commands operate on the array data type. Please see the documentation on the Adobe Web site for more information. You can create arrays with items initialized, as shown in Figure 8.11. The items have to be listed in the Value section inside square brackets. Each of the items has to be in double quotes and separated by commas.

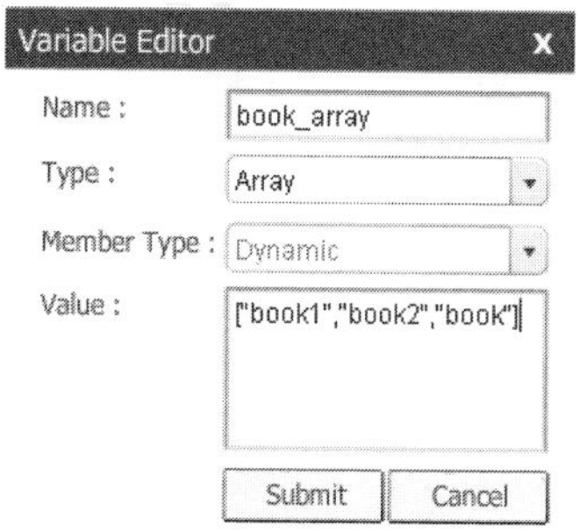

FIGURE 8.11
Creating an initialized array.

You can create arrays dynamically using AS2 commands inside an InsertScript task or by clicking the New Var button.

MASKING EXAMPLE

This last example demonstrates the power of AS2. Although GameBrix provides tasks that simplify most operations, users can leverage the power of AS2 commands to build virtually any kind of Flash game.

Start a new game and add two sprites that were used in Chapter 6 labeled CG06_cave_bg and CG06_money, as shown in Figure 8.12.

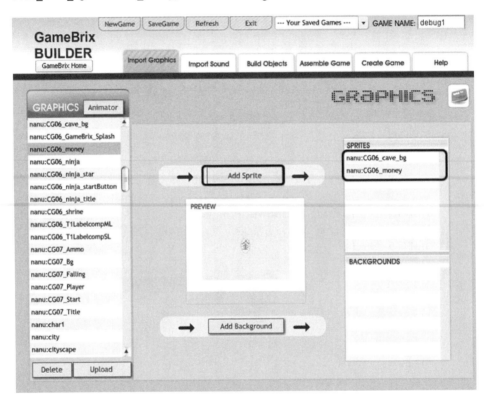

FIGURE 8.12
Masking example sprites.

Click the Build Objects tab and then the New Object button to create the following two objects shown in Figure 8.13.

■ Create an object named maskObject, and attach the sprite named CG06_money to it.
■ Create another object named imageObject, and attach the sprite named CG06_cave_bg to it.

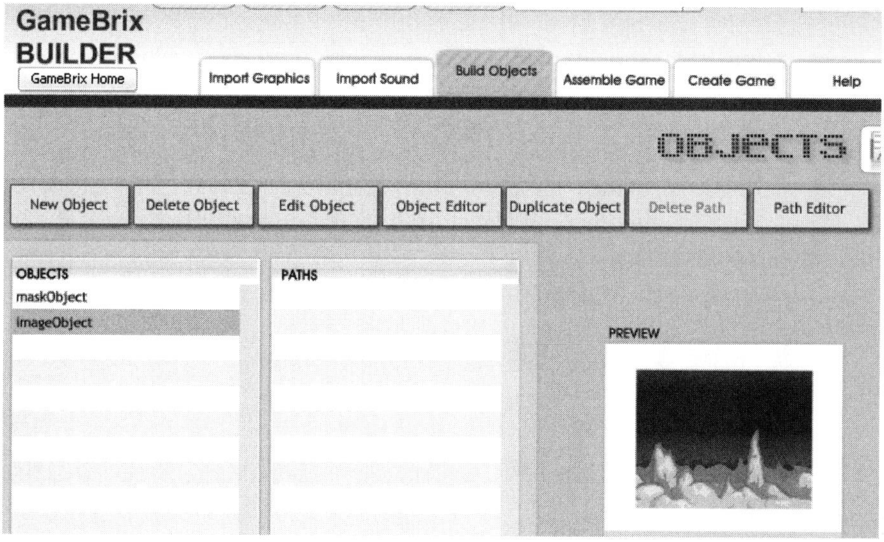

FIGURE 8.13
Objects required.

Click on the Object Editor button on the Build Objects tab and open it. Then click on the maskObject to select it, and add a Create state to it. Add a FollowMouse task with a FollowFriction value of 10. Figure 8.14 shows the maskObject with its behaviors.

FIGURE 8.14
The maskObject.

Next, click on the imageObject and add a Create state to it. Add an InsertScript task, and enter the following script to be executed, as shown in Figure 8.15.

```
setMask(_level1.myGameController.level1.maskObject_2);
```

In the previous InsertScript command, maskObject_2 corresponds to maskObject, which will be placed in the Game Assembly Area in the next step. If the name is different in the Game Assembly Area, you need to change the name in the previous InsertScript command.

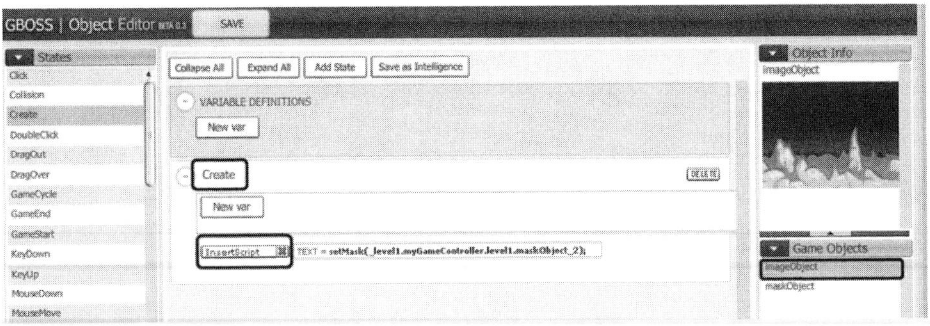

FIGURE 8.15
The imageObject.

Click the Save button in the Object Editor. Wait for the save operation to complete, and then click OK in the pop-up dialog box. Minimize the Object Editor by clicking the Microsoft Windows Minimize button, and then go back to the Game-Brix Builder screen. There should be one more dialog box that displays the message that the game is ready to build. Click OK, and close it.

Click on the Assemble Game tab, and then click and drag the imageObject onto the Game Assembly Area. Next, click and drag a maskObject onto the Game Assembly Area. After that, click the maskObject and make it a little bigger using the transformation manipulators shown in Figure 8.16. Note the name of the instance displayed in the Instance Name text box, found underneath the Game Assembly Area. If the instance name is more than 10 characters, click on the text box and scroll to see the full name. It should be set to maskObject_2 by default. If not, you need to change the setMask command to reflect this new name. If the name of the instance used in the setMask command does not match that found in the Game Assembly Area, this masking example will not work.

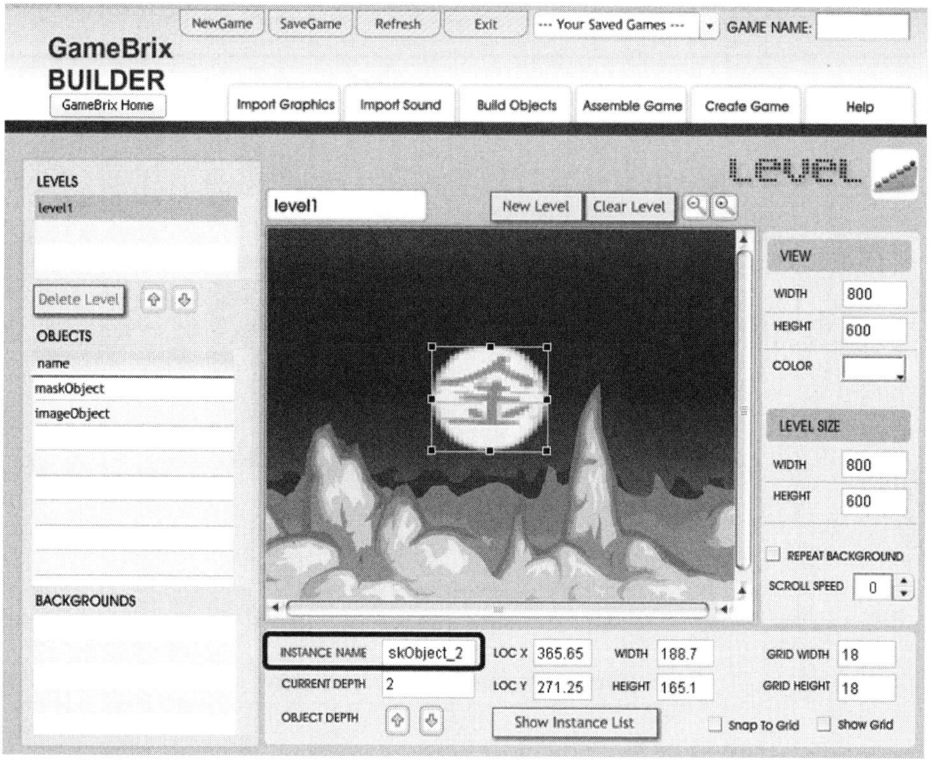

FIGURE 8.16
The assembled game.

Next, click on the Create Game tab and play the game. The image that was loaded into the Game Assembly Area will not be visible. Only the portion beneath the maskObject will be visible, as shown in Figure 8.17. Because the maskObject has been instructed to follow the mouse, you get a beautiful masking effect. That concludes the foray into the use of AS2 commands from GameBrix GameBuilder.

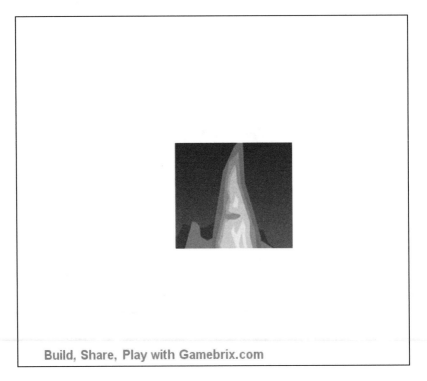

FIGURE 8.17
The masking effect.

SUMMARY

This chapter covered important aspects related to game creation. Using small examples, it introduced game objects and the use of Adobe ActionScript 2.0 to control them. The debugging and tracing facility within GameBrix were used to explore how instances of objects are named. Simple AS2 commands were used to control game objects, and variables were explored. A final example used masks. The next chapter explores the creation of a tile-based labyrinth game.

9 Building a Labyrinth Game

This chapter describes how to build a Classic Dungeon Adventure labyrinth game, whereby the player has to navigate through a maze or labyrinth to reach a goal. The labyrinth is usually filled with enemies to avoid as well as objects or coins to collect for extra points. You can use the structure of the labyrinth game to depict multiple scenarios. The labyrinth has been used in history and mythology to imprison monsters and bury kings. This history provides a rich setting for building fun games.

Many years ago, the Shamano clan created a secret test of courage to choose the new ruler of its empire. The plan was virtually flawless, except that no one could find the test! To this day, of the brave souls who have set out to complete the quest, none have succeeded. In the labyrinth game, the player is a member of a neighboring clan who accidentally comes across the courage test in a surprising location—underground! The test is composed of a long maze that contains coins, enemies, and a trophy at the end.

The objective of the game is to get to the trophy at the end of the level after collecting eight precious ancient coins that are scattered throughout. The player can lose a life by either falling off the maze path or into pools of water or graves. The player will also lose a life if he collides with one of the flaming skulls that guard the labyrinth.

BUILDING THE GAME USING THE DESIGNER'S APPROACH

The first step is to log in to GameBrix.com if you are not already logged in. The next sequence of steps involves obtaining all the images, animations, and intelligence required to build the game. A budget of 75 Brix is required to buy all these items from the online GameBrix store. If you do not have enough Brix, you can purchase them from the GameBrix Web site.

IMAGES REQUIRED

Now it's time to get the images required for the labyrinth game from the online GameBrix store. Go to the online store by clicking on the Store link. In the Search by Name text box, type in CG09 and select Images as the content type, as shown in Figure 9.1. Make sure that user coolgc owns the items.

The images required are described in Table 9.1. The name of the item might not be displayed completely if it is longer than 10 characters. Hovering your mouse over the thumbnail of the image should display the full name.

Buy all the items listed in Table 9.1 by clicking on the Add to Cart button. Make sure that coolgc owns all the items, and check page 2 to get all the required items. After all the items are in your shopping cart, click on the My Cart tab. It may take a few seconds for the system to process items in your cart. The next screen displays your cart contents. The list shows a file name and an item name. If you already have an item in your inventory by the same name, it is displayed in red text. You need to change the name of that item on this screen to avoid name conflicts and overwriting your file. If you already have purchased an item that shows up in red, you can remove it from your shopping cart using the Remove button on the same row. Figure 9.2 shows all the items in the shopping cart.

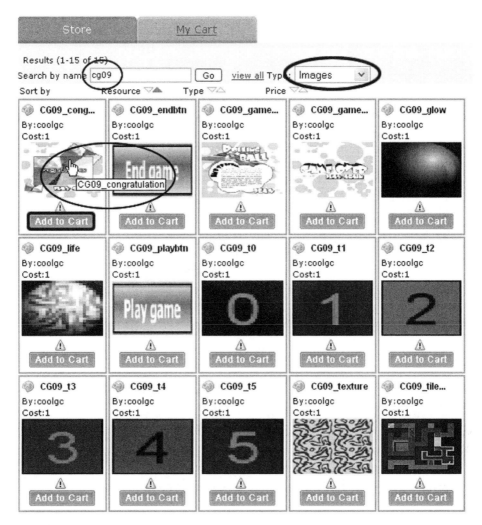

FIGURE 9.1
Some of the required images from the store.

TABLE 9.1 IMAGES REQUIRED

Item Name	Price (Brix)	Description
CG09_congratulation	1	Victory screen
CG09_endbtn	1	End button
CG09_playbtn	1	Start button
CG09_game-start	1	Start screen
CG09_gameover	1	Game Over screen
CG09_glow	1	Ball mask
CG09_life	1	Life image
CG09_t0	1	Empty tile (evil)
CG09_t1	1	Land tile (good)
CG09_t2	1	Coin tile (good)
CG09_t3	1	Enemy tile (evil)
CG09_t4	1	Water tile (evil)
CG09_t5	1	Goal tile (good)
CG09_texture	1	Ball mask image
CG09_tileguide	1	Tile guide used during game assembly

Click the Buy Now button at the bottom of the screen. The system may take a few moments to process your order. On completion of the transaction, the items are added to your inventory, and the Store screen displays. That finishes the process of assembling the images required for this game.

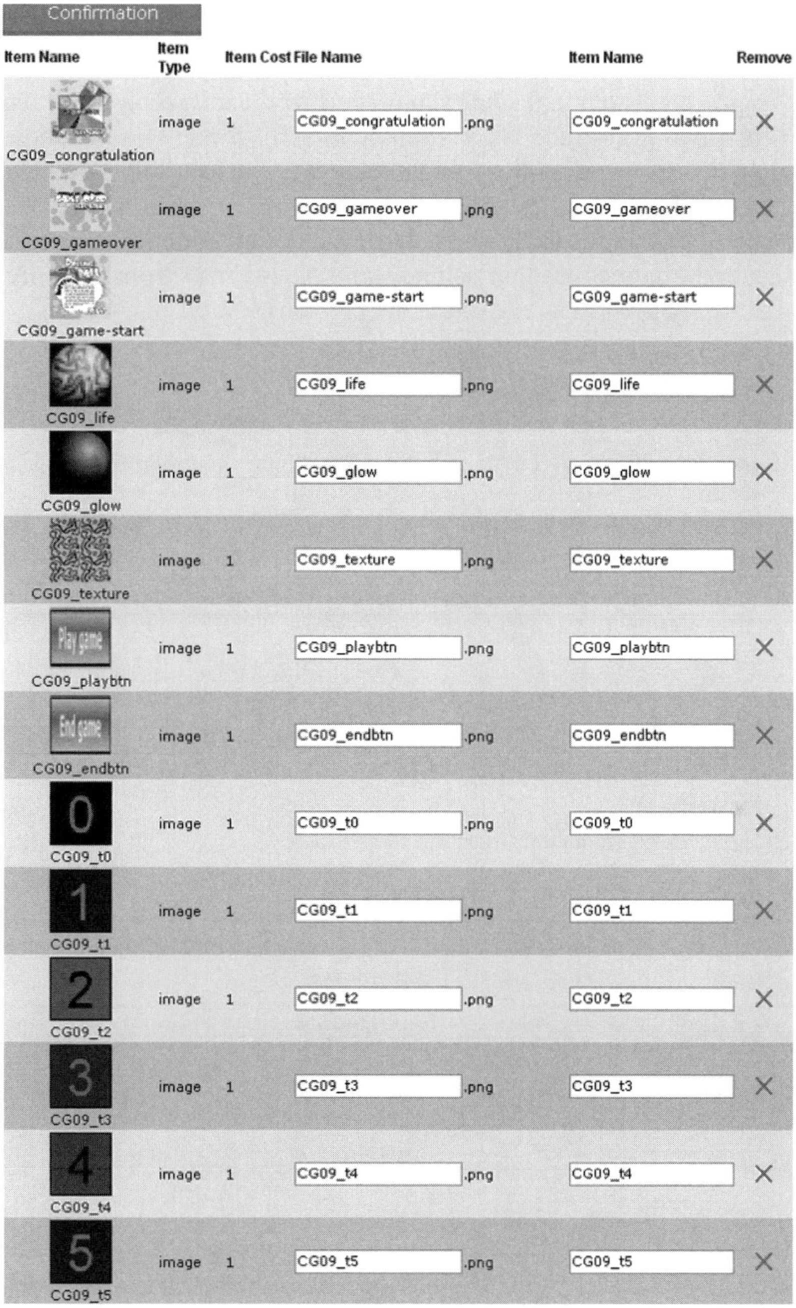

Item Name	Item Type	Item Cost	File Name	Item Name	Remove
CG09_congratulation	image	1	CG09_congratulation .png	CG09_congratulation	×
CG09_gameover	image	1	CG09_gameover .png	CG09_gameover	×
CG09_game-start	image	1	CG09_game-start .png	CG09_game-start	×
CG09_life	image	1	CG09_life .png	CG09_life	×
CG09_glow	image	1	CG09_glow .png	CG09_glow	×
CG09_texture	image	1	CG09_texture .png	CG09_texture	×
CG09_playbtn	image	1	CG09_playbtn .png	CG09_playbtn	×
CG09_endbtn	image	1	CG09_endbtn .png	CG09_endbtn	×
CG09_t0	image	1	CG09_t0 .png	CG09_t0	×
CG09_t1	image	1	CG09_t1 .png	CG09_t1	×
CG09_t2	image	1	CG09_t2 .png	CG09_t2	×
CG09_t3	image	1	CG09_t3 .png	CG09_t3	×
CG09_t4	image	1	CG09_t4 .png	CG09_t4	×
CG09_t5	image	1	CG09_t5 .png	CG09_t5	×

FIGURE 9.2
Items in the shopping cart.

ANIMATIONS REQUIRED

The next step is to get all the animations required from the online store by using a process similar to the one you used to get the images. In the Search by Name text box, type in CG09 and select Animations as the content type, as shown in Figure 9.3. Again, the owner of these assets is coolgc. The icons displayed for all animations resemble a snippet of camera film. If you are interested in previewing the animation, click on the icon, which displays the animation in a new window. Table 9.2 lists the animations that you need. Buy these items from the store, and complete the purchase just as you did in the previous section.

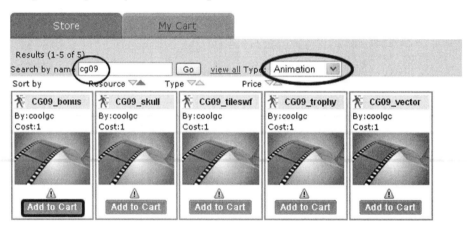

FIGURE 9.3
The required animations from the store.

TABLE 9.2 ANIMATIONS REQUIRED

Item Name	Price (Brix)	Description
CG09_bonus	1	The collectable coin
CG09_skull	1	The enemy
CG09_tileswf	1	A 144-frame SWF movie that displays the tile map
CG09_trophy	1	The goal
CG09_vector	1	A vector image of the ball used for masking purposes

TILE GAME CONCEPTS

The labyrinth game is a tile-based game created using similar-looking building blocks. The tiles are laid out in a square composed of 12 horizontal and 12 vertical tiles, thus requiring a total of 144 tiles. Building a tile-based maze game requires a mechanism for the game creator to lay out the tiles that make up the maze. After the layout is done, a game manager object reads the layout, creates an internal map, and then handles the gameplay accordingly. A general-purpose game manager object that can handle all types of layouts is the best tool to handle the situation.

You can use *marker tiles* to plan out the configuration of the maze. These are placeholders that do not necessarily display the tile they represent. A grass marker tile, therefore, does not need to look like a grass tile. Marker tiles are position indicators that inform the game manager of the existence of a particular type of tile at a particular location on the maze. Knowing about a particular tile at a particular location, the game manager can then display the appropriate image of the tile at this point in the game. He can display different types of tiles that represent grass. For example, he might use a patch of grass with weeds in addition to a healthy patch of grass. The variety increases the appeal of the game.

All marker tile objects have the same embedded logic but have different tile attribute types set within them. In the labyrinth game, marker tiles are named t0 through t5. The attribute that differentiates marker tiles is the tile type attribute. Tile t0 has its type set to a value of 0 representing an empty tile, tile t1 has this attribute set to 1 representing a land tile, and so on.

A reference background image is used as the map, and marker tiles are arranged on top of this. If the map has a water area, a water marker tile (t4) is placed there. If the map has a grassy area, land marker tiles (t1) are used. The game creator arranges 144 marker tiles of various types to create a 2-D map.

When the game is built and run, the game manager creates an empty 2-D array with 12 columns and 12 rows. Each of the 144 marker tiles loads up and runs a set of tasks in the Create state that gives the game manager a location report indicating its tile type and location. A typical report from a marker tile could be translated into a logical statement such as I'm a tile of type 3 (water), and I am located at coordinates 320, 245. The game manager receives this report from all the marker tiles and updates its 2-D array. The type of tile present at that location is updated in the appropriate row and column position within the array. The game manager keeps track of all the information received from all marker tiles. After receiving location reports from all the marker tiles, the game manager can handle the game logic because he now knows where everything is.

With the game manager acquiring a fully updated positional map of the maze, the marker tiles are no longer needed. The game manager can then start to re-create an accurate visual representation of the map for the player by attaching 144 instances of a special animation at the exact locations occupied by the marker tiles. The asset named CG09_tileswf is an example of this animation. Each frame corresponds to the appropriate image to be displayed at one specific location within the 2-D map. Frame 1 corresponds to the visual representation of the image that is to be displayed at row 1 column 1 of the tile map. Frame 2 corresponds to that of row 1, column 2 and so on.

The game manager instructs each of these animations to play and stop at the appropriate frame based on its location. The animation in row 1 and column 1 will be instructed to stop at frame 1, the animation in row 1 and column 2 will be instructed to stop at frame 2, and so on. Following this pattern, the animation on row 12 and column 12 will be instructed to stop at frame 144. Collectively, all 144 animations under the control of the game manager display the complete map that was originally designed in its entire original splendor.

To make things easier, a 144-animation of a tile map has been provided as a ready-made asset—CG09_tileswf. The steps involved in creating this animation from a raw image are described in the next section.

MAKING THE TILESWF ANIMATION

The basic procedure is to start with a PNG or JPEG image that is 960 by 960 pixels and slice it into 12 rows and 12 columns of equal size. This results in 144 images, each sized 80 pixels by 80 pixels. You need to import these 144 sliced images into 144 frames of an animation to create the tileswf animation. The easiest way to do this is by using the Sprite Editor within GameBrix Animator.

Instead of making the image from scratch, purchase the asset CG09_sparemap from the store. It is a 960 by 960 pixel PNG image. Open the GameBrix Animator by clicking on the large blue tab on the GameBrix Web site, next to the GameBrix Builder tab.

The Animator opens by default with several windows. Set the dimensions of the stage to 80 pixels by 80 pixels, as shown in Figure 9.4. Then click on the Sprite Editor button.

Click on the Load Library Image button located at the bottom of the Sprite Sheet Editor, as shown in Figure 9.5. To select the image, double-click on CG09_sparemap from the list of library images.

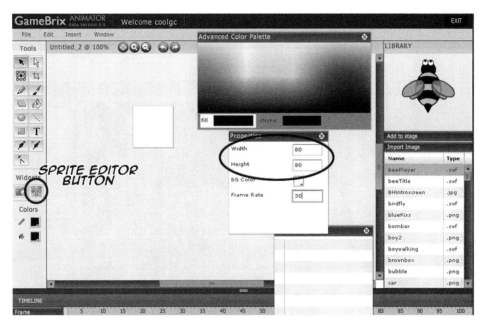

FIGURE 9.4
The Animator.

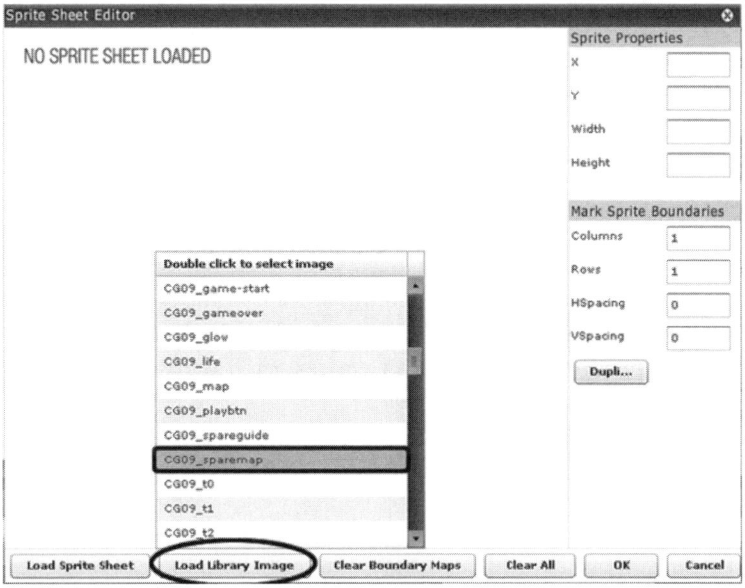

FIGURE 9.5
The Sprite Sheet Editor.

Using the mouse, click and drag a box around the first tile in the image. Set both the X and Y coordinates of the sprite bounding box to 9.5. Set both the width and height of the bounding box to 80 pixels, as shown in Figure 9.6.

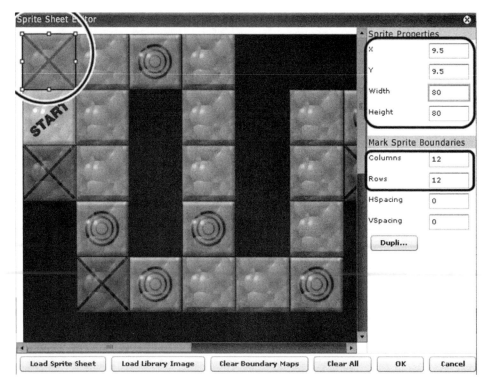

FIGURE 9.6
The Sprite Sheet Editor.

Set both the Columns and Rows fields under the Mark Sprite Boundaries section to 12, as shown in Figure 9.7. Then click on the Duplicate button. That should split the image into 144 sprites, each surrounded by a bounding box, as shown in Figure 9.7.

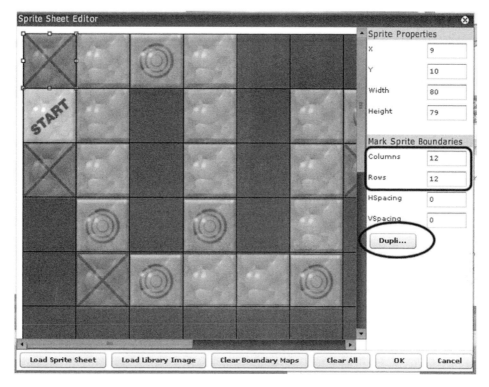

FIGURE 9.7
The 144 sliced images.

Click on the OK button to import the 144 sliced images into individual frames of an animation. The animator creates an animation with these 144 keyframes and displays the frames in the timeline, as shown in Figure 9.8. Click the Save Project button, located under the File menu. Then fill in the name of the tile game you are building. It may take a few moments to save all the frames. To export the animation for use in the Builder, click the Export Movie button located under the File menu. Be patient, because it may again take a few moments to complete the rendering process. A preview of the animation is displayed on completion. You can use this 144-frame animation as the tileswf object to create the labyrinth game. Close the window after you preview the animation.

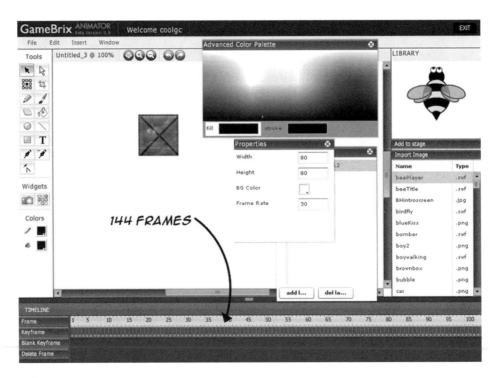

FIGURE 9.8
The imported frames.

INTELLIGENCE REQUIRED

At this point, a 144-frame tile map animation is available—which was either created manually or bought from the store. The next step is to get all the intelligence required from the online store. In the Search by Name text box, type in CG09 and select Intelligence as the content type (see Figure 9.9). As with the images and animations, coolgc owns all the intelligence. The icons displayed for all object intelligence assets resemble a single gear. You cannot view or preview object intelligence directly. You can view it only when it's used inside GameBrix GameBuilder. Table 9.3 lists the intelligence that you need. Buy these items from the store, and complete the purchase just as you did in the earlier sections.

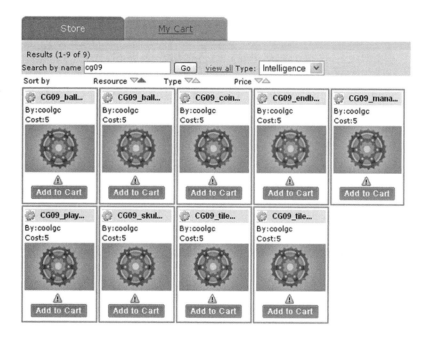

FIGURE 9.9
The required object intelligence assets from the store.

TABLE 9.3 INTELLIGENCE REQUIRED

Item Name	Price (Brix)	Description
CG09_ballglowIntl	5	Sets the height and width of the ball image glow filter
CG09_ballimageIntl	5	Sets the height and width of the ball mask
CG09_coinIntl	5	Is the bonus object intelligence
CG09_endbtnIntl	5	Is the End button
CG09_managerIntl	5	Reads marker objects, assembles tiles
CG09_playbtnIntl	5	Is the Play button
CG09_skullIntl	5	Is the enemy object intelligence
CG09_tileobjIntl	5	Contains logic to display the image of each tile
CG09_tilecodeIntl	5	Used by tiles t0 to t5

BUILDING THE OBJECTS

With all the images, animations, and intelligence in place, it's time to start building the game objects. Open the GameBrix Builder by clicking on the large tab labeled Builder. When the application loads, you are at the Import Graphics screen by default.

On the left side of the screen is a set of images and animations in your library. Select the following images, and add them to the Sprites section on the right, as shown in Figure 9.10. There are 15 images and 5 animations.

- CG09_congratulation
- CG09_endbtn
- CG09_playbtn
- CG09_game-start
- CG09_gameover
- CG09_glow
- CG09_life
- CG09_t0
- CG09_t1
- CG09_t2
- CG09_t3
- CG09_t4
- CG09_t5
- CG09_texture
- CG09_tileguide
- CG09_bonus
- CG09_skull
- CG09_vector
- CG09_trophy
- CG09_tileswf

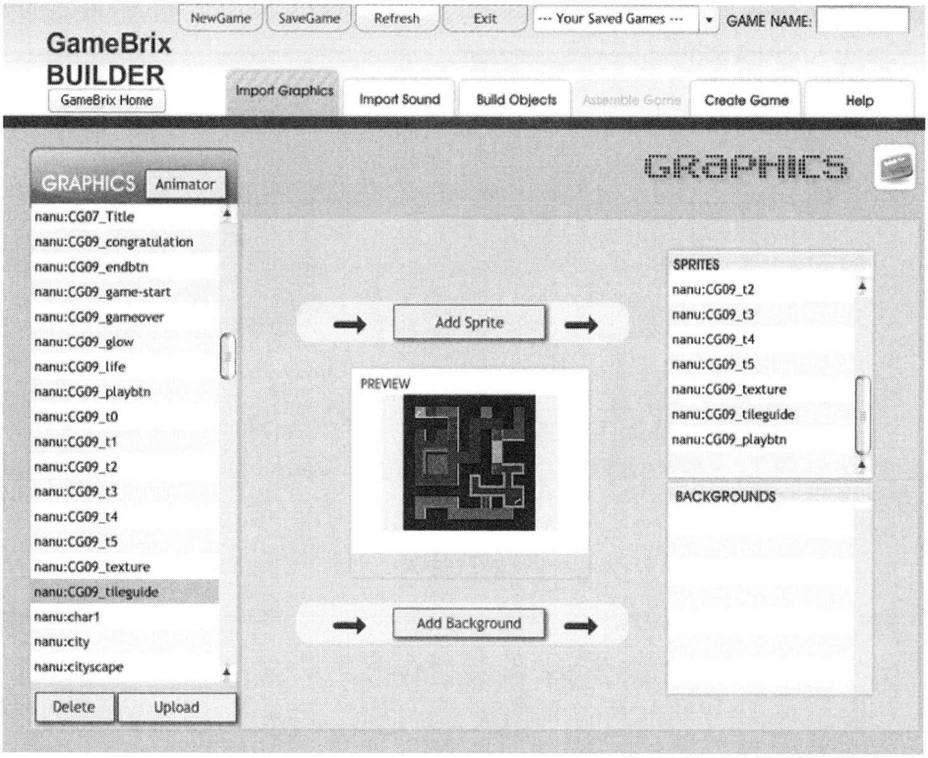

FIGURE 9.10
Assembling the sprites.

Now it's time to build game objects. Click on the Build Objects tab and then on the New Object button to go to the screen shown in Figure 9.11. Choose the image named CG09_t0 from the list of images displayed under the Select Graphics label. Name the object t0 by typing it in the text box labeled Object Name, and then click the Done button. You just created an object named t0.

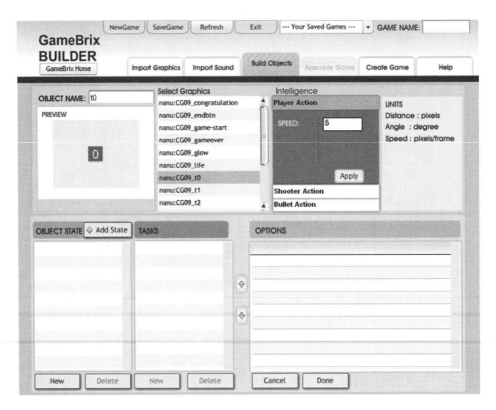

FIGURE 9.11
Object creation process.

Repeat this step and create the other objects listed in Table 9.4. The table lists their object names and the images or animations that are attached to them. Please note that the object names are case sensitive. Your game will not function with incorrect object names.

TABLE 9.4 OBJECTS REQUIRED

Object Name	Image/Animation Required
t0	CG09_t0
t1	CG09_t1
t2	CG09_t2
t3	CG09_t3
t4	CG09_t4
t5	CG09_t5
Tileobj	CG09_tileswf
skull	CG09_skull
playgame_btn	CG09_playbtn
endgame_btn	CG09_endbtn
playerlife	CG09_life
gamemanager	CG09_texture
finishgame_screen	CG09_congratulation
coin	CG09_bonus
ball_won	CG09_congratulation
ball_trophy	CG09_trophy
ball_texture	CG09_texture
ball_start	CG09_game-start
ball_image	CG09_vector
ball_glow	CG09_glow
ball_end	CG09_gameover
guide	CG09_tileguide

After creating all the objects, click the SaveGame button shown in Figure 9.12. Always provide a title and description when you save. Make sure the file name does not contain spaces or special symbols. A dialog box signals the completion of the save game process. Click the OK button to proceed.

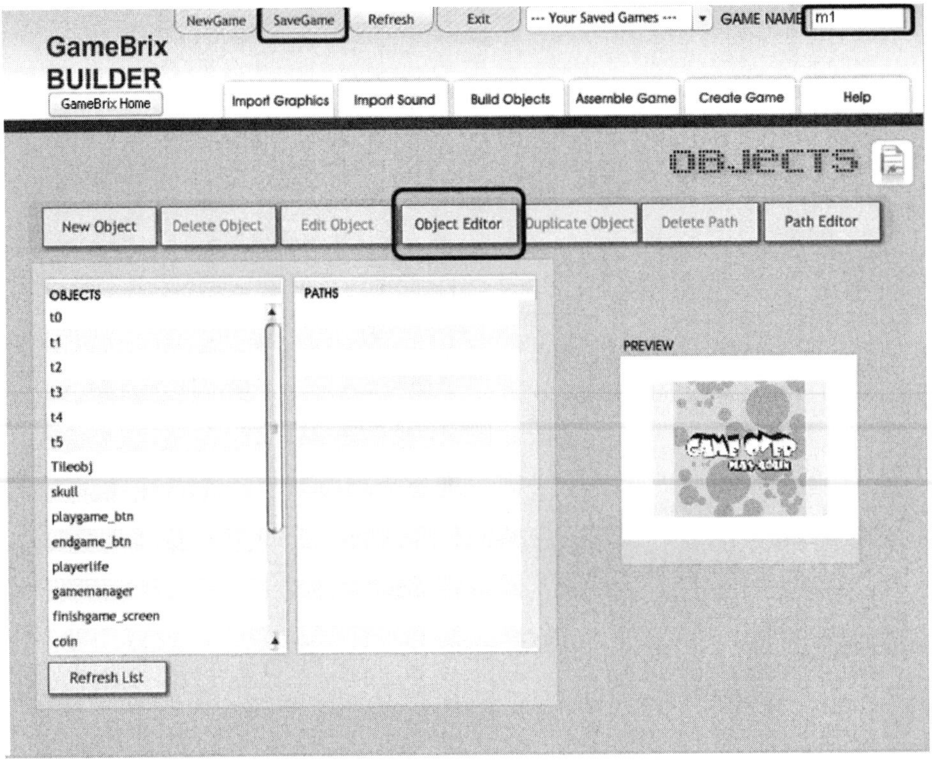

FIGURE 9.12
Object creation process.

It's time to use the Object Editor to add behavioral intelligence to your objects. Click on the Object Editor button shown in Figure 9.12 to open the Object Editor window. Descriptions of all areas of the Object Editor were provided in Chapter 6, "Building a Platform Game." See Figure 6.8 to refresh your memory.

The areas of importance are

- The list of objects present in the Game Objects section
- The contents of the Intelligence section
- The empty section labeled World Vars

Select the coin object by clicking on it in the Game Objects section. Next search for the intelligence labeled CG09_coinIntl in the Intelligence section. Double-click on it. You should be prompted with a dialog box asking if you want to overwrite your object's behavior. Click Yes. That should populate the object with one or more states and tasks, as shown in Figure 9.13.

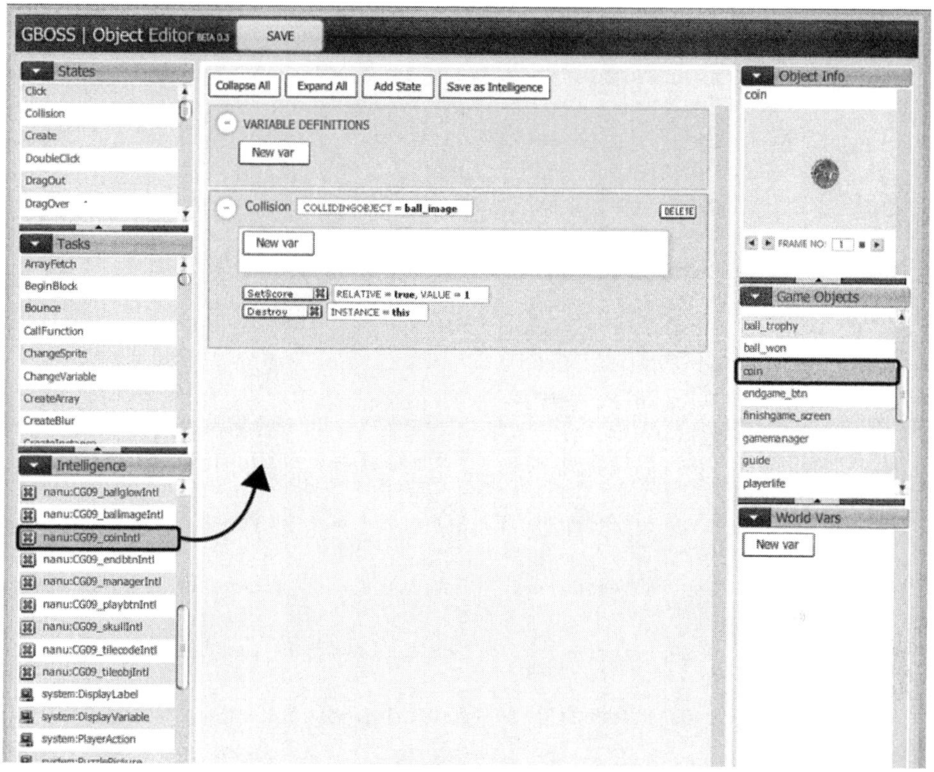

FIGURE 9.13
Populated Object Editor screen.

That completes the creation of the coin object.

Perform the same sequence of steps to create all the other objects listed in Table 9.5. Keep in mind that different objects require different intelligence assigned to them. Allow about 10 to 15 minutes to complete this intelligence assignment process for all the objects. Table 9.5 lists all the objects and the appropriate intelligence they require.

TABLE 9.5 INTELLIGENCE ASSIGNMENT

Object Name	Intelligence Required	Required Configuration
coin	CG09_coinIntl	
Tileobj	CG09_tileobjIntl	
skull	CG09_skullIntl	
playgame_btn	CG09_playbtnIntl	
endgame_btn	CG09_endbtnIntl	
gamemanager	CG09_managerIntl	Set totalcoins = 8
ball_image	CG09_ballimageIntl	
ball_glow	CG09_ballglowIntl	
t0	CG09_tilecodeIntl	Set value = 0 [in Variable Definition section]
t1	CG09_tilecodeIntl	Set value = 1 [in Variable Definition section]
t2	CG09_tilecodeIntl	Set value = 2 [in Variable Definition section]
t3	CG09_tilecodeIntl	Set value = 3 [in Variable Definition section]
t4	CG09_tilecodeIntl	Set value = 4 [in Variable Definition section]
t5	CG09_tilecodeIntl	Set value = 5 [in Variable Definition section]

CONFIGURATION

In this tile game, although several objects share the same intelligence, each of them needs different behaviors. The objects t0, t1, t2, t3, t4, and t5 fall into this category. For them to behave differently, the class variable named value is assigned different numbers. A value of 0 signifies an empty tile. All the possible values for this class variable are shown in Table 9.6.

TABLE 9.6 TILE CONFIGURATION VARIABLE

Object Name	Variable Value	Description
t0	0	Empty tile (evil)
t1	1	Land tile (good)
t2	2	Coin tile (good)
t3	3	Skull tile (evil)
t4	4	Water tile (evil)
t5	5	Trophy tile (good)

Configure the class value variable starting with the object t5. Click on the t5 object in the Game Objects list, shown in Figure 9.14. Then click on the class variable named value, and the Variable Editor dialog is displayed. Change the value of this variable to 5 and then click the Submit button, as shown in Figure 9.14.

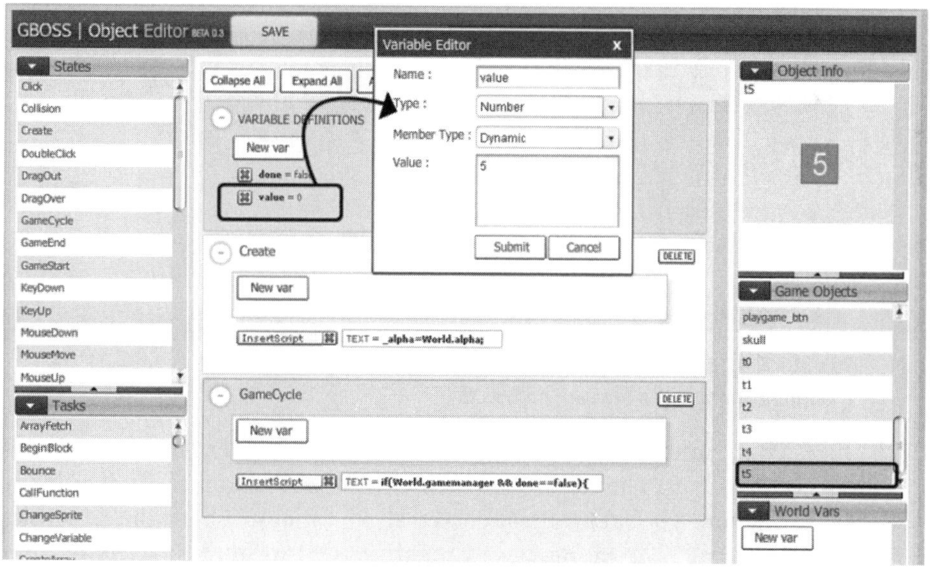

FIGURE 9.14
Configuring tile objects.

Repeat the process for objects t4, t3, t2, t1, and t0 by assigning the class variable value the numbers 4, 3, 2, 1, and 0, respectively. Incorrect assignments change the behavior of the tile.

You also need to configure the gamemanager object, so click on it in the Game Objects list. The gamemanager object is a complex object that contains several tasks occupying more than a page of information. Click the Collapse All button to hide all the tasks, as shown in Figure 9.15. Expand the Class Variable Definitions section by clicking on the circular button shown in Figure 9.15. The gamemanager object has many class variables. The totalcoins variable defines the total number of coins to be picked up before collecting the trophy to complete the game. Click the totalcoins variable, and check to see if its value is 8.

FIGURE 9.15
Configuring the gamemanager object.

That completes the object creation process. The next step is the creation of six world variables. The world variable named level is an array that holds all the tile information. The ballwidth and ballheight variables define the dimensions of the labyrinth ball. The gamemanager variable is used to store a variety of information. The soundon variable controls whether the music is on or off. The alpha variable controls the transparency of certain objects.

To create world variables, click the New Var button in the World Vars section in the lower-right corner of the Object Editor. The Variable Editor dialog box is displayed. Carefully enter data into this dialog box using information provided in Table 9.7. Figure 9.16 shows several existing world variables and the procedure to create the `level` world variable. The value assigned to the `level` world variable is a set of square brackets. This signifies an empty array with no items in it. Note that variable names are case sensitive. The game will not work with incorrect variable names.

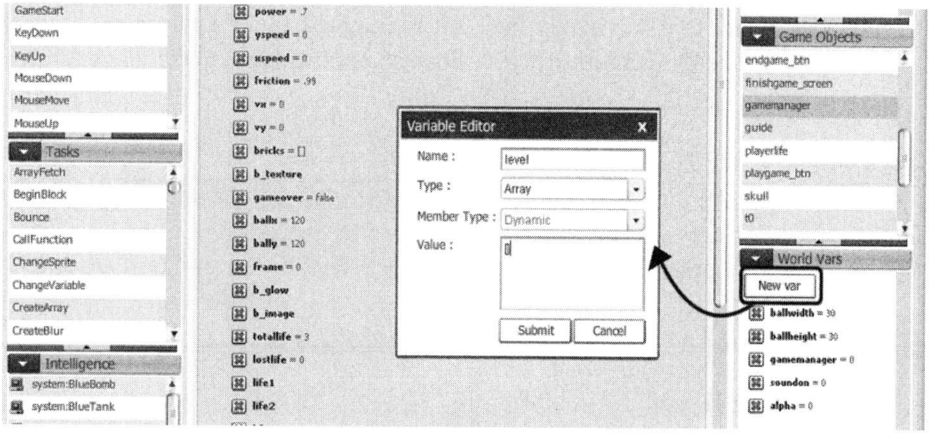

FIGURE 9.16
Creating world variables.

TABLE 9.7 WORLD VARIABLES

Variable Name	Variable Type	Member Type	Value
ballwidth	Number	Dynamic	30
ballheight	Number	Dynamic	30
gamemanager	Object	Dynamic	0
soundon	Number	Dynamic	0
alpha	Number	Dynamic	0
level	Array	Dynamic	[ ]

After you've created the six world variables, click the Save button at the top of the Object Editor screen. This is an important step, so don't skip it. A message box displays the message Save complete. You can close the message by clicking the OK button. Minimize the Object Editor window using the standard Minimize button, which brings you back to the Build Objects screen in the GameBrix Builder that displays the message Game ready to build. Click the OK button here to continue the game creation process. If the Game ready to build message does not display when you return to the Build Objects screen, your GameBrix session likely timed out. This means that you need to log out and log back in. Any unsaved progress you've made in the Object Editor will be lost, so be sure to save often!

ASSEMBLING THE GAME

All the objects are ready. Next comes the fun part of assembling the game and testing it. Click the Assemble Game tab. This screen has several buttons and fields. The area on the left labeled Levels lists all the levels you have created. Level 1 is always created by default.

LEVEL DESCRIPTION

In the Assemble Game tab, the area labeled Objects lists all the objects that you've created. These are all the toys you have at your disposal to play with. In the center is the Game Assembly Area. Figure 6.12 in Chapter 6 described all areas of the Assemble Game tab.

This game has four levels, so you need to create three new levels in addition to Level 1. The first level is a Title screen, and the second is the actual game. The third level is the Game Over screen, and the fourth is the Victory screen. After the player plays the game, either the third or the fourth level is displayed, depending on whether he won or lost.

ASSEMBLING LEVEL 1

Assembling the title screen that has the Start button embedded in it is a simple process. Change the name of Level 1, shown on top of the Level Editor, to Startgame. Change the width and height of both the View and Level Size areas to 400 pixels by 400 pixels. Then set the Grid Width and Height options to 40. Also, enable the Snap to Grid and Show Grid options (see Figure 9.17). Check marks appear in enabled options.

In this game, objects are used as background images. Click and drag the object named `ball_start` onto the Game Assembly Area. It is used as the background image for the first level. Click on the `ball_start` object to verify that the `ball_start` object's LOC X and LOC Y coordinates are 200, 200. Click and drag the `playgame_btn` object onto the Game Assembly Area. Then position it at the coordinates 320, 360 using the LOC X and LOC Y fields, as shown in Figure 9.17.

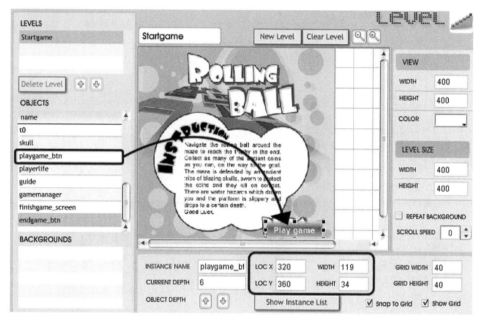

FIGURE 9.17
Level 1 assembled.

That completes the Level 1 assembly process.

ASSEMBLING LEVEL 2

Create a second level by clicking the New level button. This level will house the actual game. Name the level `Begingame`, and set the level size to 800 pixels by 800 pixels. Then set the view size to 400 pixels by 400 pixels. Next, set the grid width and height options to 40. Also, enable the Snap to Grid and Show Grid options. Check marks appear in enabled options.

Click and drag the object named `guide` onto the Game Assembly Area. Set the LOC X and LOC Y coordinates for this object to 260, 300. The guide object is used as a reference for correctly positioning the different types of marker tiles. The guide object has an image named CG09_tileguide attached to it. The dimensions are 480 pixels by 480 pixels, and the image is a replica of the tile map picture. Marker tiles do not look like the labyrinth pieces they represent. The marker tiles t0 through t5 are just placeholders that define the tile's location and type. The tileswf object (which is controlled by the gamemanager object) renders the areas covered by marker tiles.

Next, click and drag a t0 tile onto the Game Assembly Area. Position it at 40, 80 by using the LOC X and LOC Y fields, if required. Next, place 11 more t0 tiles horizontally next to it by holding down the Shift key and clicking and dragging the first tile. The result is shown in Figure 9.18.

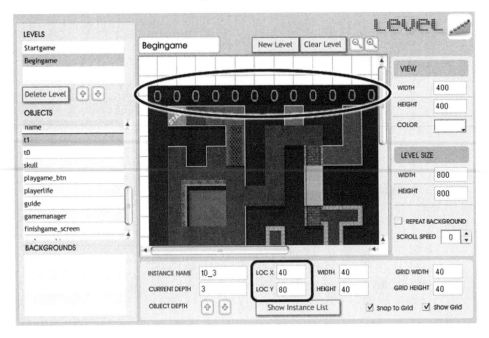

FIGURE 9.18
The top row of t0 tiles.

Populate all the areas colored black over the guide object with t0 tiles. The level populated with t0 objects is shown in Figure 9.19.

The next step is to place at least eight t2 coin marker objects in the labyrinth. The number of coins should equal what you set earlier in the totalcoins class variable in the gamemanager object. Click and drag eight t2 coin marker objects into locations of your choice. During this process, do not remove any t0 objects or overlay any of them with other objects. Next, click and drag six t3 enemy marker tiles onto appropriate locations in the level. Continue by placing four t4 water marker tiles and one t5 marker trophy tile into the locations shown in Figure 9.20.

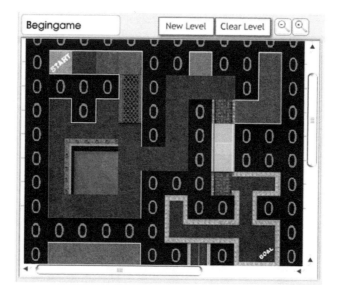

FIGURE 9.19
The completed placement of t0 tiles.

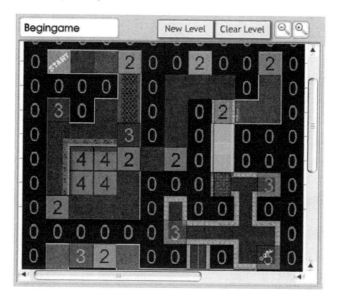

FIGURE 9.20
The completed placement of other tiles.

The only tiles remaining to be placed are the t1 land marker tiles. No guide is needed from this point on. Right-click on the guide object and delete it. Then fill in the remaining blank areas with t1 land marker tiles, as shown in Figure 9.21.

The last step to complete this level is placing the gamemanager object. Click and drag the gamemanager object into the Game Assembly Area. Position it at the location 80, 40. Set the width and height to 40 pixels by 40 pixels, and then click on any area outside the level to enable it to take the values shown in Figure 9.21.

FIGURE 9.21
The completed Level 2.

This completes the assembly of the main level.

ASSEMBLING LEVEL 3

Level 3 is the Game Over level that a player reaches when he loses the game. Click the New Level button, and change the name of the level to Endgame. Change the width and height of both the Level and View areas to 400 pixels by 400 pixels. Then set the grid width and height options to 40. Also, enable the Snap to Grid and Show Grid options. Check marks appear in enabled options.

In this level, objects are used as background images. Click and drag the object named `ball_end` onto the Game Assembly Area. It forms the background image for this level. Then verify that the `ball_end` object is positioned at 200, 200. Click and drag the object named `endgame_btn` onto the Game Assembly Area. Position it at 250, 250, and set its width to 210, as shown in Figure 9.22.

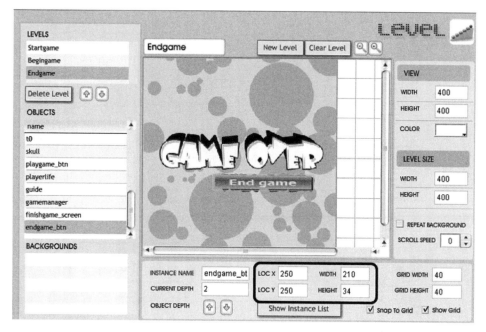

FIGURE 9.22
Level 3 assembled.

That completes the Level 3 assembly process.

ASSEMBLING LEVEL 4

Level 4 is the victory screen that a player reaches when he wins the game. Click the New Level button, and change the name of the level to `Finish`. Change the width and height of both the Level and View areas to 400 pixels by 400 pixels. Set the Grid Width and Height options to 40. Also, enable the Snap to Grid and Show Grid options. Check marks appear in enabled options.

In this level, objects are used as background images. Click and drag the `finishgame_screen` object onto the Game Assembly Area. It is the background image for the third level. Verify that the `ball_end` object is positioned at the coordinates 200, 200. Click and drag the object named `playgame_btn` onto the Game Assembly Area. Position it at the coordinates 250, 335, and set its width to 180, as shown in Figure 9.23.

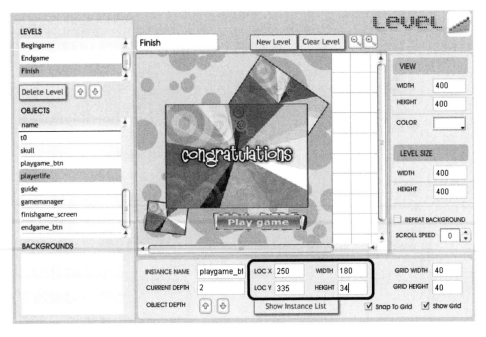

FIGURE 9.23
Level 4 assembled.

That completes the Level 4 assembly process.

Congratulations! You have completed the hard part of building the game. Next, proceed to the Create Game tab, and click the Preview button to play your game.

BUILDING THE GAME USING THE PUBLISHER'S APPROACH

The second method to build this labyrinth game is to use a black-box approach and buy the complete source for the game. The game source is kept in the GameBrix system as a Game Definition Format (GDF) file. Click on Store and search for `CG09_labyrinth`. Then change the asset type to GDF. In the search results, look for the file owned by coolgc, and add this asset to your shopping cart. Then click on the tab labeled My Cart. After you've loaded the shopping cart, scroll down and click the button labeled Buy Now. After the transaction is complete, this GDF file is added to your inventory. You can see this file when you load GameBrix GameBuilder—it appears in the Your Saved Games section. Open this file and build it directly from the Create Game tab. The game builds with all its glory in one step. You can customize this game by going into the Build Objects tab and modifying each object with the knowledge gained in the step-by-step game creation process.

Summary

In this tutorial, you used the GameBrix Builder and GameBrix Animator to create a labyrinth game. With this knowledge, you can create variations of the labyrinth game and publish them for use on Web sites. The next chapter looks at how to build a game collaboratively using the GameBrix portal.

10 Collaboration—Join Forces with Friends and Build Games

In This Chapter

- Creating a Group
- Inviting Friends
- Uploading Art Assets
- Sharing Game Assets
- Building a Game with Shared Game Mechanics

This chapter describes the process involved in building a game as a group activity. Creating games that are compelling and engaging requires artists, programmers, audio specialists, marketers, and distributors collaborating as a group. GameBrix.com delivers an interactive distributed and shared environment that enables users to form groups, invite friends, upload digital assets, share game mechanics, build, and publish games.

CREATING A GROUP

Creating groups in GameBrix.com is easy. The first step is to log in to Gamebrix.com if you haven't already done so. The next sequence of steps involves creating a group and obtaining shared images, animations, and intelligence required for building the game. Images and animations are the basic raw materials required for building games. Images can be in the PNG or JPG format. Animations can only be in the flash SWF format.

Select the Groups button. The Groups feature displays information on groups created at GameBrix.com, members of each group, and group assets, as shown in Figure 10.1.

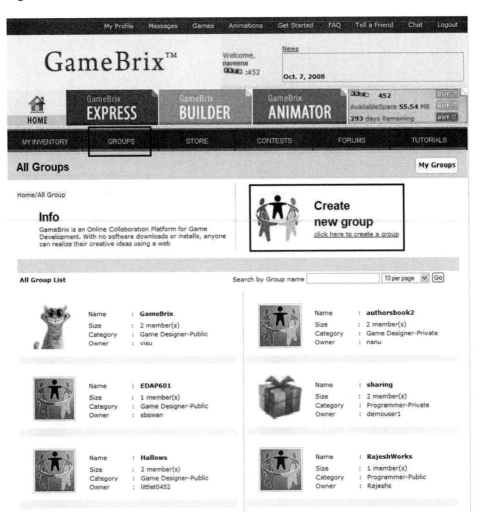

FIGURE 10.1
Select groups.

Selecting the Create New Group option allows you to create a new group. By creating a group, you assume the role of a manager of this group. You control membership privileges and access to shared assets of the group. Select Create Group, as shown in Figure 10.2.

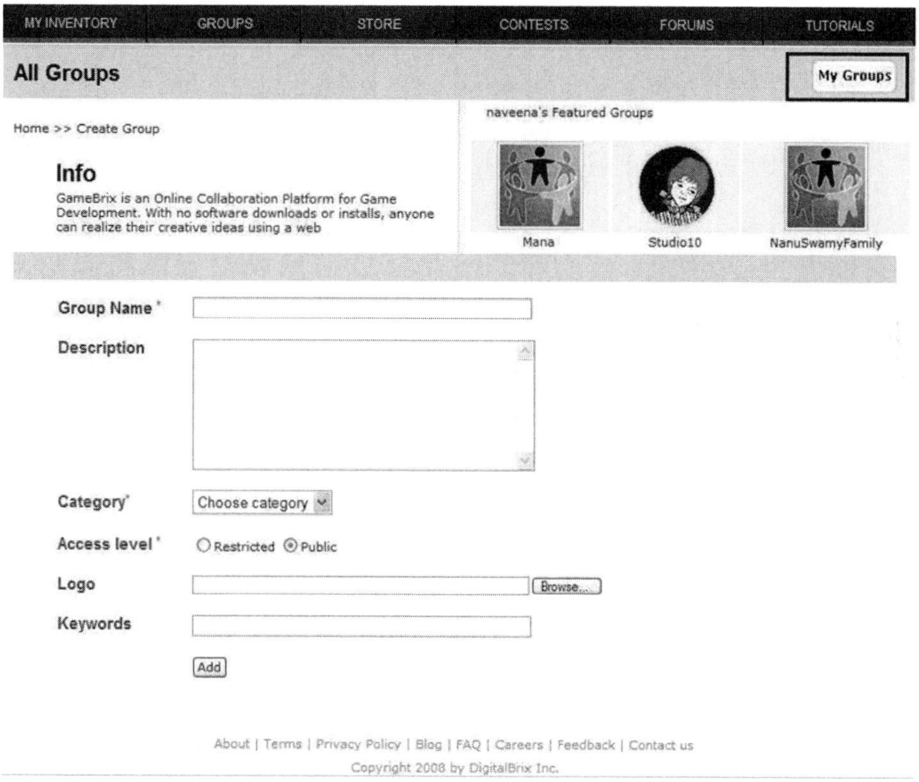

FIGURE 10.2
Create group form.

This opens the Create Group form, which you should complete with the details of the group. The group categories, which describe the nature of the group, are shown in Figure 10.3.

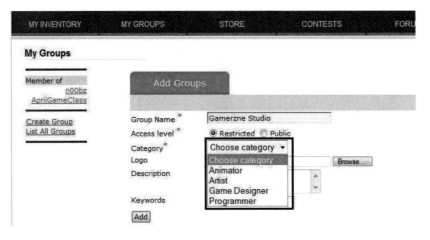

FIGURE 10.3
Add group category.

Groups can be public or restricted. With a restricted group selection, users can keep the work confidential and restricted to the members of the group. This feature allows control of group membership and the ability to share group assets like images, animations, and games with members of the group. The public option of the group feature allows other GameBrix users to see the group and join it if they'd like. Game-Brix registered users can become members of the public group. They just need to complete the form with their group name, group description, category, access level, category, logo, and keywords, as shown in Figure 10.4.

Use the Logo option to upload logo graphics from an external source, as shown in Figure 10.5. Then describe the group. Use of key words is important to set tags on the group feature. This enables easy access to the group through search filters, if the group's intent is to invite community members.

A message is displayed on the portal to indicate that the group has been added, as shown in Figure 10.6.

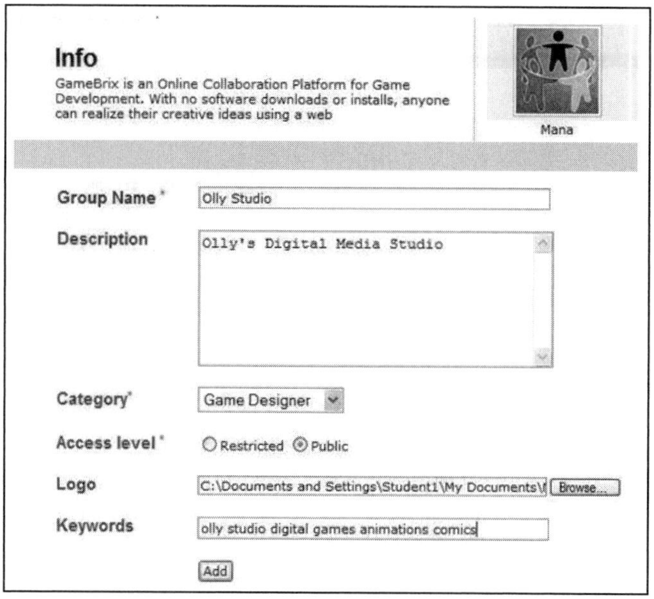

FIGURE 10.4
Create a public group.

FIGURE 10.5
Upload logo for the group.

FIGURE 10.6
Group addition status.

Select the My Groups option; you see the new group listed in the menus on the left, as shown in Figure 10.7.

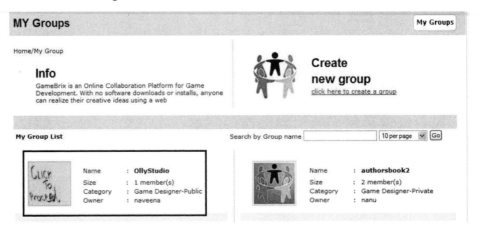

FIGURE 10.7
Group menu.

Left-click on the OllyStudio group. This opens the group page that has options to list members, invite new members, show assets of the group, and indicate the group status (whether public or restricted), as shown in Figure 10.8.

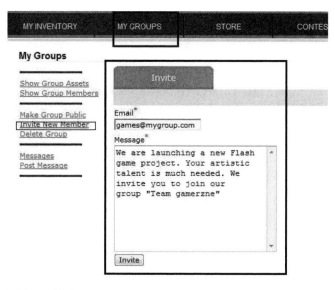

FIGURE 10.8
New group features.

INVITING FRIENDS

Friends share ideas, have common interests, and enjoy the pursuit of creative endeavors. Creating games with them is an exciting activity because it combines the diverse talents in the group to transform an idea into a working, playable game that all the members of the group can have fun with. Friends enjoy refining concepts and turning them into prototypes and finally into finished products. GameBrix enables this social creative interaction with friends.

It's easy to invite a friend to join a group. Just left-click the group name, as indicated in the text label, and select the Invite New Member link on the left. This opens a new form that requires your friend's e-mail address and a message from you. Complete the form and click Invite (see Figure 10.8). A confirmation message appears, as shown in Figure 10.9.

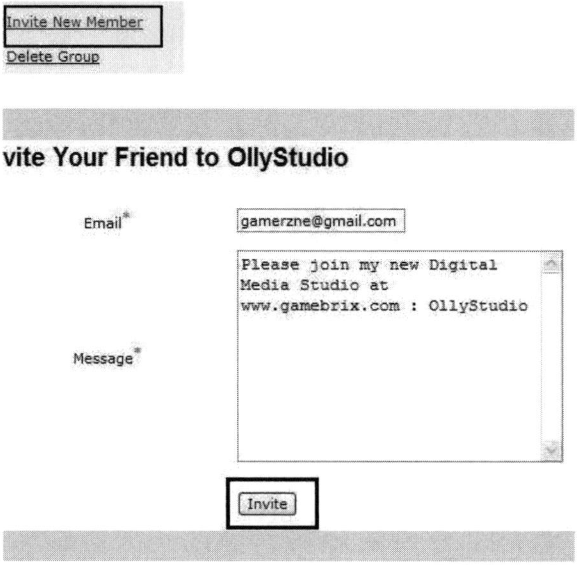

FIGURE 10.9
Invite group member.

UPLOADING ART ASSETS

When you're designing games, interactive advertisements, or banners, art assets are key ingredients. The art assets can be of multiple formats. The formats that GameBrix supports are listed in Table 10.1.

TABLE 10.1 IMAGE FORMAT DESCRIPTIONS

Image Type	Description	File Format
PNG	Portable Network Graphics	PNG
SWF	Shockwave Flash Format	SWF
JPEG	Joint Photographic Experts Group	JPG or JPEG

Select the My Inventory tab in GameBrix and then the Upload Assets link on the left. Complete the form with the asset resource to upload, the asset name and the value in Brix you want to assign, and a description of the asset, as shown in Figure 10.10.

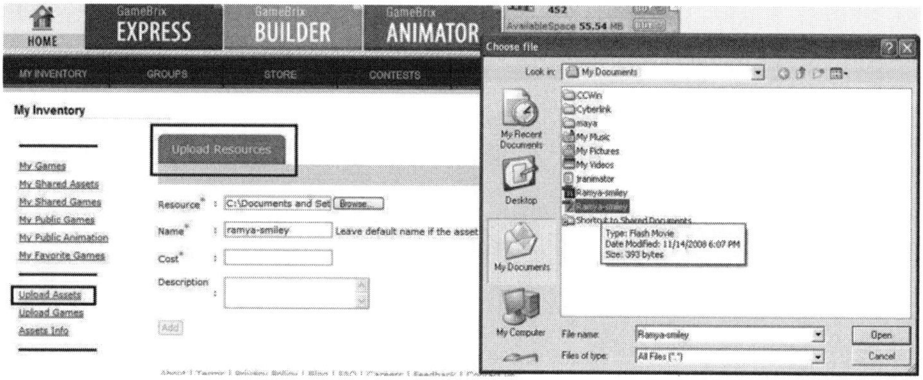

FIGURE 10.10
Upload Assets menu.

A message appears indicating that the addition of the resource was successful. If the format of the assets is incompatible or the file size is too large, you are informed that the action was not completed.

SHARING GAME ASSETS

GameBrix allows users to share game assets between members and groups. It supports many types of assets, including animations, images, games, and game definition files. To share game assets, select the My Inventory tab. In the My Inventory form, use the filter to specify the asset name in the Search by Name field, as shown in Figure 10.11.

The searched asset is displayed, as shown in Figure 10.12.

Select the Share icon at the bottom of the displayed asset. Selecting this option enables the sprite ramya-smiley to be shared with a group, as shown in Figure 10.13.

Selecting a group displays summary information on the group, as shown in Figure 10.14.

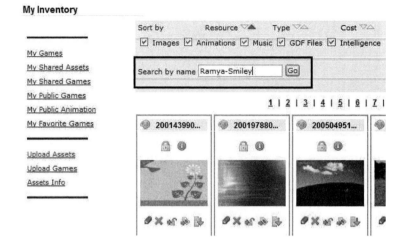

FIGURE 10.11
Search graphic assets.

FIGURE 10.12
Display selected graphics.

FIGURE 10.13
Display selected graphics.

My Inventory

| MY INVENTORY | GROUPS | STORE | CONTESTS | FORUMS | TUTORIALS |

OllyStudio   **My Groups**

Click
To
Product.

GroupName: **OllyStudio**
Description: Olly\'s Digital Media Studio
Category :   Game Designer-Public
Size: 1 member(s)
Total Games Shared: 0
Total Assets Shared: 1
Owner Name: naveena
Owner Email: naveena@digitalbrix.com

Show Group Assets
Show Group Games
Show Group Members
Messages
PostMessage
Make Group Private
Invite New Member
Delete Group

Group Games   **Group Members**

FIGURE 10.14
Group summary information.

Select the Share with Group tab and then OllyStudio to enable the asset to be shared with the OllyStudio group, as shown in Figure 10.15.

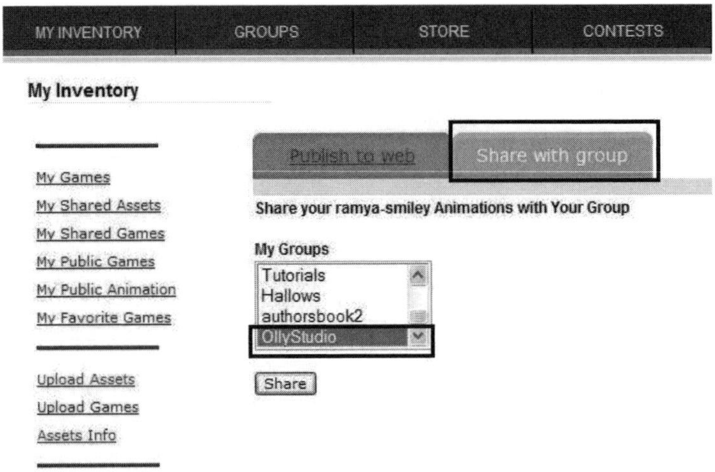

FIGURE 10.15
Share assets with the group.

A validation indicates that the resource has been shared with the group. Select the Groups option and the OllyStudio group. Choose the Show Group Assets link, and notice that the asset has been shared with the selected group. The group creator of OllyStudio has to select the pending check box and click on the Update Assets button to enable the asset to be shared within the group, as shown in Figure 10.16.

GroupName: **OllyStudio**

Description: Olly\'s Digital Media Studio

Category :   Game Designer-Public

Size: 1 member(s)

Total Games Shared: 0

Total Assets Shared: 1

Owner Name: naveena

Owner Email: naveena@digitalbrix.com

Show Group Assets

Show Group Games

Show Group Members

Messages

PostMessage

Make Group Private

Invite New Member

Delete Group

Group Gallery

| Image | Animations | Music | GDF Files | Intelligence |

Name   : ramya-smiley
Tye   : animation
AssetFile   : Ramya-smiley.swf
Owner   : naveena
Created Date : Nov-14-2008
Status   : Approved

✕ ☑ Accepted

Update Assets

FIGURE 10.16
Asset accepted status.

BUILDING A GAME WITH SHARED GAME MECHANICS

Now it's time to create a casual game that allows players to match patterns of colored tiles. Select the Groups option and type coolgc into the search box. Then click the coolgc logo to view the assets of the group. Select the Show Group Assets link on the left. The coolgc group assets are shown in Figure 10.17.

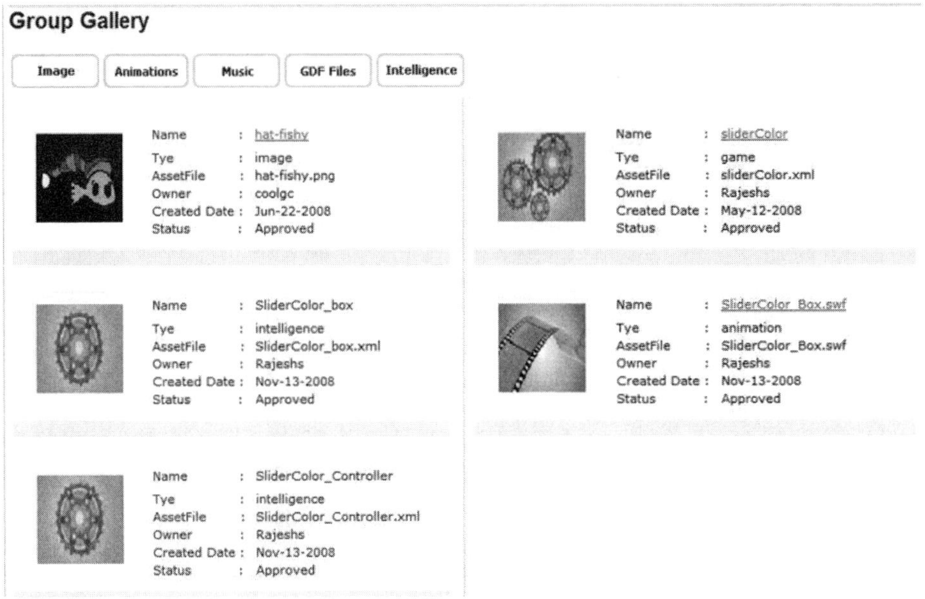

FIGURE 10.17
Coolgc group assets.

You see the assets as listed in Table 10.2.

TABLE 10.2 COOLGC GROUP ASSETS

Item Name	Description
Hat-fishy	Graphics image
SliderColor_box	Game mechanics
SliderColor_Controller	Game intelligence
sliderColor	Game definition file
SliderColor_Box.swf	Animation

Join the group coolgc so you can share assets of the group. After you are approved as a member of the coolgc group, launch the GameBrix Builder. Then select the sliderColor game from the Saved Games section, as shown in Figure 10.18.

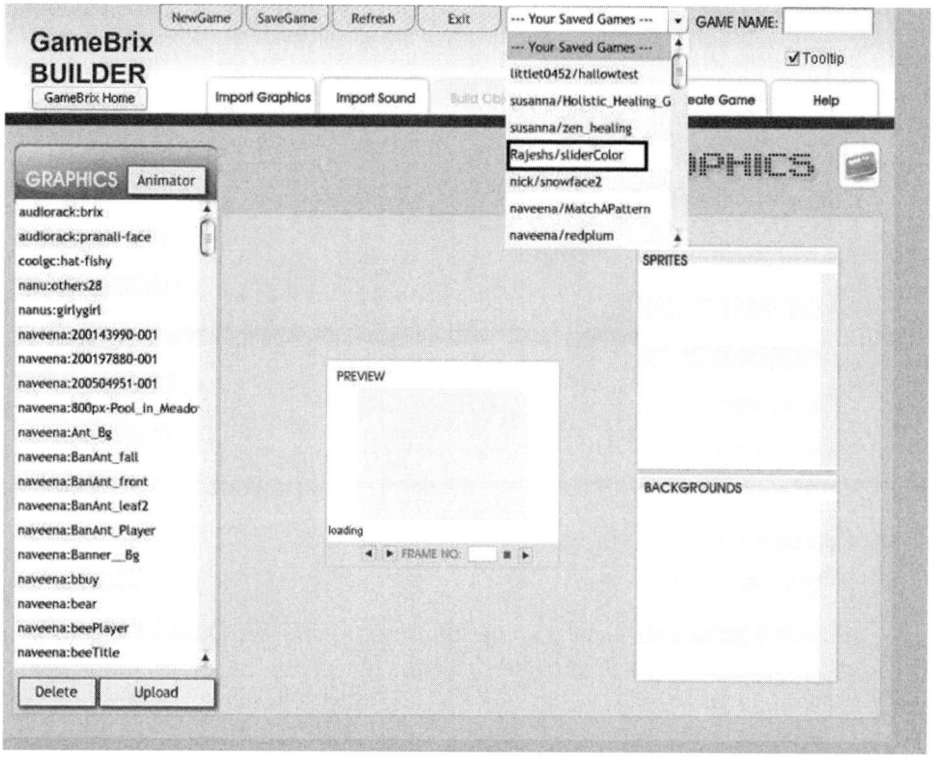

FIGURE 10.18
Shared game in Builder.

Select the Create Game tab and preview the game. You will see the game open in a new window, as shown in Figure 10.19. The game challenges the player to move the tiles with the mouse and match the pattern shown on the separated tile. Enjoy playing the game.

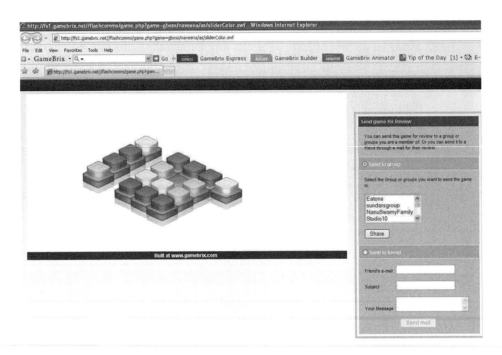

FIGURE 10.19
Color Slider game.

To modify the game, explore the objects using the Object Editor. The game has two objects: box and controller. The box object uses the SliderColor_Box sprite that belongs to the coolgc group, and the controller uses the bubble sprite. Exploring the sprites with the Import Graphics tab shows that the SliderColor_Box sprite consists of five frames. Use the arrow keys on the preview window to view the graphics on each frame, as shown in Figure 10.20.

GameBrix member Rajeshs created the sprites used in the game. Add your graphics to the game to modify it. Invite friends to join your group, and enjoy building custom games as a group activity. To share your completed games with your group, select the group name, as shown in Figure 10.21.

You see a message indicating that the game was shared successfully.

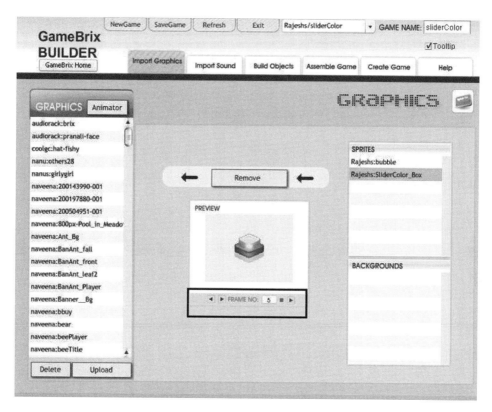

FIGURE 10.20
View of `SliderColor_Box` animated sprite.

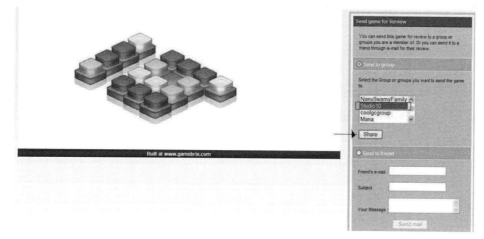

FIGURE 10.21
Sharing games with a group.

SUMMARY

In this tutorial, you explored the process of creating groups, joining groups, sharing assets, employing gaming mechanics, and sharing games with members. Game-Brix enables online collaboration and distribution of Flash games. In the next chapter, you learn to build a puzzle game.

11 Building a Puzzle Game

In This Chapter

Puzzle games, such as *Tetris*, are fun to play because they engage your mind and improve your memory. You can easily create online puzzle games using GameBrix Builder, and then you can share the games you create with your friends. Building puzzle games requires knowledge of dynamic masking capabilities available in ActionScript. Masking concepts are covered in detail with an example before creating the puzzle game.

Building a puzzle game requires two objects: a puzzle `manager` object and a `picture` object. The puzzle `manager` object handles all the major functions, whereas the `picture` object handles the functionality that an individual puzzle piece requires. Two images that represent these two objects are required. In this example, a small dot represents the puzzle manager. The final picture of the completed puzzle represents the puzzle piece. It might seem strange to have each puzzle piece represented by the picture of a completed puzzle, but this works well when used with movie clip–masking tricks.

WHAT IS MASKING?

A term originally derived from photography, *masking* defines the method to protect specific portions of a photograph from alteration. Masking can also be described from a painter's perspective. It is the process of using masking tape to mask out the parts of the painting that you want to protect from accidental damage.

ActionScript provides a mechanism for creating masks to hide pictures, just as painters use masking tape to hide areas. Masking is an important concept used in building puzzle games. You need to have a solid grasp of how masks are created and manipulated with ActionScript. You can apply masking techniques to hide or show different parts of a picture. Figure 11.1 shows a picture without a mask.

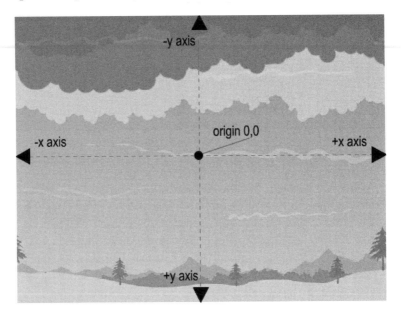

FIGURE 11.1
A sample picture without the application of a mask.

To mask that picture selectively, you need a new MovieClip object. Ideally, it should be sized equally to the picture. You can create this new MovieClip object by using ActionScript. An enclosed area within that movie clip can be defined to be the visible portion of the mask. You can then attach this movie clip to the original picture using the setMask function to selectively change the visibility of the original picture.

The sequence of instructions required to create a mask using ActionScript are shown here:

```
var mask = this.createEmptyMovieClip("myMask", this.getNextHighestDepth());
mask.beginFill(0xFF0000);
mask.moveTo(maskxpos, maskypos);
mask.lineTo(maskxpos + maskwidth, maskypos);
mask.lineTo(maskxpos + maskwidth, maskypos + maskheight);
mask.lineTo(maskxpos, maskypos + maskheight);
mask.lineTo(maskxpos, maskypos);
this.setMask(mask);
```

A brief description of the code warrants discussion here. Four variables define the rectangular mask area. maskxpos and maskypos define the X and Y coordinates of the top-left corner of the mask. maskheight and maskwidth define the height and width of the mask. Keep in mind that GameBrix objects have their origin at the center, as shown in Figure 11.1.

To mask a picture object, first create a new (empty) movie clip. Think of it as a brand new sheet of paper. Next, define the color of the pen to use for drawing on this movie clip. You draw using the Flash drawing functions beginfill, moveTo, and lineTo. The rectangular area drawn becomes the transparent portion of the mask. Using the paper analogy, this is similar to making a portion of the paper transparent so that images behind it are visible. All other areas of the image are masked out. The line of code this.setMask(mask) is the glue that attaches the new movie clip to the original picture object for masking purposes.

A mask with its top-left corner at 0, 0, with a height and width of 150 pixels, is shown in dotted lines in Figure 11.2. Notice that the enclosed area within the rectangle is visible.

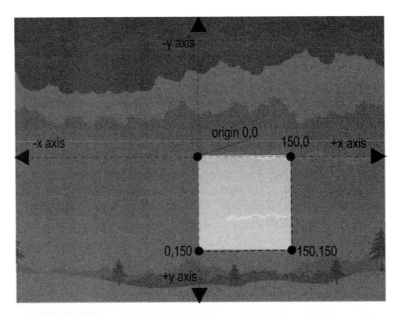

FIGURE 11.2
A rectangular region 150 pixels wide and 150 pixels high.

The masking sequence is done using ActionScript code. Four variables named `maskxpos`, `maskypos`, `maskheight`, and `maskwidth` are initialized with a value of either 0 or 150. You can do this by either creating new variables using the New Var button within the Script Editor or using the `ChangeVariable` task. This example uses the New Var button.

The line

```
var mask = this.createEmptyMovieClip("myMask", this.getNextHighestDepth())
```

creates a movie clip named `myMask`. The new movie clip created is placed above all the others by the function `this.getNextHighestDepth()`. You have to place the mask on top of all the other movie clips for it to work correctly in this example.

The next line of code

```
mask.beginFill(0xFF0000);
```

defines the color that fills the mask area.

With the variables `maskxpos` and `maskypos` set to 0, the line of code `mask.moveTo(maskxpos, maskypos)` moves the drawing pen to the location 0, 0, which is the origin.

`mask.lineTo(maskxpos + maskwidth, maskypos)` moves the pen to the location 150, 0 and draws a line. Note that the sum of the variables `maskxpos` and `maskwidth` is 150.

`mask.lineTo(maskxpos + maskwidth, maskypos + maskheight)` moves the pen to the location 150, 150 and draws the second line. Note that the sum of the variables `maskxpos` and `maskwidth` is 150, as is the sum of the variables `maskypos` and `maskheight`.

`mask.lineTo(maskxpos, maskypos + maskheight)` moves the pen to the location 0, 150 and draws the third line. Note that the sum of the variables `maskypos` and `maskheight` is 150.

`mask.moveTo(maskxpos, maskypos)` moves the drawing pen back to the origin and draws the fourth line that completes a rectangle.

`this.setMask(mask)` sets the defined rectangular region to be the mask. This makes only the image behind this rectangular area visible, as shown in Figure 11.3. All other areas are masked out. You can visualize the `setMask` ActionScript function as having the opposite effect of the painter's masking tape. The areas masked using the painter's masking tape become invisible, whereas the areas masked using the ActionScript function call `setmask()` make the designated area transparent.

FIGURE 11.3
Visible rectangular region 150 pixels wide and 150 pixels high after the application of the mask.

IMPLEMENTING MASKS

To begin experimenting with masks, log in to the GameBrix portal, go to the store, and buy the item labeled Fig11_1. You can access the store by clicking on the Store menu item highlighted in Figure 11.4. The store has many items, making it hard to find the one you need. The easiest way to find what you're looking for is to use the Search by Name feature and type Fig11_1 in the Search box. Buy the picture by clicking on the Buy button, and then complete the transaction.

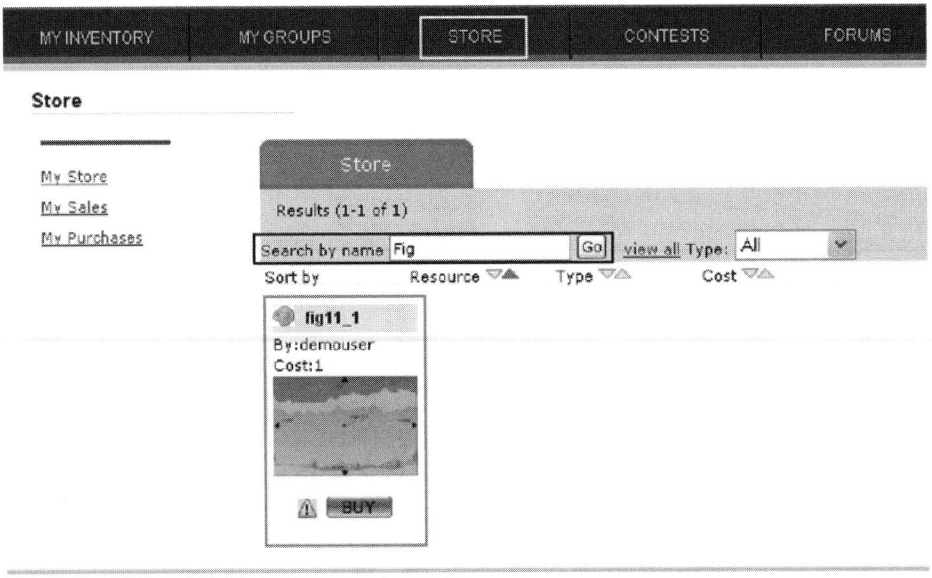

FIGURE 11.4
The GameBrix store.

Open the GameBrix GameBuilder Web application and locate the graphic labeled Fig11_1, as shown in Figure 11.5. Click on it in the Graphics window on the left, and then click the Add Sprite button to move it to the selected Sprites window on the right.

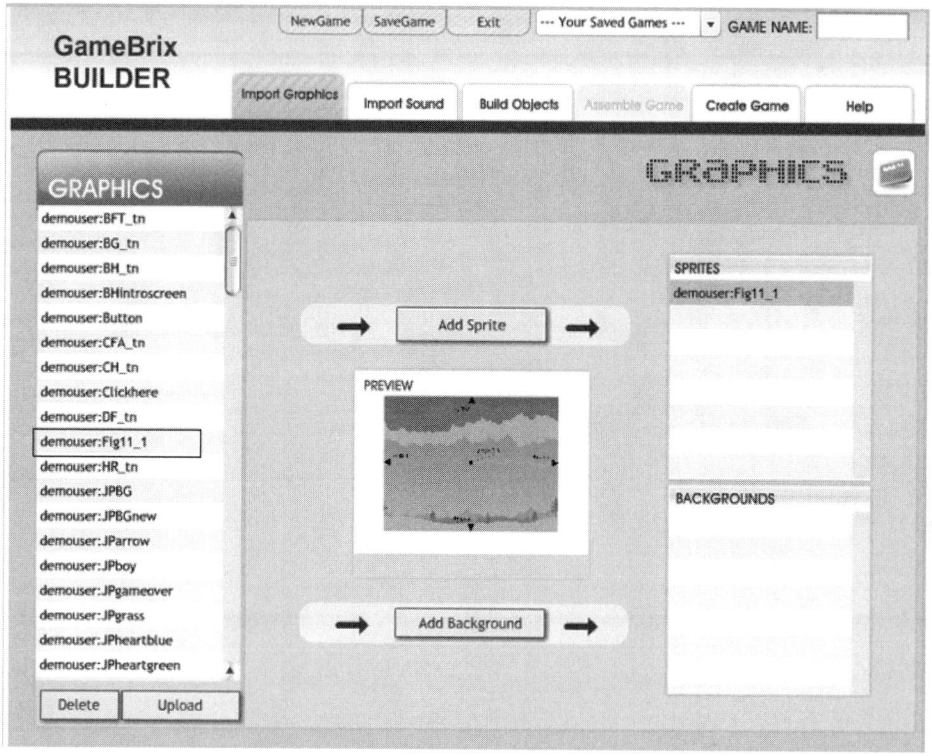

FIGURE 11.5
Selecting the image.

The next step is to build an object. Click on the Build Objects tab and then on the New Object button. That brings you to the screen shown in Figure 11.6. In the object's Name field, type `picture`, and click on the `Fig11_1` graphic so that it is displayed in the preview window. To complete the object creation process, click the Done button. That takes you back to the Build Objects tab.

To begin creating the mask, click on the Object Editor button. This opens the Script Editor window. Add a `Click` state to the object by double-clicking it on the States list, as shown in Figure 11.7. Create the four variables one by one by clicking on the New Var button. Create the first variable named `maskxpos` of type `number` with an initial value of `0`, and fill in the values shown in Figure 11.8. Then click the Submit button to complete creation of the first variable. After that, create the other three required variables. Their names, datatypes, and initial values are shown in Table 11.1.

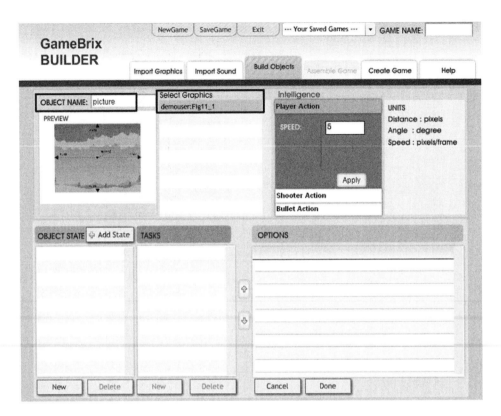

FIGURE 11.6
Building the `picture` object.

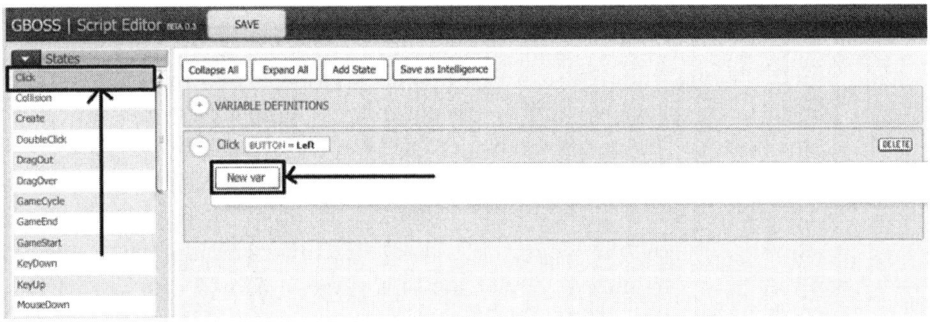

FIGURE 11.7
The New Var button.

FIGURE 11.8
Creating a variable.

TABLE 11.1 VARIABLES: THEIR DATA TYPE AND VALUES

Variable Name	Variable Type	Member Type	Variable Value
maskypos	Number	Dynamic	0
maskxpos	Number	Dynamic	0
maskwidth	Number	Dynamic	150
maskheight	Number	Dynamic	150

After you create the four variables with their initial values, the Script Editor screen should look similar to Figure 11.9.

FIGURE 11.9
Variables definition.

The next step is to add the InsertScript task highlighted in Figure 11.10. Click and drag the InsertScript task to the object's Click state.

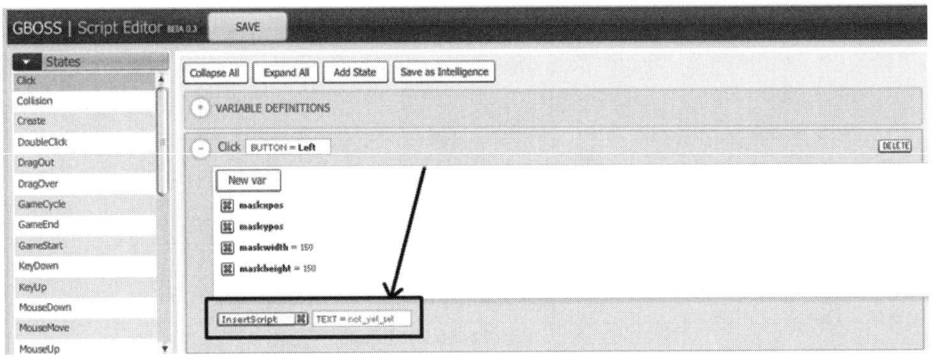

FIGURE 11.10
Adding the `InsertScript` task.

In the next step, enter the text (code) required by the `InsertScript` task. There are two ways to do this. You can put all the code inside one `InsertScript` task, or you can put each line of ActionScript code on individual ActionScript tasks. It is easier to debug the code under the `InsertScript` task using the first approach. The masking script required is shown here:

```
var mask = this.createEmptyMovieClip("myMask", this.getNextHighestDepth());
mask.beginFill(0xFF0000);
mask.moveTo(maskxpos, maskypos);
mask.lineTo(maskxpos + maskwidth, maskypos);
mask.lineTo(maskxpos + maskwidth, maskypos + maskheight);
mask.lineTo(maskxpos, maskypos + maskheight);
mask.lineTo(maskxpos, maskypos);
this.setMask(mask);
```

The steps that follow put all the script inside one task. Click on the argument for the `InsertScript` task, shown as Step 1 in Figure 11.11. This opens the Text options box for the `InsertScript` task. Next, click on the empty value field highlighted as Step 2. This opens the `InsertScript` Value box highlighted as Step 3. Type all the masking code into this box, as shown in the figure. Be careful, because even a small mistake can cause the compiler to generate an error. Click the Apply button, and then close the Options box.

To make the code readable and easier to understand at a later point, have one `InsertScript` task for each line of code. If you use multiple `InsertScript` tasks, your screen will look like the one shown in Figure 11.12.

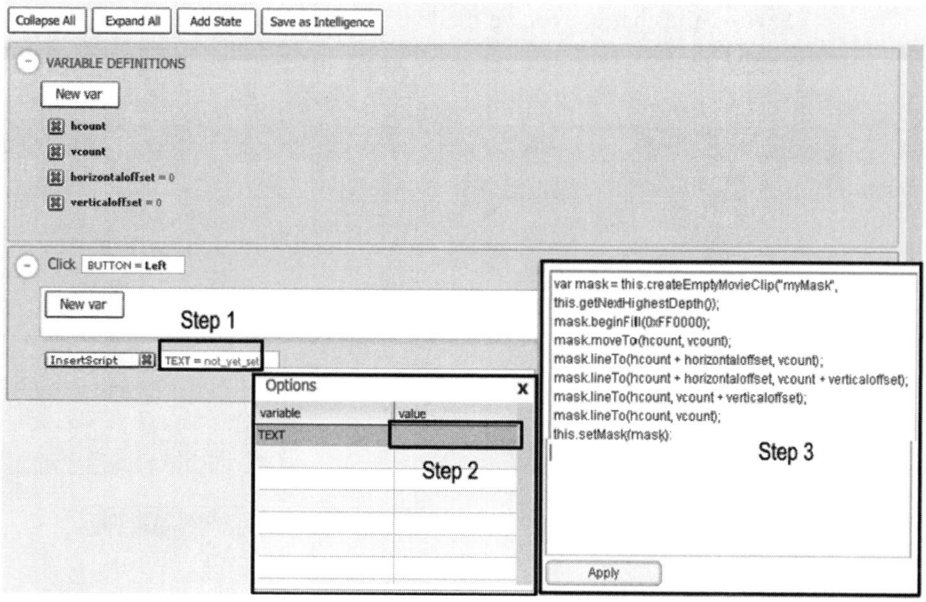

FIGURE 11.11
Using a single `InsertScript` task.

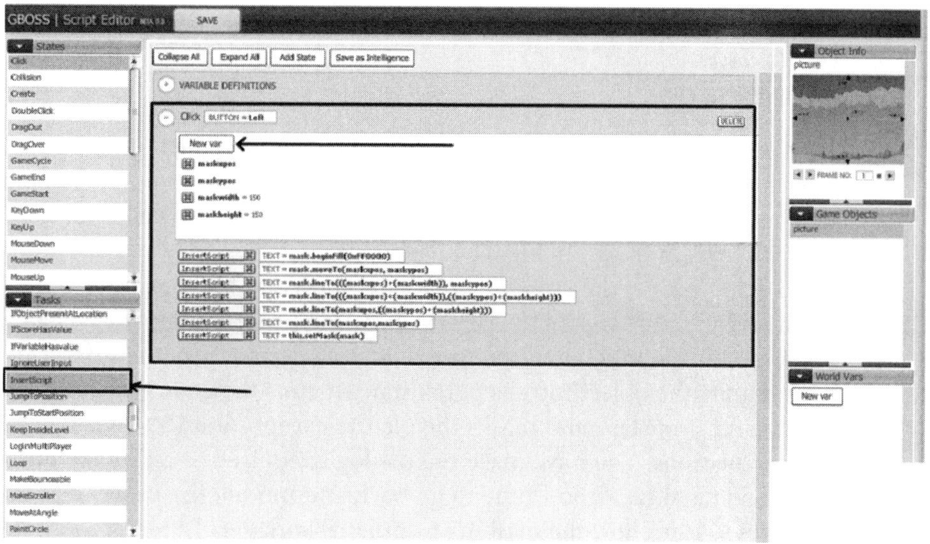

FIGURE 11.12
Using multiple `InsertScript` tasks.

Save all the changes you've made with the Script Editor using the Save button shown in Figure 11.13. Then wait for the pop-up box that displays the Save Complete message.

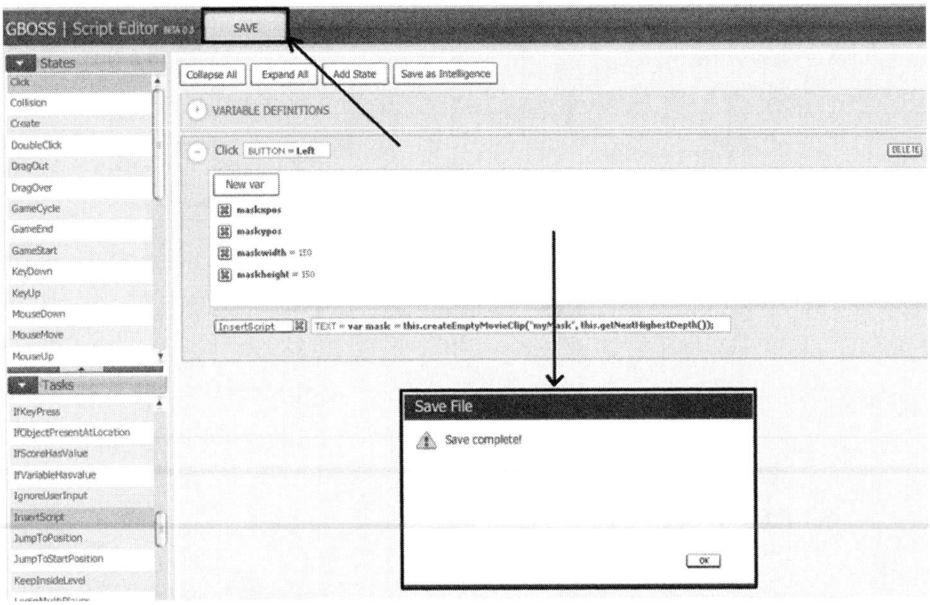

FIGURE 11.13
Saving the script.

Close the Script Editor window and then go back to the GameBuilder window. You should see a pop-up box that displays the message Game ready to build. Close that box and click on the Assemble Game tab. Click and drag a picture object onto the first level, as shown in Figure 11.14.

Next, click on the Create Game tab, and click the Generate Game button. Then save your file and let the game generation process complete. When the game is loaded, you should see the picture that you selected from the store. Clicking the picture puts the object into its Click state. It runs the code you embedded using the InsertScript task and masks the picture except for a 150 by 150 pixel square. Congratulations! You have mastered the logic required to create the puzzle game.

Now might be a good time to go back and modify the values set for the four variables to learn how the masking technique works.

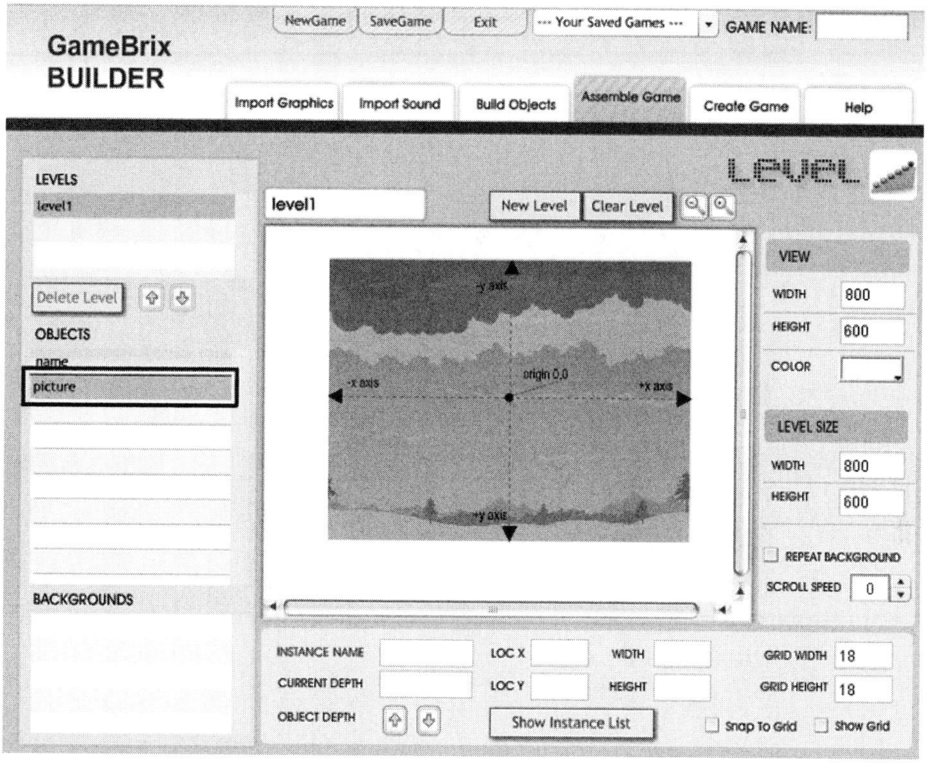

FIGURE 11.14
Assembling the game room.

BUILDING THE GAME

To start creating the puzzle game, you need a picture and a red dot. The picture used in this example is shown in Figure 11.15. Go to the GameBrix store and buy the picture named Fig11_15. To find the asset named Fig11_15, type Fig in the search box on the Store page to narrow your choices. Alternatively, you can create a picture using the GameBrix Animator. Be sure to set the size of the picture to 640 pixels by 480 pixels in that case.

FIGURE 11.15
Puzzle game picture.

Before building complex puzzle games, think about the logic required to create a simple puzzle that has two rows and two columns. For a 2-column-by-2-row puzzle, you need four instances of the picture. You create and place them at random distances from the center of the game level, as shown in Figure 11.16. These four instances are marked as piece1, piece2, piece3, and piece4. Based on the piece, a mask is created, as shown in Figure 11.17. To create four puzzle pieces, you need four masks. Each mask has a different offset from the top-left corner of the image. For example, in piece1, the mask is on the top-left corner of the image, and for piece4, it is on the bottom right of the image. More pieces require more masks. The random placement of these masked images will look like a broken-up jigsaw puzzle. Each of these pieces is a GameBrix object that you can drag and drop. If the pieces are close to the final destination, they snap in place. If all the pieces are positioned correctly, the player wins and the game is over.

FIGURE 11.16
Four pictures to create a 2-by-2 jigsaw puzzle.

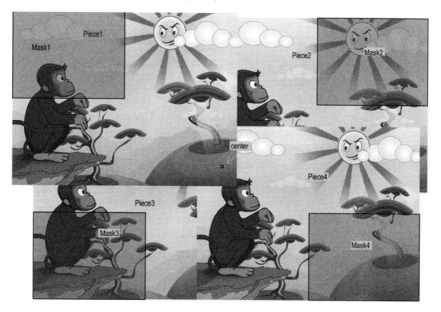

FIGURE 11.17
Four pictures with their masks.

With an understanding of the basics of puzzle game creation, it's time to create one. Log in to the GameBrix portal and load the online GameBrix Builder application. In the Import Graphics tab, choose two images. One of them is a small dot, and the other is a picture of the completed puzzle. Figure 11.18 shows the two images that you need.

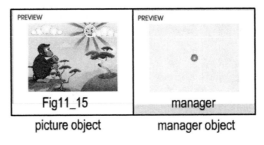

picture object   manager object

FIGURE 11.18
Images required for the puzzle game.

Create two objects: one called manager that is attached to the small red dot, and the other named picture that is attached to the jigsaw picture. The two objects are shown in Figure 11.18. No tasks or states are assigned to either of these objects at this point.

CREATING THE MANAGER OBJECT

Open the Script Editor by clicking the Script Editor button located on the Objects tab. There should be two object listed in the Game Objects window on your right. Click on the manager object to start working with it. Begin creating the seven world variables by clicking on the New Var button in the World Vars panel on your right. The details of each of these variables are listed in Table 11.2. The variables managerxpos and managerypos keep track of the manager object's X and Y coordinates. The rows and columns variables define the number of rows and columns to break the puzzle picture into. picturewidth and pictureheight define the puzzle picture's actual width and height in pixels. The initialized world variables are shown in Figure 11.19. Verify that your work has the same variables as shown there.

TABLE 11.2 MANAGER OBJECTS AND WORLD VARIABLES: THEIR DATA TYPE AND VALUES

Variable Name	Variable Type	Member Type	Variable Value
managerxpos	Number	Dynamic	0
managerypos	Number	Dynamic	0
rows	Number	Dynamic	4
columns	Number	Dynamic	4
picturewidth	Number	Dynamic	0
pictureheight	Number	Dynamic	0
count	Number	Dynamic	0

FIGURE 11.19
Initialized global variables.

THE MANAGER OBJECT'S CREATE TASK LIST

Initialization of variables for the manager object is done in the object's Create state. You can add the Create state by double-clicking it, as shown in Figure 11.20.

FIGURE 11.20
Adding the Create state.

Add two ChangeVariable tasks to use the manager object's X and Y coordinates into the world variables managerxpos and managerypos. Use Table 11.3 and Table 11.4 to set the options for the two ChangeVariable tasks. Figure 11.21 shows the two completed ChangeVariable tasks.

TABLE 11.3 CHANGEVARIABLE TASK

Variable	Value
VARIABLENAME	World.managerxpos
VARIABLEVALUE	this._x
EXPRESSION	true
RELATIVE	true

TABLE 11.4 CHANGEVARIABLE TASK

Variable	Value
VARIABLENAME	World.managerypos
VARIABLEVALUE	this._y
EXPRESSION	true
RELATIVE	true

The `manager` object creates several instances of the `picture` object. You do this by using the `CreateInstance` task inside a `Loop` task. For each instance of the piece object that is created, a function named `initialize` is invoked. Click and drag a `Loop` task from the taskbar on the left, which drags an `EndLoop` task along with it. A `Loop` task always accompanies an `EndLoop` task. The parameters used for the `Loop` task are shown in Table 11.5.

TABLE 11.5 LOOP TASK

Variable	Value
CONDITION	<
VARIABLENAME	i
INCVALUE	true
ENDVALUE	World.columns*World.rows
INITIALVALUE	0

Next, create instances of the `picture` object inside the `Loop` task by clicking and dragging the `CreateInstance` task inside the `Loop` task. The options used for the `CreateInstance` task are shown in Table 11.6. Instances created are a maximum of 100 pixels away in the X and Y directions from the center of the `manager` object. The ActionScript function `Math.floor(Math.random() * 200) -100` returns a value between −100 and +100.

TABLE 11.6 CREATEINSTANCE TASK

Variable	Value
VARIABLENAME	piece
INSTANCENAME	picture
RELATIVE	true
XLOC	Math.floor(Math.random() * 200) -100
YLOC	Math.floor(Math.random() * 200) -100

The initialize() function is invoked on the newly created picture object. The next step is to click and drag the CallFunction task below the CreateInstance task, as shown in Figure 11.21. The parameters required for this task are shown in Table 11.7.

TABLE 11.7 CALLFUNCTION TASK

Variable	Value
ARGS	(i%World.rows),Math.floor(i/World.columns)
OBJECT	piece
FUNCTION	initialize

The last task to add is SetTimer. Click and drag a SetTimer task beneath the EndLoop task. The timer number 0 is set to be activated after 1,000 milliseconds. The complete set of tasks for the Create event is shown in Figure 11.21. This is a good time to compare the tasks you've created with those depicted in Figure 11.21. Make sure they are identical before proceeding.

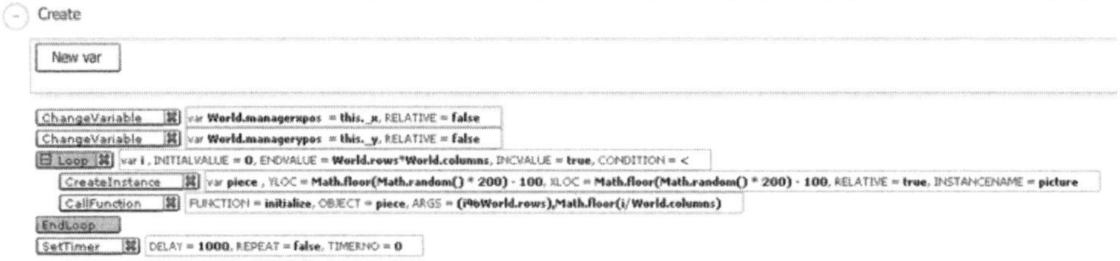

FIGURE 11.21
The manager object's Create task list.

THE MANAGER OBJECT'S TIMER TASK LIST

The manager object needs to perform certain tasks when it enters the timer state. Add a timer state with its number parameter set to 0. Inside this state, ActionScript code is used to draw out a red background. This is done using the ActionScript code snippet shown here:

```
this.beginFill(0xFF0000);
this.moveTo(-World.picturewidth/2,-World.pictureheight/2);
this.lineTo(World.picturewidth/2,-World.pictureheight/2);
this.lineTo(World.picturewidth/2,World.pictureheight/2);
this.lineTo(-World.picturewidth/2,World.pictureheight/2);
this.lineTo(-World.picturewidth/2,-World.pictureheight/2);
this.endFill(0xFF0000);
```

You can insert each of these lines as separate tasks using multiple InsertScript tasks, or you can put them all inside one InsertScript task. It is more readable if each line of ActionScript is embedded inside one InsertScript task, as shown in Figure 11.22.

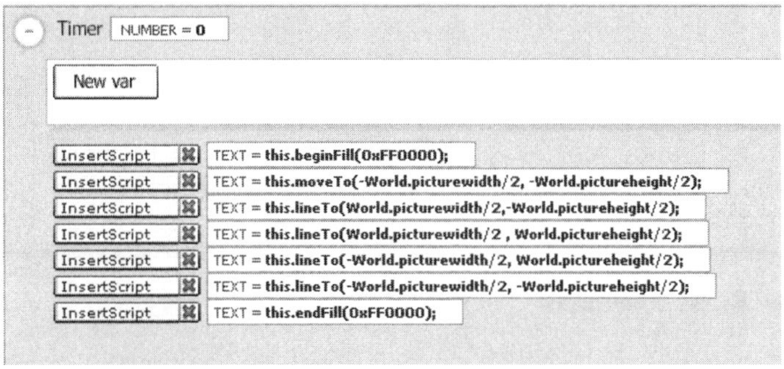

FIGURE 11.22
The timer tasks for the manager object.

With that, your manager object is complete. It can create multiple instances of the picture object. The picture object implements the masking and checking functionality for the jigsaw puzzle.

CREATING THE PICTURE OBJECT

The picture object has to perform several tasks during the mouse Click and mouse Press states. It also has to perform initialization tasks in the Create event and requires two custom states to perform other tasks. Now it's time to create all these states for the picture object. With the picture object selected, double-click on the Create state to move it over. Then double-click the Click state and the Press state to add them to the picture object. Create a custom state named initialize by clicking the Add State button. Next, click on its empty argument list and type cw,ch.

These two variables denote column width and column height, respectively. Create another custom state and name it slice. Then change its argument to num to signify the jigsaw puzzle piece number.

After you create these states for the picture object, the Script Editor screen should look like that shown in Figure 11.23.

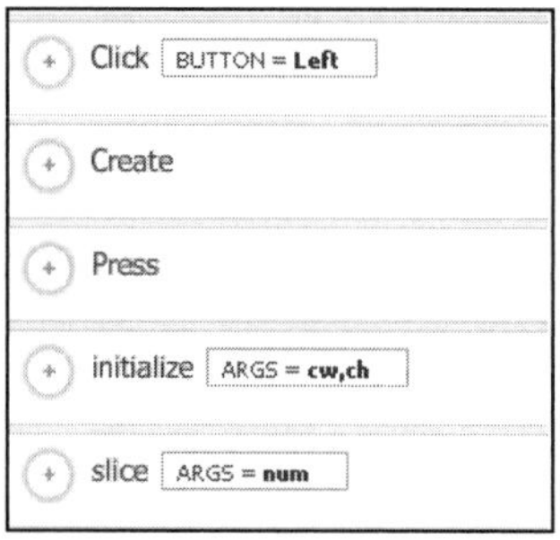

FIGURE 11.23
All the states required for the
picture object.

CREATING THE CLASS VARIABLES

A couple of variables that are visible only to the picture object are required. You can create class variables for this purpose using the New Var button found at the top of the Object Definition window. Create four class variables named hcount, vcount, horizontaloffset, and verticaloffset of type number (see Figure 11.24).

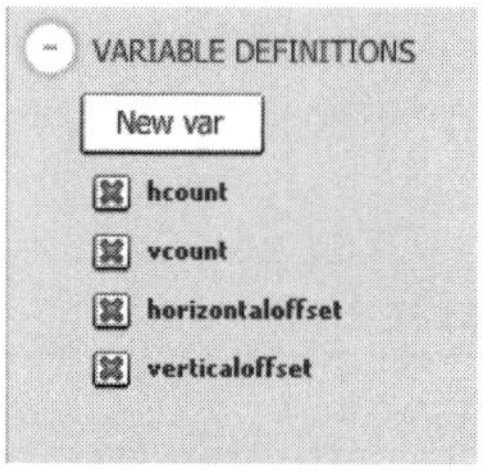

FIGURE 11.24
picture object's class
variables.

THE PICTURE OBJECT'S CREATE STATE

The different tasks to add in the Create state are listed next.

Add two ChangeVariable tasks to save the picture width and height in world variables named pictureheight and picturewidth, as shown in Figure 11.25. Table 11.8 lists the options for these two ChangeVariable tasks.

TABLE 11.8 CHANGEVARIABLE TASK

Variable	Value	Value
VARIABLENAME	World.picturewidth	World.pictureheight
VARIABLEVALUE	this._width	this._height;
EXPRESSION	true	true
RELATIVE	false	false

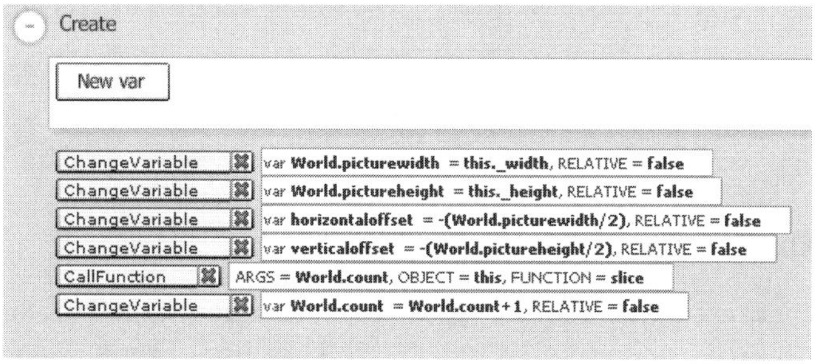

FIGURE 11.25
The picture object's complete Create state.

Add two more ChangeVariable tasks to save the offset to the left border and top border in class variables horizontaloffset and verticaloffset.

Add a CallFunction task to call a slice function. The slice function requires the current value to be assigned to the count world variable. The count variable indirectly provides positioning information to the slice function on where the picture will be loaded.

Add a ChangeVariable task to increment the count world variable. This is in preparation for passing the next new number when slicing the next picture.

All information required for completing the task list for the `Create` state is shown in Figure 11.25. Once again, this is a good time to stop and check whether the information shown in the figure matches the information on your screen.

THE PICTURE OBJECT'S PRESS STATE

The `picture` object needs the click-and-drag behavior in the jigsaw puzzle. As soon as a user presses the left mouse button on that object, the `picture` object should start following the mouse, and when the user releases the button, the `picture` object should stop moving. The `picture` object should snap onto the jigsaw puzzle's frame if it is placed within 20 pixels of its correct destination.

You can use the tasks `StartDrag` and `PlaceAboveAll` to accomplish this. Figure 11.26 shows the tasks in the `Press` state. Add the tasks `StartDrag` and `PlaceAboveAll` to the `picture` object's `Press` state.

FIGURE 11.26
The `picture` object's complete `Press` state.

THE PICTURE OBJECT'S CLICK STATE

The `picture` object requires four local variables named `minXpos`, `minYpos`, `maxXpos`, and `maxYpos`, shown in Figure 11.27. They are of type `number` and can be created by clicking the New Var button beneath the `Click` state. The tasks in the `Click` state work in conjunction with the tasks in the `Press` state. Add the `StopDrag` task to disable the `picture` object from following the mouse.

Add four `ChangeVariable` tasks to set the minimum and maximum X and Y positions that the `picture` object can be positioned at to snap into position. If the jigsaw puzzle piece is less than 20 pixels to its final destination, it is snapped into position. Four nested `IfVariableHasvalue` tasks determine if the `picture` object's distance is less than 20 pixels away from its destination. If the conditions match, the `picture` object is snapped into place. Add a `StopDrag` task inside the innermost loop. Then, using two `ChangeVariable` tasks, set the X and Y coordinates to be the same as the `manager` object's X and Y coordinates. Verify whether your work matches the completed `Click` state shown in Figure 11.27 before proceeding further.

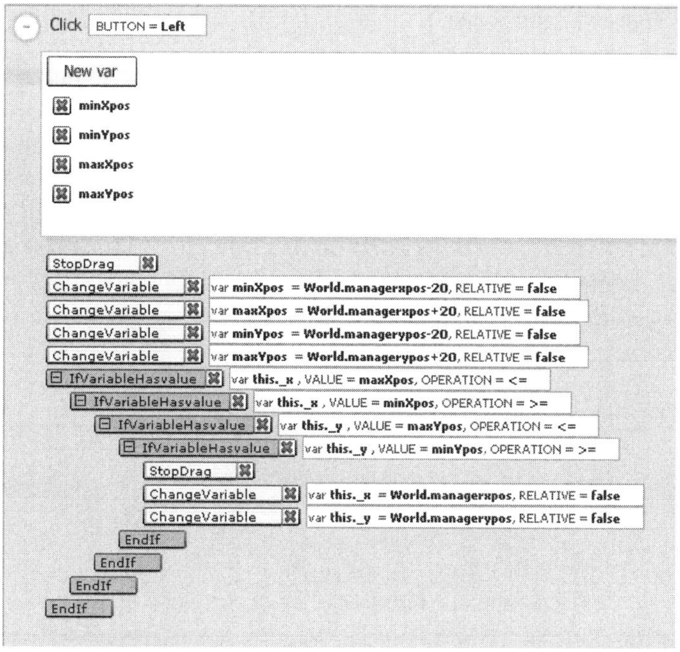

FIGURE 11.27
The picture object's complete Click state.

THE PICTURE OBJECT'S INITIALIZE STATE

Add two ChangeVariable tasks to the initialize state to set the hcount and vcount variables, as shown in Figure 11.28. They refer to the row and column location within the picture object that has to be masked.

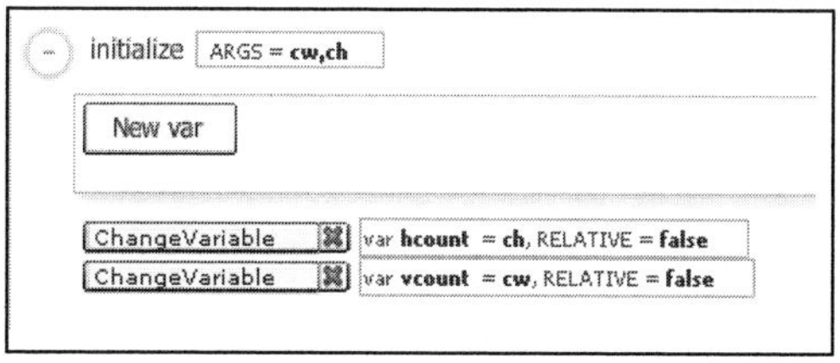

FIGURE 11.28
The picture object's complete initialize state.

THE PICTURE OBJECT'S SLICE STATE

This custom state handles the masking of the picture object based on its row and column position. Create four local variables of type Number by clicking the New Var button in the slice state. Name the first two variables maskxpos and maskypos; they refer to the X and Y offsets of the mask. Name the next two variables maskwidth and maskheight; they are the mask's dimensions. Next create an Object variable and name it mask. It is an object that holds a reference to the masking movie clip. Table 11.9 defines the mask variable, and Figure 11.29 shows the complete variable and task list for the slice state. Add the tasks to your work by using Figure 11.29 as a reference. An explanation of the tasks follows.

TABLE 11.9 MASK VARIABLE DEFINITION

Field Name	Field Value
Name	mask
Type	Object
Member Type	Dynamic
Value	

The first two ChangeVariable tasks within the slice (Figure 11.29) state set values for variables maskwidth and maskheight to the dimensions of a single puzzle piece within a picture object. The third and fourth ChangeVariable tasks set the variables maskxpos and maskypos to the X and Y positions of the mask with respect to the top-left corner of the picture object. The fifth ChangeVariable task creates an empty movie clip on top of all other objects. The MovieClip object is stored in the mask variable. The six InsertScript tasks that follow draw the rectangular area, and the last InsertScript task sets this area as the mask. Ensure that your work matches what's shown in Figure 11.29 before proceeding further.

This completes the creation of the picture object. Save your work by clicking the Save button found at the top of the Script Editor window. You will see a small image displayed while the save operation is in progress and then an OK box signifying its completion. Click the OK button and switch back to the GameBrix Builder window that was opened before the Script Editor was launched. You should see a dialog box that displays the message Game ready to build, as shown in Figure 11.30.

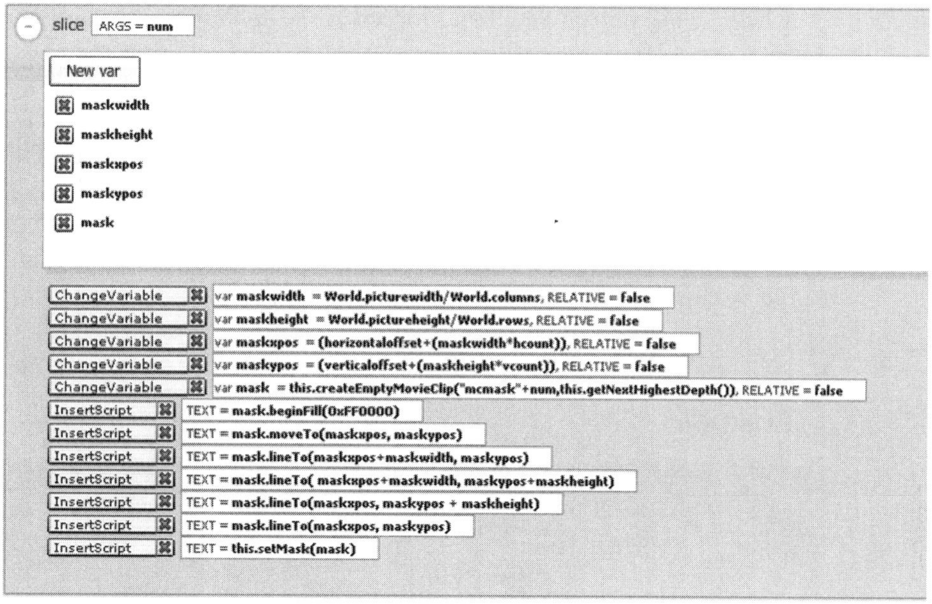

FIGURE 11.29
The `picture` object's complete `slice` state.

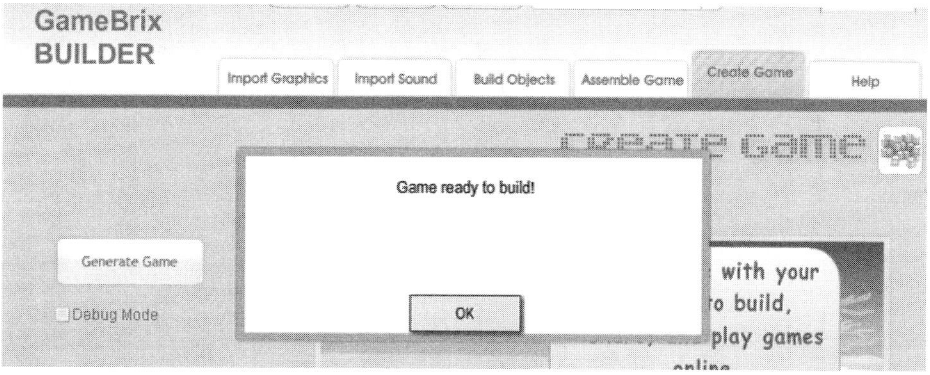

FIGURE 11.30
`Game ready to build` **dialog box.**

Click the OK button and then proceed to the Assemble Game tab. You should see the two available objects displayed on the left. Click and drag the manager object to the center of the level, as shown in Figure 11.31. Set the width of the level to 800 pixels and the height to 600 pixels, as shown in Figure 11.31. If the manager object is not at the right position, click on it after it is placed on the level. The manager object should have manipulators displayed around it when it is selected. You can change the manager object's location by modifying the values in the LOC X and LOC Y text boxes shown in Figure 11.31. The two values for LOC X and LOC Y should be close to 400 and 300, respectively.

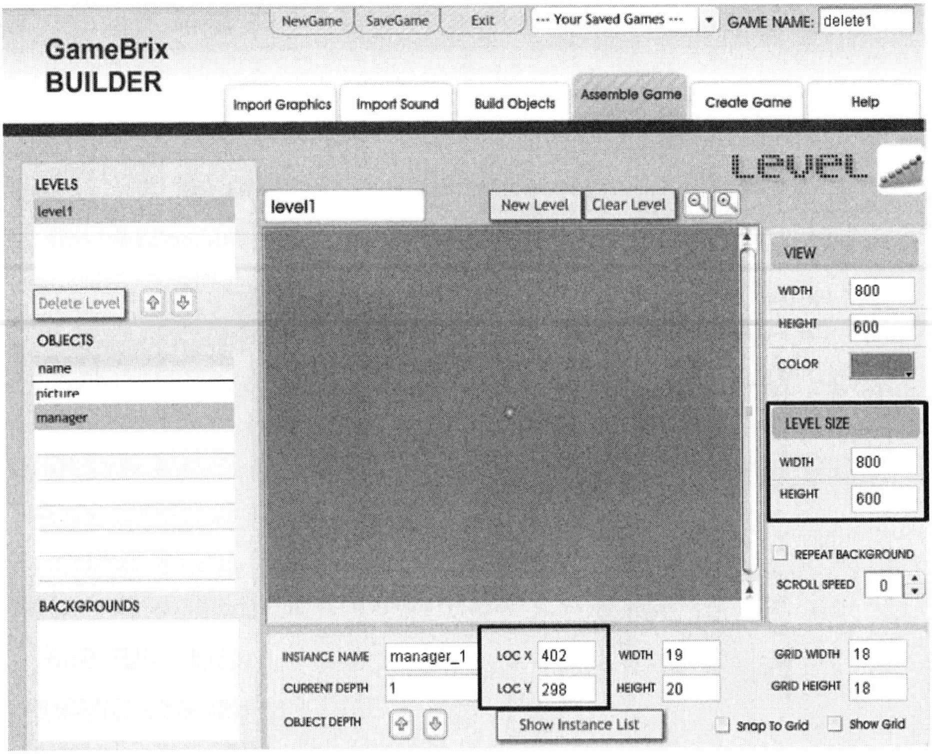

FIGURE 11.31
Positioning the Game manager object inside the level.

Now it's time to build the game. Click on the Create Game tab, and then click the Generate button. Save your game. Your generated game is displayed on a new window. Click and drag the pieces. They should snap into their slots when they are positioned and released about 20 pixels away from their correct position.

ADDING THE FINISHING TOUCHES

To make this a complete game, you need a few different elements:

- An introductory screen that enables users to play this game at multiple levels
- A message that displays the number of pieces that have been positioned correctly
- A message that congratulates the user when the game is completed successfully

These assets are available in the store. You need an introductory screen as shown in Figure 11.32, a Restart button as shown in Figure 11.33, and a flash label component. You can find these in the store labeled `Fig11_32`, `Fig11_33`, and `Fig11_34`, respectively. The item labeled `Fig11_34` is the flash label component that is in the SWF format. Go to the store, search for these items, and buy them. You can now use them to complete the game.

FIGURE 11.32
Puzzle game introductory screen.

FIGURE 11.33
Restart button.

ADDING IMAGES AND BACKGROUNDS

Click on the GameBuilder icon on the GameBrix portal to start the game creation Web application. Move the items labeled Fig11_33 and Fig11_34 to the active sprite list by clicking on them in the Graphics list and then clicking the Add Sprite button. Move the item labeled Fig11_32 to the Backgrounds list by clicking on it in the Graphics list and then clicking the Add Background button. After completing this step, the screen should look like Figure 11.34.

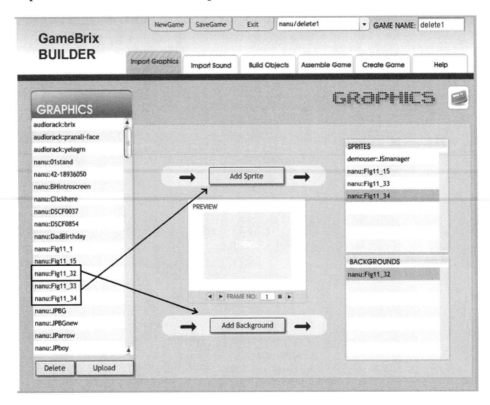

FIGURE 11.34
Images and background for finishing the game.

BUILDING NEW OBJECTS

New objects are required for completing the game. Three objects are required for choosing three levels of difficulty. Create LevelEasy, LevelMedium, and LevelHard. Let all of them use the Restart image labeled Fig11_33 as their sprite. Lay these objects over the areas labeled Easy, Medium, and Hard in the introductory screen, and then make them invisible using the TransformObject task as defined in Table 11.10. This will make the circular button-like shapes to the left of these labels behave like real buttons.

TABLE 11.10 SETTINGS FOR MAKING OBJECTS INVISIBLE

Object State	Task	Options Setting
Create	TransformObject	VISIBLE=False

Two more objects are required. A Restart object is required to restart the game, and an InfoLabel object is required to display the status of the game. You create the Restart object by clicking on the New Object button and then choosing Fig11_33 as its sprite. You create the InfoLabel object by clicking on the New Object button and then choosing Fig11_34 as its sprite. Note that Fig11_34 is actually a compiled flash file.

All the objects required for the puzzle game are shown in Figure 11.34. You'll use the Script Editor to customize the behavior of these objects.

Click on the Script Editor. The objects listed in the Build Objects tab shown in Figure 11.35 should also be visible in the Script Editor, as shown in Figure 11.36. Start building the LevelEasy object. Click on it in the Game Objects list to select it. Then add two object states: Create and Click.

FIGURE 11.35
Objects in the puzzle game.

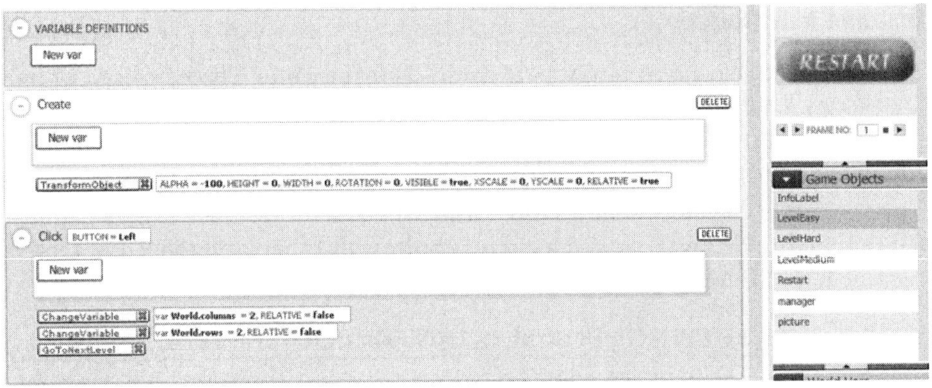

FIGURE 11.36
LevelEasy object.

You need a new world variable to keep track of the number of pieces that have been correctly placed within the puzzle. Create a world variable called matchCount of type number and initialize it to 0. There should be eight world variables at this point, as shown in Figure 11.37.

FIGURE 11.37
Summary of eight world variables required.

In the Create state of the LevelEasy object, add a TransformObject task and set the _alpha to −100 to make the object transparent. In the Click state, add two ChangeVariable tasks that assign the world variables columns and rows to a value of 2. Add a GoToNextLevel task that will take the user to the game. Figure 11.36 shows the completed LevelEasy object.

The LevelMedium object is an exact replica of the LevelEasy object except for the setting of the two ChangeVariable tasks. For medium complexity, the world row and column variables are set to a value of 6. For the hardest level, these variables are set to a value of 12.

Complete building the LevelMedium and LevelHard objects using the same procedure you used to build the LevelEasy object. Make sure the columns and rows world variables are set to the right values in each of those cases. Save your game and continue.

The function of the Restart object is to reset all variables and enable the user to restart the game. Click on the Restart object in the Game Objects list in the Script Editor. Then add a Click state. In the Click state, add two ChangeVariable tasks that set the world variables count and matchCount to a value of 0. Add a GotoNextLevel task. Figure 11.37 shows the completed Restart object.

The InfoLabel object displays information about the games progress. It is a flash component that displays a count of the pieces that have been matched and the total number of pieces in the puzzle. Click on the InfoLabel object in the Game Objects list within the Script Editor. Then add a GameCycle task.

Add the SetLabel task, and set the display message to that shown in Figure 11.38. It displays the number of pieces matched and the total number of pieces. The message to display is shown here:

```
World.matchCount + " pieces matched out of "+ World.rows*World.columns
+ " pieces."
```

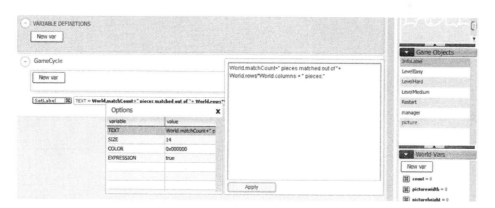

FIGURE 11.38
InfoLabel object.

The last object to modify before the game is tested is `picture`. Click on the `picture` object, and then move to the `Click` event shown in Figure 11.39. Following are the changes you need to make:

■ Disable the drag/drop capability of the `picture` object after it has been placed at the correct location.
■ If all the pieces have been placed in the right location, reset the `matchCount` variable to 0, display a message congratulating the player, and then go back to the start level.

Tasks that perform these operations are shown in Figure 11.39.

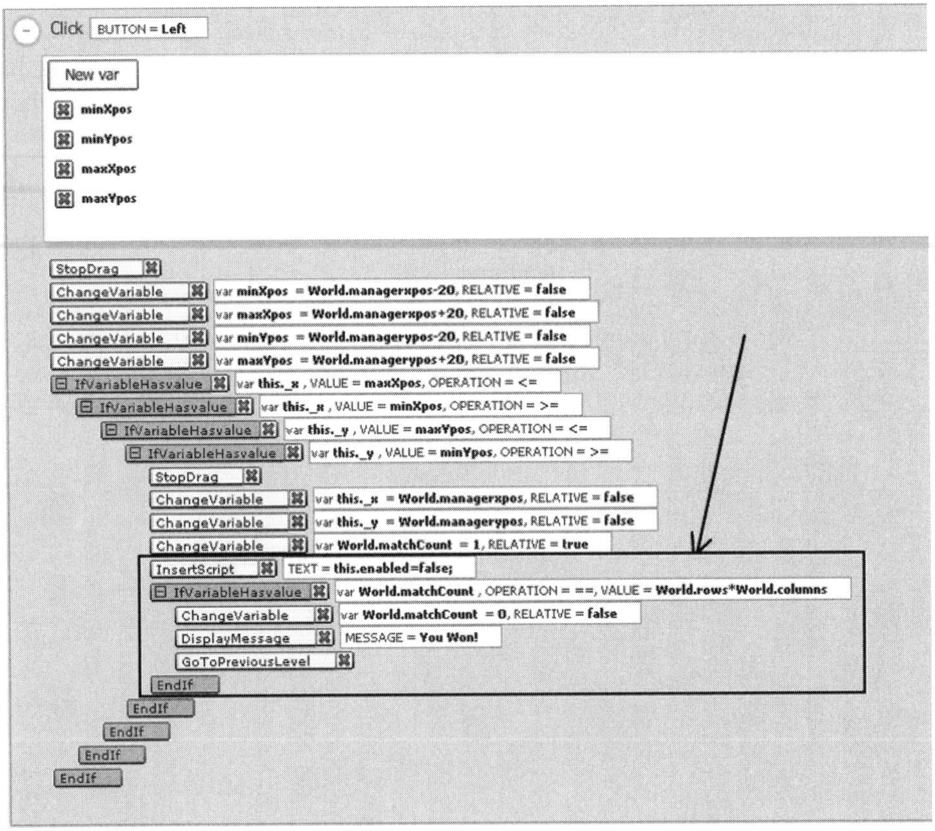

FIGURE 11.39
`Picture` object.

The first task to add is `InsertScript`. The command to execute is `this.enabled=false`. This ActionScript command disables the object from any user interaction.

The next task to add is `IfVariableHasValue`. It verifies whether the variable `World.matchCount` has the same value as the product of `World.rows` and `World.columns`.

The next three tasks are executed only if the game is over. The `ChangeVariable` task sets the `matchCount` variable back to 0 because you are starting a new game.

The `DisplayMessage` task congratulates the player on winning the puzzle game.

The `GoToPrevious` task enables the player to play the game again.

It's a good time to stop and check whether the work you have completed matches that shown in Figure 11.39.

Save your work by clicking the Save button in the Script Editor.

ASSEMBLING THE LEVELS

Move back to the GameBuilder screen and click on the Assemble Game tab. Follow steps 1 through 8 to assemble the title page for the game, as described next and shown in Figure 11.40.

1. Create a new level by clicking on the New Level button. This results in the creation of a new level named `Level2`. It will be your title page that should be displayed before the game starts.
2. Click on the level named `Level2` in the Levels list box.
3. Click the up arrow button to move `Level2` above `Level1`, as shown in Figure 11.40. This ensures that `Level2` runs before `Level1`.
4. Click the background. It moves to the right onto the level.
5. Click and drag the `Restart` object to the location ideal for a Restart button.
6. Click and drag the `LevelEasy` object to the top of the button labeled Easy in the background image.
7. Click and drag the `LevelMedium` object to the top of the button labeled Medium in the background image.
8. Click and drag the `LevelHard` object to the top of the button labeled Hard in the background image.

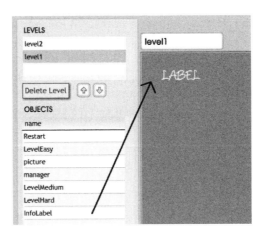

FIGURE 11.40
Assembling the title page.

Next, move to the level named Level1 by clicking on it, as shown in Figure 11.41. Click and drag the InfoLabel onto the top-left corner of the level, as shown in Figure 11.41.

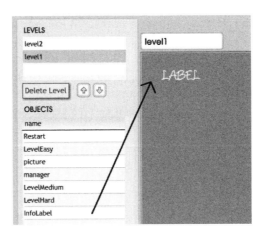

FIGURE 11.41
Assembling the game page.

Congratulations!

That completes the creation of the puzzle game. Now it's time to build the game again, so click on the Create Game tab and then click the Generate button. Save your game, which is displayed on a new window. In the title page, choose the level you want to play, and click and drag the pieces. They should snap into their slots when they are positioned and released about 20 pixels away from their correct position. The message in the top-left corner should display the number of pieces that have been placed correctly. You might also notice that pieces positioned correctly do not respond either to the mouse or to the keyboard. They have been disabled and cannot be moved.

SUMMARY

In this tutorial, you learned to build a puzzle game using GameBrix Builder. You also imported graphics into the game and used the graphics to create objects with intelligence. In addition, you learned how to import ActionScript code using the InsertScript tasks with different object states. The next chapter takes an in-depth look at creating an educational math game.

12 Building an E-Learning Math Game

This chapter describes how to build an e-learning math game. E-learning games are short and fun games that teach concepts in an engaging fashion. There are games that teach history, math, logic, English, and many other subjects. Reenacting the historical events and playing a central role in the game enables players to learn concepts that are traditionally hard to understand by reading books.

DESIGNING A MATH GAME

In this game, floating bubbles fall randomly from the sky. Each of these bubbles holds a one- or two-digit number. These numbers are either regular or prime numbers. The object of the game is to selectively throw pellets at bubbles holding prime numbers and break them. The player is awarded 10 points for breaking open a bubble holding a prime number. If the bubble hit is not a prime number, 5 points are deducted from the player's health and 10 points are deducted from his score. If a bubble holding a prime number escapes and hits the bottom of the screen, the same number of points is deducted from the score and health. The game ends when the player's health becomes 0.

CREATING THE GAME

The first step is to log in to GameBrix.com if you are not already logged in. The next sequence of steps involves obtaining all the images, animations, and intelligence required for building the game. A budget of 80 Brix is required to buy all these items from the online GameBrix store. If you do not have enough Brix, you can purchase them from the GameBrix Web site.

IMAGES REQUIRED

Now it's time to get the images required for the math game from the online GameBrix store. Go to the online store by clicking on the Store link. In the Search by Name text box, type in CG12 and select Images as the content type, as shown in Figure 12.1. Make sure that the items are owned by user coolgc.

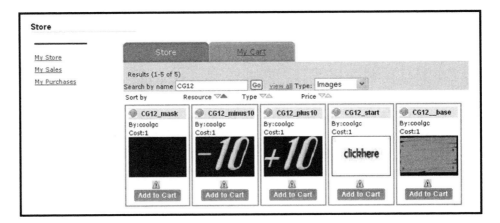

FIGURE 12.1
Some of the required images from the store.

The required images are described in Table 12.1. The name of the item might not be displayed completely if it is longer than 10 characters, as shown in Figure 12.1. The full name of the image is displayed when the mouse hovers over the thumbnail of the image.

TABLE 12.1 IMAGES REQUIRED

Item Name	Price (Brix)	Description
CG12_mask	1	Is the mask used to mask the player
CG12_minus10	1	Displays when the player loses points
CG12_plus10	1	Displays when the player wins points
CG12_start	1	Is the Start button
CG12_base	1	Defines the bottom of the game level

Buy all the items listed in Table 12.1 by clicking on the Add to Cart button. You need to ensure that coolgc owns all the items. After you add all the items to your shopping cart, click on the My Cart tab. It might take a few seconds for the system to process items in your cart. The next screen displays your cart contents. The list displays a file name and an item name. If you already have an item in your inventory by the same name, it is displayed in red text. You need to change the name of that item on this screen to avoid name conflicts and overwriting your file. If you already have purchased an item that shows up in red, you can remove it from your shopping cart using the Remove button on the same row. Figure 12.2 shows the items in the shopping cart.

Click the Buy Now button at the bottom of the screen. The system might take a few moments to process your order. On completion of the transaction, the items are added to your inventory and the Store screen displays. This finishes the process of assembling the images required for this game.

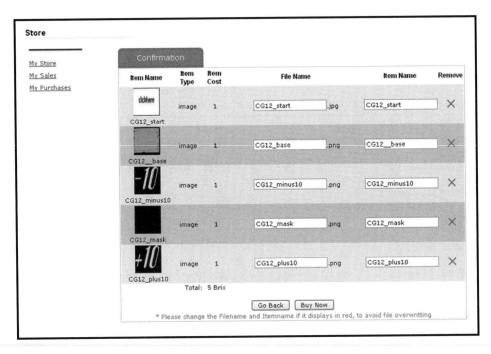

FIGURE 12.2
Items in the shopping cart.

ANIMATIONS REQUIRED

The next step is to get the animations required from the online store by using a process similar to the one you used to get the images. In the Search by Name text box, type in CG12 and select Animations as the content type, as shown in Figure 12.3. Again, the owner of these assets is coolgc. The icons displayed for all animations resemble a snippet of camera film. If you are interested in previewing the animation, click on the icon, which displays the animation in a new window. Table 12.2 lists the animations that you need. Buy these items from the store, and complete the purchase just as you did in the previous section.

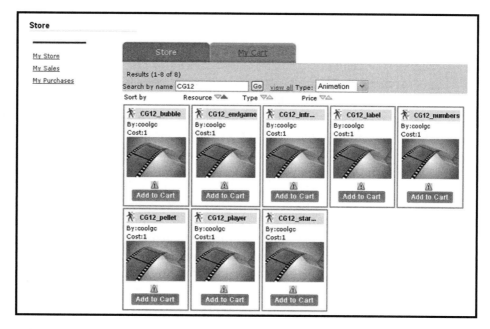

FIGURE 12.3
Animations required from the store.

TABLE 12.2 ANIMATIONS REQUIRED

Item Name	Price	Description
CG12_bubble	1	The container that holds the numbers
CG12_endgame	1	The end game background screen
CG12_introgame	1	The game introduction background screen
CG12_label	1	The text box that holds the score and health
CG12_numbers	1	A 10-frame animation to display numeric digits
CG12_pellet	1	The pellet thrown by the player
CG12_player	1	The player
CG12_startgame	1	The start game background screen

MATH GAME CONCEPTS

This math game enables players to learn to differentiate prime numbers from others. Numbers descend from the sky inside bubbles while the player is on a boat floating in the water. The aim of the game is to break bubbles holding prime numbers. The player can move left or right by using the cursor keys and shoot pellets using the spacebar. If the pellets strike a prime number and break the bubble, the player is awarded 10 points. If the player misses striking the bubble holding a prime number and the bubble touches the water unhurt, the player loses 10 points from his score and 5 health points.

The manager object initially creates five bubbles. These containers hold either one- or two-digit numbers. They are programmed to move down vertically from hidden locations above the game level. Just before the bubbles start the descent, a random number picked up from a prepopulated array is assigned to them. The one- or two-digit number is displayed using one or two number objects.

The number object is a 10-frame flash animation that can be created in Flash or using the GameBrix Animator. Frame 1 holds the image of the number 0, frame 2 holds the image of the number 1, and Frame 10 holds the image for the number 9. The number object is a flash file that can be controlled to display any digit of choice by using the flash gotoAndStop function. In simple terms, if a number object is programmed to gotoAndStop at frame 4, it displays the number 3. To display the prime number 37 inside the bubble, two number objects are required for displaying two digits. The first number object executes the command gotoAndStop on frame 4 to display the number 3. The second number object executes the command gotoAndStop on frame 8 to display the number 7. Both of these objects are attached to the bubble and move along with it. A mathematical sinusoidal function is used to make the vertical motion of the bubble objects wavy.

INTELLIGENCE REQUIRED

At this point, all images and animations have been bought from the store. The next step is to get all the intelligence required from the online store. In the Search by Name text box, type in CG12 and select Intelligence as the content type, as shown in Figure 12.4. As with the images and animations, coolgc owns all the intelligence. The icons displayed for all intelligence object assets resemble a single gear. You cannot view or preview object intelligence directly. You can view it only when it's used inside GameBrix GameBuilder. Table 12.3 lists the intelligence that you need. Buy these items from the store and complete the purchase just as you did in the earlier section.

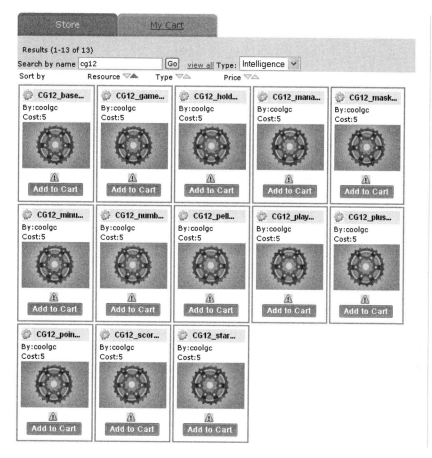

FIGURE 12.4
Object intelligence assets.

TABLE 12.3 INTELLIGENCE REQUIRED

Item Name	Price (Brix)	Description
CG13_StartIntl	5	Used for the Start button
CG13_ScoreIntl	5	Sets the score
CG13_PointsIntl	5	Sets the health
CG13_PlusIntl	5	Displays the plus-10 image
CG12_NumberIntl	5	Displays the number
CG12_HolderIntl	5	Handles collisions and manipulates the number objects
CG12_MinusIntl	5	Displays the minus-10 image
CG12_MaskIntl	5	Selectively masks the player
CG12_ManagerIntl	5	Manages the creation of the holder objects and the game
CG12_GameOverIntl	5	Used for the Play Again button
CG12_PlayerIntl	5	Has all the player logic
CG12_PelletIntl	5	Has logic to handle the pellet motion
CG12_BaseIntl	5	Simulates an invisible lower boundary for the game

BUILDING THE OBJECTS

With all the images, animations, and intelligence in place, it's time to start building the game objects. Open the GameBrix GameBuilder by clicking on the large tab labeled Game Builder. When the application loads, it displays the Import Graphics screen.

On the left side of the screen is a set of images and animations in your library. Select the following images and add them to the Sprites section on the right, as shown in Figure 12.5. There are five images and five animations:

- CG12_start
- CG12_label
- CG12_plus10
- CG12_numbers
- CG12_bubble

- CG12_minus10
- CG12_wave
- CG12_player
- CG12_pellet
- CG12_base

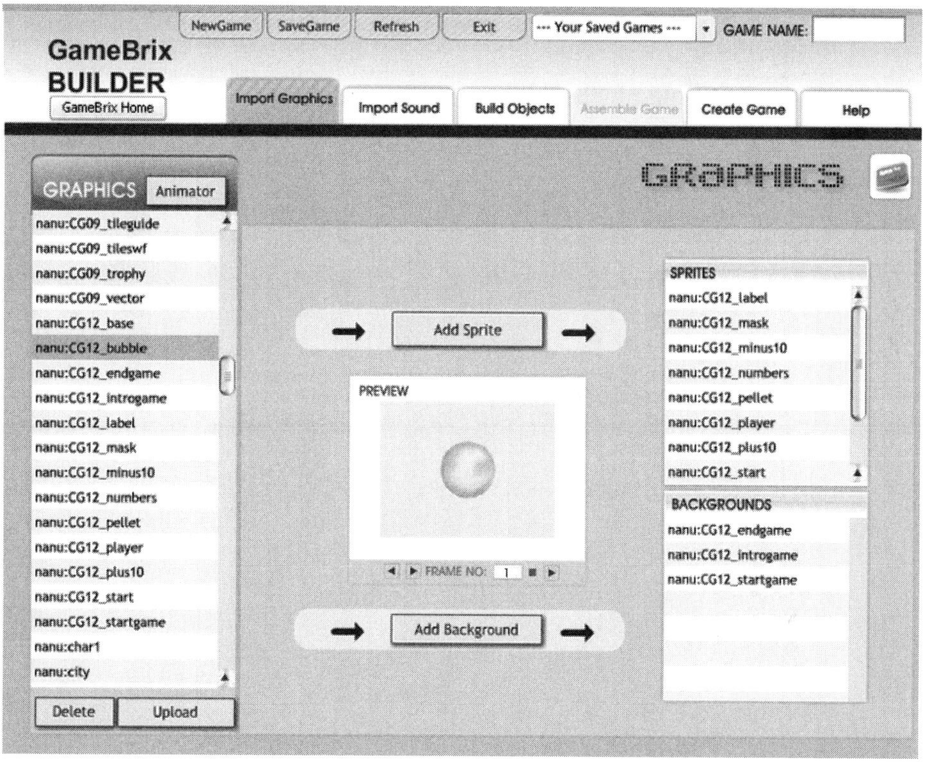

FIGURE 12.5
Assemble sprites and backgrounds.

Next, select the following three animations and add them to the Backgrounds section on the right:

- CG12_introgame
- CG12_startgame
- CG12_endgame

To build game objects, click on the Build Objects tab and then on the New Object button. That takes you to the screen shown in Figure 12.6. Choose the image named CG12_start from the list of images displayed under Select Graphics. Name the object startObj by typing it in the Object Name text box. Then click the Done button. This creates an object named startObj.

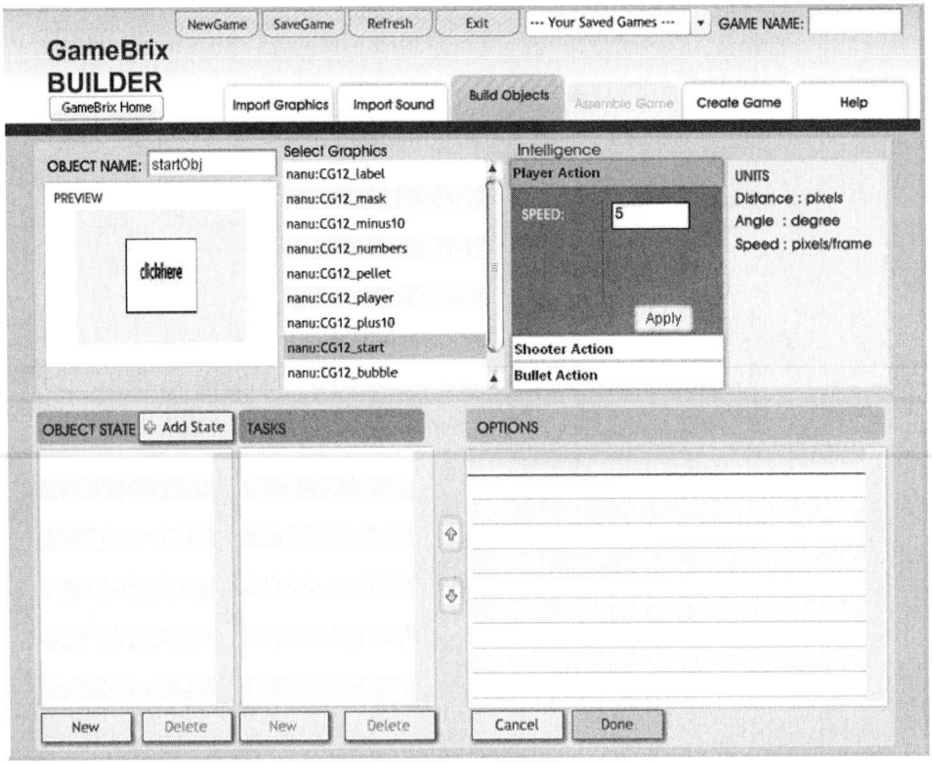

FIGURE 12.6
Object creation process.

Repeat this step and create the other objects listed in Table 12.4, which lists the object names and the images or animations that are attached to them. Note that the object names you type are case sensitive. Your game will not function with incorrect object names.

TABLE 12.4 OBJECTS REQUIRED

Object Name	Image/Animation Required
startObj	CG12_start.jpg
scoreObj	CG12_label.swf
pointsObj	CG12_label.swf
plusObj	CG12_plus10.png
numbersObj	CG12_numbers.swf
holderObj	CG12_bubble.swf
minusObj	CG12_minus10.png
maskObj	CG12_mask.png
managerObj	CG12_start.jpg
gameoverObj	CG12_start.jpg
playerObj	CG12_player.swf
pelletObj	CG12_pellet.swf
baseObj	CG12_base.png

After creating all the objects, click the SaveGame button shown in Figure 12.6. Provide a title and description when you save. Make sure the file name does not contain spaces or special symbols. A dialog box signals the completion of the save game process. Click the OK button to proceed.

It's time to use the Object Editor to add behavioral intelligence to your objects. Click on the Object Editor button in the Build Objects tab. This opens the Object Editor window. Descriptions of all areas of the Object Editor were provided in Chapter 6, "Building a Platform Game." See Figure 6.8 to refresh your memory.

The notable areas of importance are

- The list of objects present in the Game Objects section
- The contents of the Intelligence section
- The empty section labeled World Vars

In the Game Objects section, select the startObj object by clicking on it. Then search for the intelligence labeled CG12_StartIntl in the Intelligence section. Double-click on it. You should be prompted with a dialog box asking you if you want to overwrite your object's behavior. Click Yes. That should populate the object with one or more states and tasks, as shown in Figure 12.7.

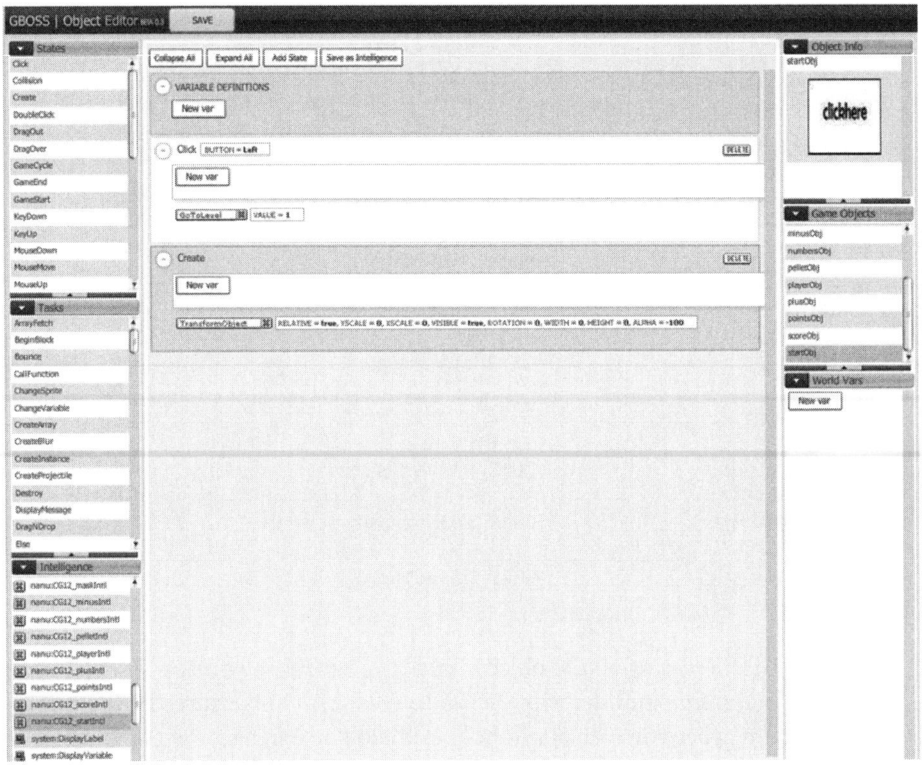

FIGURE 12.7
Populated Object Editor screen.

That completes the creation of the first object.

Perform the same sequence of steps to create all the other objects listed in Table 12.5. Keep in mind that different objects require different intelligence assigned to them. Allow about 10 to 15 minutes to complete this intelligence assignment process for all the objects. Table 12.5 lists all the objects and the appropriate intelligence they require.

TABLE 12.5 INTELLIGENCE ASSIGNMENT

Object Name	Intelligence Required
startObj	CG12_StartIntl
scoreObj	CG12_ScoreIntl
pointsObj	CG12_PointsIntl
plusObj	CG12_PlusIntl
numbersObj	CG12_NumberIntl
holderObj	CG12_HolderIntl
minusObj	CG12_MinusIntl
maskObj	CG12_MaskIntl
managerObj	CG12_ManagerIntl
gameoverObj	CG12_GameOverIntl
playerObj	CG12_PlayerIntl
pelletObj	CG12_PelletIntl
baseObj	CG12_BaseIntl

CREATING WORLD VARIABLES

To create world variables, click the New Var button in the World Vars section in the lower-right corner of the Object Editor. The Variable Editor dialog box is displayed. Carefully enter data into this dialog box using information provided in Table 12.6. Figure 12.8 shows several existing world variables and the procedure to create the world variable named p. The value assigned to the p world variable is a set of comma-separated numbers inside square brackets. Be sure to terminate it with a semicolon and no carriage return at the end. p is an array populated with several numbers, some of which are prime numbers. Note that variable names are case sensitive. The game will not work with incorrect variable names.

FIGURE 12.8
Creating world variables.

TABLE 12.6 WORLD VARIABLES

Variable Name	Variable Type	Member Type	Value
player	Object	Dynamic	
pellet	Object	Dynamic	
movey	Number	Dynamic	
health	Number	Dynamic	
gameover	Object	Dynamic	
mask	Object	Dynamic	
points	Number	Dynamic	
p	Array	Dynamic	[2, 4, 5, 32, 23, 47, 67, 89, 63, 27, 8, 7, 5, 97, 39, 87, 47, 4, 69, 79, 43, 27, 3, 11, 13]

After you've created the eight world variables, click the Save button found at the top of the Object Editor screen. This is an important step, so don't skip it. A message box displays the message Save complete. You can close it by clicking the OK button. Minimize the Object Editor window using the standard Minimize button. That brings you back to the Build Objects screen in the GameBrix Builder. You see a message box displaying the message Game ready to build. Click the OK button here to continue the game creation process. If the Game ready to build message does not display when you return to the Build Objects screen, your GameBrix session likely timed out. This means that you need to log out and log back in. Any unsaved progress you've made in the Object Editor will be lost, so be sure to save often!

ASSEMBLING THE GAME

All the objects are ready. Next comes the fun part of assembling the game and testing it. Click the Assemble Game tab, whose resulting screen has several buttons and fields. The area on the left labeled Levels lists all the levels that you've created. Level 1 is always created by default.

There are three levels in this game. The first level is a title screen, the second is the game, and the third is the Game Over screen.

ASSEMBLING LEVEL 1

Assembling the title screen that has the Start button is simple. First change the name of the level, shown on top of the level editor, to IntroGame. Then change the width and height of both the View and Level Size areas to 800 pixels by 600 pixels.

In this level, CG12_introgame is used as the background. Click on it. It should move to the Game Assembly Area and form the background.

Next, scroll the Game Assembly Area horizontally to view the top-right corner of the background. Click and drag the startObj object onto the Game Assembly Area. You should position it above the area displaying the image resembling the Play button. The coordinates should be close to 730, 60, as shown in Figure 12.9.

That completes the Level 1 assembly process.

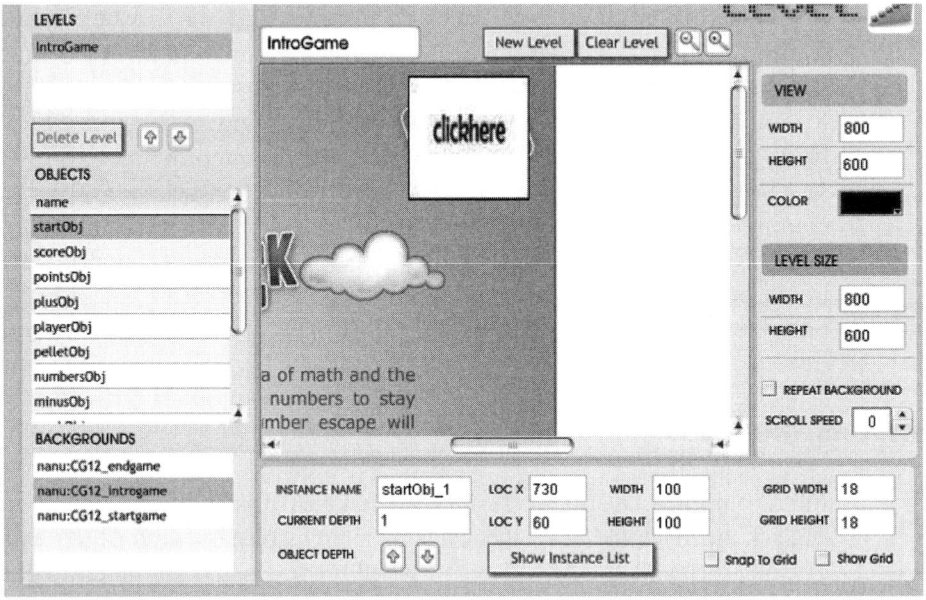

FIGURE 12.9
Level 1 assembled.

ASSEMBLING LEVEL 2

Create a second level by clicking the New Level button. This level houses the actual game. Name the level startGame, and set the level and view size to be 800 pixels by 800 pixels.

In this level, CG12_startgame is used as the background. Click on it. It should move to the Game Assembly Area and form the background.

Click and drag the maskObj object onto the Game Assembly Area. Set the LOC X and LOC Y coordinates for this object to 400, 500. Then move the playerObj to the same location.

Click and drag the pointsObj object onto the Game Assembly Area. Set the LOC X and LOC Y coordinates for this object to 690, 560. Then move the scoreObj to the location 690, 590, as shown in Figure 12.10.

Click and drag the baseObj object onto the Game Assembly Area. Set the LOC X and LOC Y coordinates for this object to 400, 590. Next, move managerObj to the location 80, 80, as shown in Figure 12.11.

This completes the assembly of the main game level. Save the game.

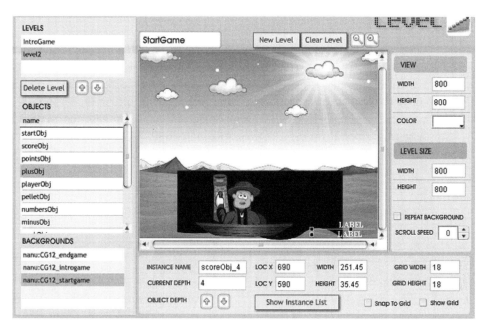

FIGURE 12.10
Level 2 partially assembled.

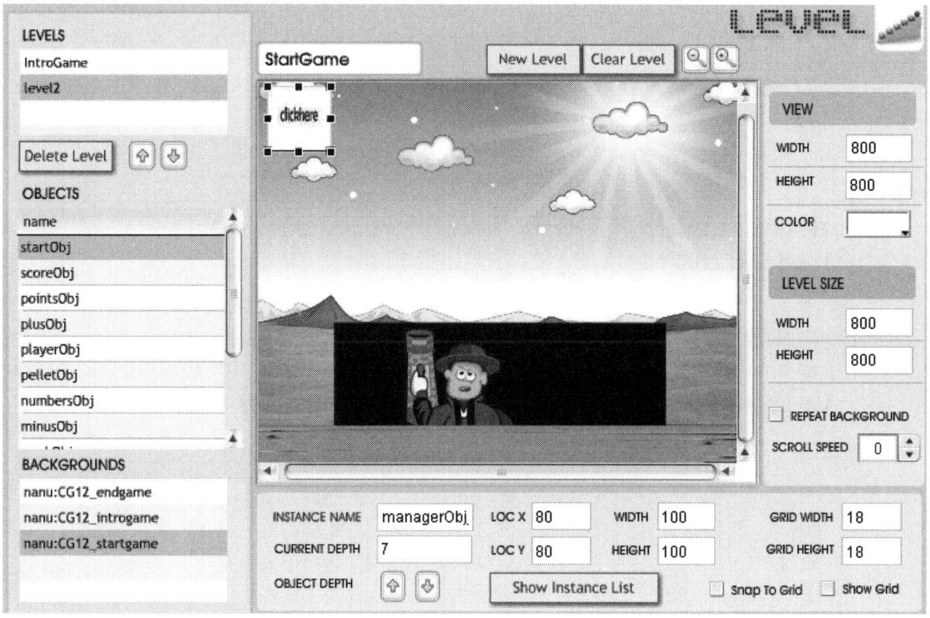

FIGURE 12.11
Level 2 partially assembled.

ASSEMBLING LEVEL 3

Level 3 is the last level of the game. Change the width and height of both the Level and View areas to 800 pixels by 600 pixels. Change the name of the level to Endgame.

In this level, CG12_endgame is used as the background. Click on it. It should move to the Game Assembly Area and form the background.

Click and drag the gameoverObj object onto the top-right corner of the Game Assembly Area. Position it at the coordinates 690, 75, as shown in Figure 12.12.

FIGURE 12.12
Level 3 assembled.

That completes the Level 3 assembly process.

Congratulations! You have completed building the game. Next proceed to the Create Game tab, and click the Preview button to play your game.

CUSTOMIZING THE GAME USING A GAME TEMPLATE

The second method to build the math game is to use a black-box approach and buy the complete source for the game. The game source is kept in the GameBrix system as a Game Definition Format (GDF) file. Click on Store and search for CG12_mathgame. Change the asset type to GDF. In the search results, look for the file owned by coolgc, and add this asset to your shopping cart. Then click on the My Cart tab. After you've loaded the shopping cart, scroll down and click the button labeled Buy Now. After the transaction is complete, this GDF file is added to your inventory. You can see this file when you load GameBrix GameBuilder; it appears in the Your Saved Games section. Open this file and build it directly from the Create Game tab. The game builds with all its glory in one step. You can customize this game by going into the Build Objects tab and modifying each object with the knowledge you gained in the step-by-step game creation process.

SUMMARY

In this tutorial, you used the GameBrix Builder and GameBrix Animator to create a math game. With this knowledge, you can create variations of the prime numbers game and publish them for use on Web sites. The next chapter looks at how to build another game using the GameBrix portal.

13   Going Green–Building a Recycling Game

In This Chapter

- The Recycling Game
- Creating the Game Plan
- Building the Objects
- Assembling the Game
- Creating the Game
- Building the Game Using the Publisher's Approach

This chapter describes the process involved in building a fun casual game that enables the player to recycle objects. In this era of technological advancement, it has become more and more important to protect the environment. This process starts at home, with everyone doing whatever they can to keep the planet pristine. One of the easiest and most powerful ways to do this is by recycling. Thousands of products that could have been recycled are thrown away each year. Creating a recycling game may communicate a message to the game player to recycle; after all, games are one of the most influential and widespread forms of media today. The game concept has the game player recycle paper, glass, and plastic into the appropriate bins to gain points. When the game timer stops, an end screen is displayed that indicates the game is over.

THE RECYCLING GAME

In this game, your role as a player is to sort paper, plastic, and glass into recycle bins. The challenge element of the game is to read a hint displayed above the recycling bin and pick the appropriate object needed with the mouse. If you select an incorrect object, you lose health. At the game start, your health is initialized to 100 points. When the health score becomes 0, the game ends.

CREATING THE GAME PLAN

The first step in creating any game is to lay out a plan for building it. You need graphics for the recyclable objects, colored bins for sorting, and some animations to acknowledge the game players' accomplishment. In addition, standard graphics to start and end the game are required. Background graphics are required for the title and end screens. You can create your own graphics or use the assets available at the GameBrix store. The easiest way to create the game is to follow the step-by-step process. After you build and preview the game, you can spend time creating custom graphics, modifying the game options in terms of health, score, or behaviors to create a unique experience from your ideas.

IMAGES REQUIRED

Now it's time to get the images required for the recycling game. You can create your own graphics or purchase assets from the online GameBrix store. If you are creating your own assets, you need the specific sizes of the graphics to build this game.

The images required with size specifications are described in Table 13.1.

TABLE 13.1 IMAGES REQUIRED

Item Name	Graphics Size (Pixels)	File Format	Description
CG13_Recycle_ClickHere	150×100	JPEG	Any Image; not visible at runtime
CG13_Recycle_Bg	800×600	JPEG	Background image for gameplay
CG13_Recycle_EndGame	800×600	JPEG	Background image for game end
CG13_Recycle_StartGame	800×600	JPEG	Background image for game start
CG13_Recycle_Explode	75×85	SWF	Animation with 2 keyframes
CG13_Recycle_Bin	100×100	SWF	Animation with 3 keyframes
CG13_Recycle_PowerBar	100×12	SWF	Animation with 100 keyframes
CG13_Recycle_Plastic	75×85	SWF	Animation with 2 keyframes
CG13_Recycle_Paper	75×85	SWF	Animation with 2 keyframes
CG13_Recycle_Glass	75×85	SWF	Animation with 2 keyframes

IMAGES DESCRIPTION

To create your own graphics, use the list in Table 13.1 for the naming convention and size attributes. The CG13_Recycle_ClickHere image is a placeholder and can be any image that you choose, because it will not be visible to the game player. Create the graphic for the CG13_Recycle_ClickHere image using Microsoft Paint or the GameBrix Animator with attributes of 100×150 pixel size, as shown in Figure 13.1.

```
CLICK
HERE
```

FIGURE 13.1
CG13_Recycle_ClickHere
image.

This game will have three levels. Create three background graphics to be used for each level with a 800×600 pixel size. The first background is for the start level, the second for the game level, and the third for the end level. Create a background image for the title level, and name it CG13_Recycle_StartGame, as shown in Figure 13.2.

FIGURE 13.2
CG13_Recycle_StartGame image.

The second background you need to create is used for the gameplay level. Save the file as CG13_RecycleBg. A background with light colors is suggested to showcase the elements being recycled.

The background for the last level is CG13_Recycle_EndGame, and it is shown in Figure 13.3.

FIGURE 13.3

CG13_Recycle_EndGame image.

The next step is to create animations with keyframes. Each keyframe holds an image of a specific size. Simple keyframe animations can be created with Adobe Flash or GameBrix Animator. An example would be a flip book where you draw the character moving between the pages and then flip the book to watch the animation. Create the animation for the CG13_Recycle_Explode asset used in the game. When the recyclable material touches the bin, program the builder to display the CG13_Recycle_Explode animation. The CG13_Recycle_Explode animation has an 85×75 pixel size, and two keyframes are used to create the animated effect. The first keyframe of the CG13_Recycle_Explode asset is shown in Figure 13.4.

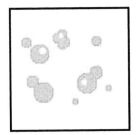

FIGURE 13.4
CG13_Recycle_Explode
animated keyframe.

CG13_Recycle_Bin is an animation with three keyframes. This animation consists of colored bins that are used as receptacles for the recycled materials. Create each keyframe with a unique colored bin to collect a specific recyclable material, as shown in Figure 13.5.

FIGURE 13.5
CG13_RecycleBin
animated image.

The CG13_Recycle_PowerBar animated graphic displays the progress bar for health. Health is initialized to 100 and serves as a timer in the recycle game; for each second elapsed, the health decreases by one. When the health gets to 0, the game ends. The PowerBar animation is made up of 100 keyframes; a single keyframe is shown in Figure 13.6.

FIGURE 13.6
CG13_Recycle_PowerBar
animated image.

CG13_Recycle_Plastic is an animated image with two keyframes. Each frame holds an image that is 75×85 pixels to showcase a type of plastic that needs to be recycled. This enables the player to view two types of plastic material that need to be recycled. The first keyframe of the animated CG13_Recycle_Plastic image is shown in Figure 13.7.

FIGURE 13.7
CG13_Recycle_Plastic
animation keyframe
image.

CG13_Recycle_Paper is an animated image with two keyframes. Each frame holds a 75×85-pixel image. The player is shown two types of CG13_Recycle_paper images. The first keyframe of the animated CG13_Recycle_Paper image is shown in Figure 13.8. You can create a similar image with the same size attributes for the second keyframe.

FIGURE 13.8
CG13_Recycle_Paper
animation keyframe
image.

CG13_Recycle_Glass is an animated image with two keyframes. Each frame holds an image of a type of glass that is 75×85 pixels. To enable the game player to view two types of glass material, you need two images in two keyframes. The first keyframe of the animated CG13_Recycle_Glass image is shown in Figure 13.9. You can create a similar image with the same size attributes for the second keyframe.

FIGURE 13.9
CG13_Recycle_Glass
animation keyframe 1
image.

Alternatively, you can buy all the images required for the game, listed in Table 13.1, from the GameBrix store. The items in the store have a CG13_prefix. Use the search filter to purchase all items listed in the table by entering CG13_ in the search box. Purchase all items that GameBrix user coolgc owns. After you place all the items in your shopping cart, click on the My Cart tab. It may take a few seconds for the system to process items in your cart.

The next screen displays your cart contents. The list shows a file name and an item name. If you already have an item in your inventory by the same name, it is displayed in red text. You need to change the name of that item on this screen to avoid name conflicts and overwriting your files. If you already have purchased an item that shows up in red, you can remove it from your shopping cart using the Remove button on the same row. Figure 13.10 shows all the items in the shopping cart.

Please change the file name and item name if it displays in red to avoid file overwriting. Click the Buy Now button at the bottom of the screen. The system may take a few moments to process your order. On completion of the transaction, the items are added to your inventory, and the store screen displays. That completes the process of assembling the images required for this game.

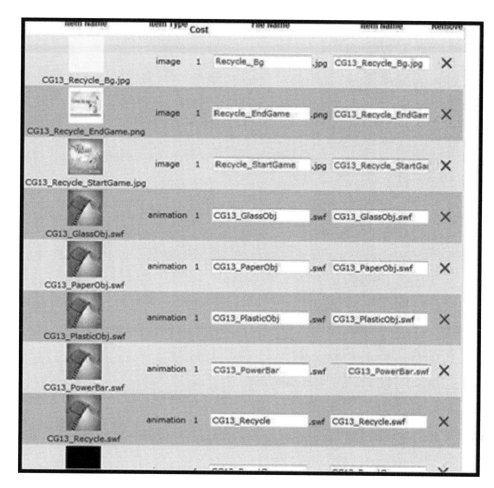

FIGURE 13.10
Recycle game assets in the shopping cart.

INTELLIGENCE REQUIRED

The next step is to get all the intelligence required from the online store. In the Search by Name text box, type in CG13 and select Intelligence as the content type, as shown in Figure 13.11. All the intelligence assets are owned by coolgc. The icons displayed for all object intelligence assets resemble a single gear. You cannot view or preview object intelligence directly. You can view it only when you use it inside GameBrix GameBuilder. Table 13.2 lists the intelligence that you need. Buy these items from the store, and complete the purchase just as you did in the earlier section.

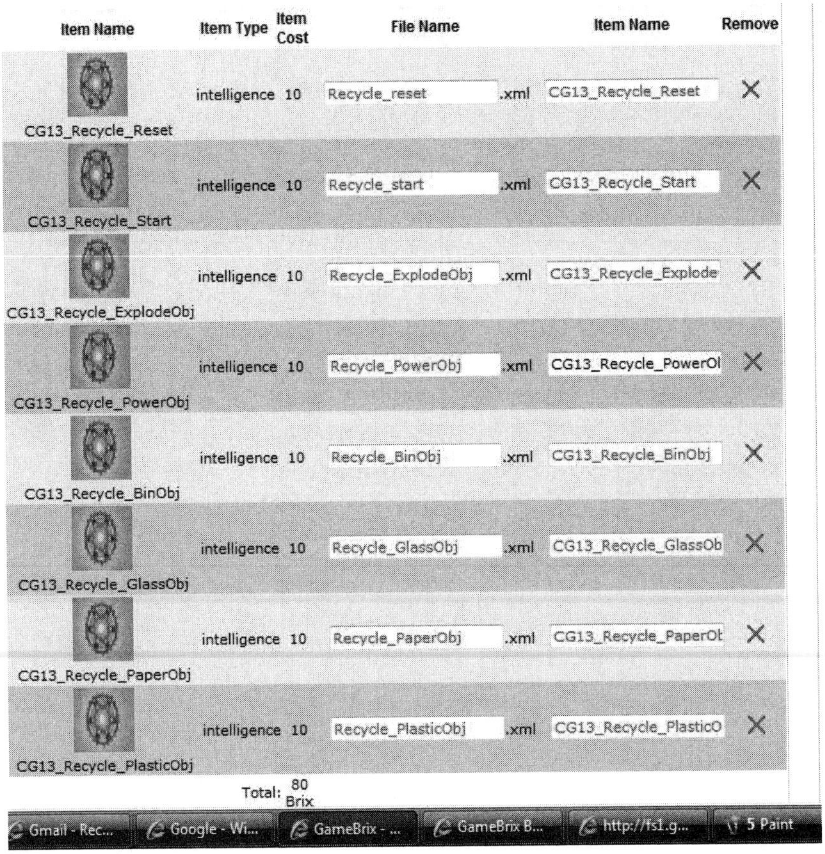

Item Name	Item Type	Item Cost	File Name		Item Name	Remove
CG13_Recycle_Reset	intelligence	10	Recycle_reset	.xml	CG13_Recycle_Reset	✕
CG13_Recycle_Start	intelligence	10	Recycle_start	.xml	CG13_Recycle_Start	✕
CG13_Recycle_ExplodeObj	intelligence	10	Recycle_ExplodeObj	.xml	CG13_Recycle_Explode	✕
CG13_Recycle_PowerObj	intelligence	10	Recycle_PowerObj	.xml	CG13_Recycle_PowerOl	✕
CG13_Recycle_BinObj	intelligence	10	Recycle_BinObj	.xml	CG13_Recycle_BinObj	✕
CG13_Recycle_GlassObj	intelligence	10	Recycle_GlassObj	.xml	CG13_Recycle_GlassOb	✕
CG13_Recycle_PaperObj	intelligence	10	Recycle_PaperObj	.xml	CG13_Recycle_PaperOl	✕
CG13_Recycle_PlasticObj	intelligence	10	Recycle_PlasticObj	.xml	CG13_Recycle_PlasticO	✕

Total: 80 Brix

| Gmail - Rec... | Google - Wi... | GameBrix - ... | GameBrix B... | http://fs1.g... | 5 Paint |

FIGURE 13.11

The recycle game object intelligence assets from the store.

TABLE 13.2 INTELLIGENCE REQUIRED

Item Name	Description
CG13_Recycle_PlasticObj	Plastic recyclable material intelligence
CG13_Recycle_PaperObj	Paper recyclable material intelligence
CG13_Recycle_GlassObj	Glass recyclable material intelligence
CG13_Recycle_BinObj	Bin recyclable material intelligence
CG13_Recycle_PowerObj	Progressive power bar intelligence
CG13_Recycle_ExplodeObj	Explosion animation intelligence
CG13_Recycle_Reset	Reset button
CG13_Recycle_Start	Start button

BUILDING THE OBJECTS

With all the raw materials in place, it's time to start building the game objects. Open the GameBrix GameBuilder by clicking on the large Game Builder tab. When the application loads, you are, by default, at the Import Graphics screen.

On the left side of the screen is a set of images and animations in your library. Select the following images and add them to the Sprites section on the right, as shown in Figure 13.12. You can replace store-purchased graphics with the ones you created by using the Upload button in Builder.

- CG13_Recycle_StartGame or Recycle_ClickHere
- CG13_Recycle_ResetGame
- CG13_Recycle_Explode
- CG13_Recycle_Plastic
- CG13_Recycle_Paper
- CG13_Recycle_Glass
- CG13_Recycle_Explode
- CG13_Recycle_PowerBar
- CG13_Recycle_Bin

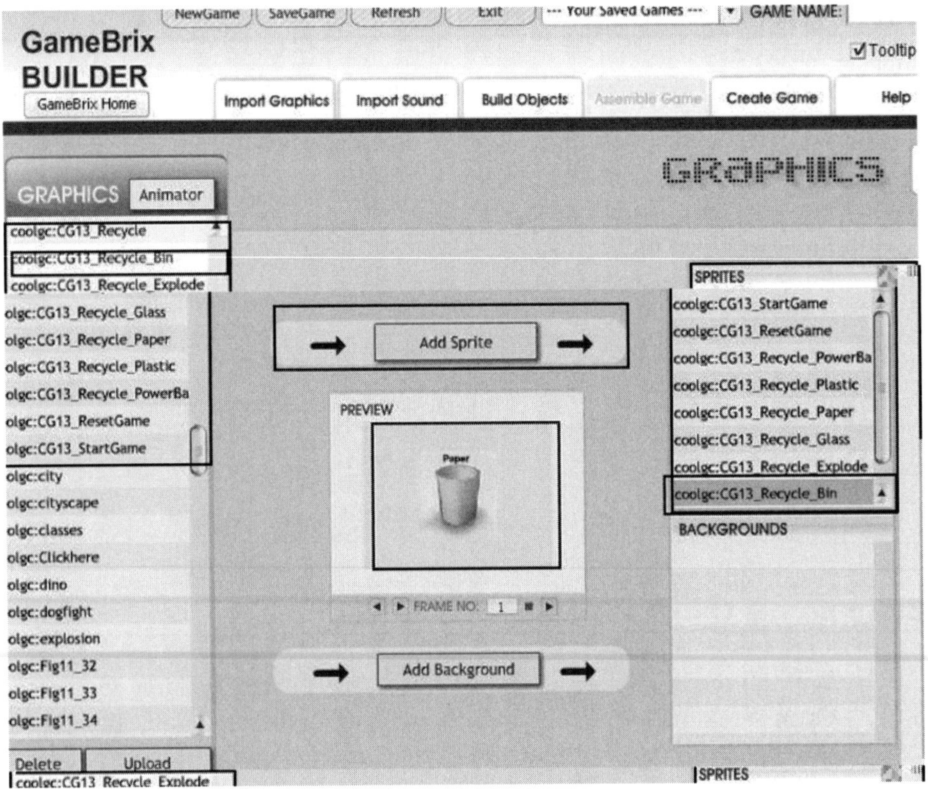

FIGURE 13.12
Recycle game sprites in Builder.

Select the following images, and move them to the Backgrounds section on the right, as shown in Figure 13.13.

■ RecycleBg
■ RecycleStartGame
■ RecycleEndGame

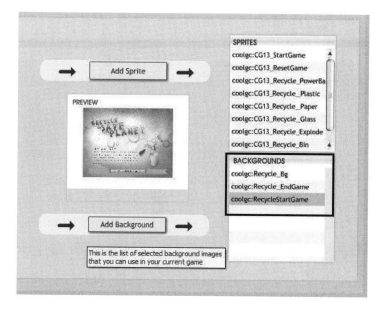

FIGURE 13.13
Adding the recycle backgrounds.

It's time to build game objects. Click on the Build Objects tab and then on the New Object button. That takes you to the screen shown in Figure 13.14. Choose the image named CG13_Recycle_Plastic from the list of images displayed under the Select Graphics label. Name the object PlasticObj by typing it in the Object Name text box. Then click the Done button to complete creation of the PlasticObj object.

Repeat this step and create the other objects listed in Table 13.3. The table lists their object names and the images or animations that are attached to them. Please note that the object names you type are case sensitive and have to match the ones provided in the table. Your game might not function with incorrect object names.

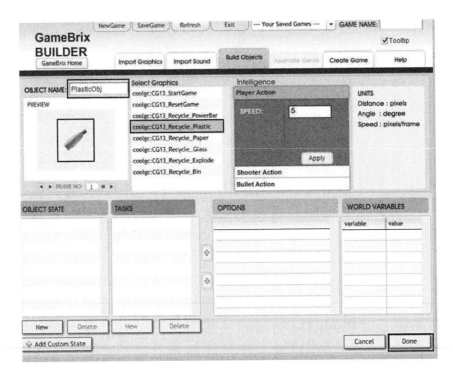

FIGURE 13.14
Recycle game object creation process.

TABLE 13.3 OBJECTS REQUIRED

Object Name	Image/Animation Required
StartGame	CG13_CG13_Recycle_ClickHere
ResetGame	CG13_ResetGame
Explode	CG13_Explode
PlasticObj	CG13_PlasticObj
PaperObj	CG13_PaperObj
GlassObj	CG13_GlassObj
Explode	CG13_Explode
PowerBar	CG13_PowerBar
Recycle	CG13_Recycle

After creating all the objects, click the SaveGame button shown in Figure 13.15. Provide a title and description when you save. The file name specified should not contain spaces or special symbols. A dialog box signals the completion of the SaveGame process. Click OK to proceed.

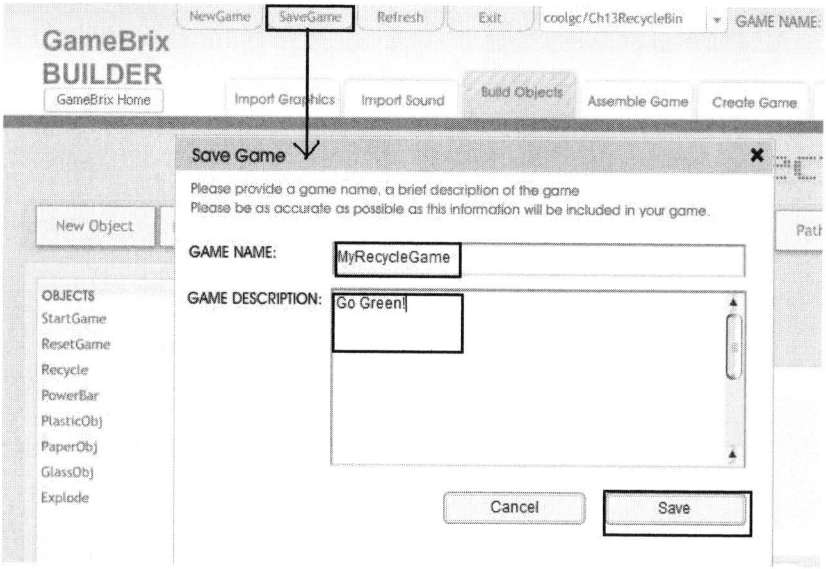

FIGURE 13.15
Save Recycle game.

It's time to use the Object Editor to add behavioral intelligence to your objects. On the Build Objects screen, click on the Object Editor button. This opens the Object Editor window. Descriptions of all areas of the Object Editor were provided in Chapter 6, "Building a Platform Game." See Figure 6.8 to refresh your memory.

Here you will find the important areas of the Object Editor screen:

▪ The list of objects present in the Game Objects section
▪ The contents of the Intelligence section
▪ The empty section labeled World Vars

Select the `Explode` object by clicking on it in the Game Objects section. Then double-click on `CG13_Recycle_Explode` in the Intelligence section. You are prompted with a dialog box asking you if you want to overwrite your object's behavior, as shown in Figure 13.16. Click Yes.

Tasks
Do you want to overwrite all the actions?
YES
NO
CANCEL
Timer
New var
Destroy
Intelligence
Game Objects
World Vars
New var

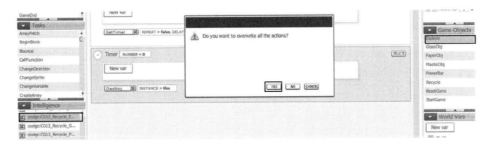

FIGURE 13.16
Adding intelligence in Object Editor.

That should populate the object with one or more states and tasks, as shown in Figure 13.17.

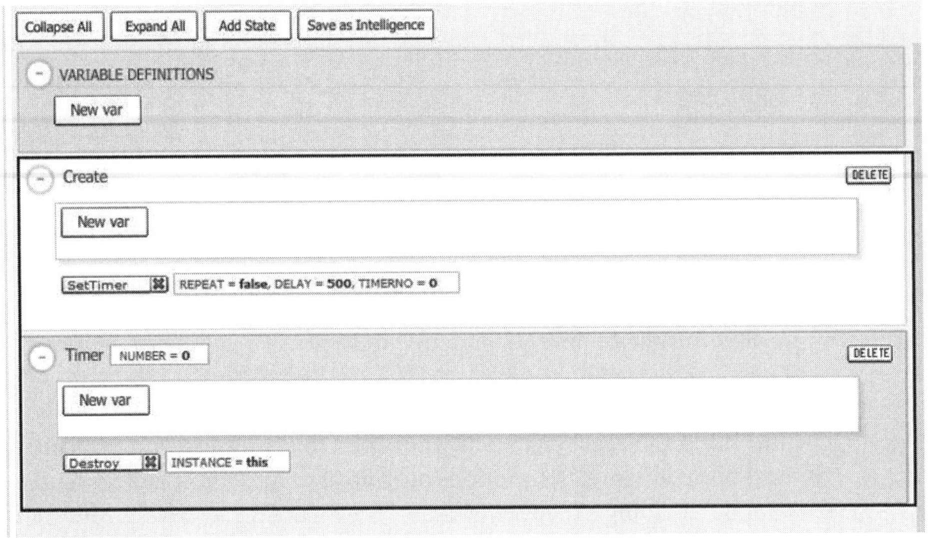
Collapse All
Expand All
Add State
Save as Intelligence
VARIABLE DEFINITIONS
New var
Create
DELETE
New var
SetTimer
REPEAT = false, DELAY = 500, TIMERNO = 0
Timer
NUMBER = 0
DELETE
New var
Destroy
INSTANCE = this

FIGURE 13.17
Populated Object Editor screen.

That completes the creation of the `CG13_Recycle_Explode` object.

Perform the same sequence of steps to create all the other objects listed in Table 13.4. Keep in mind that different objects require different intelligence assigned to them. Table 13.4 lists all the objects and the appropriate intelligence they require.

TABLE 13.4 INTELLIGENCE ASSIGNMENT

Object Name	Intelligence Required
GlassObj	CG13_Recycle_GlassObj
PlasticObj	CG13_Recycle_PlasticObj
PaperObj	CG13_Recycle_PaperObj
Explode	CG13_Recycle_ExplodeObj
PowerBar	CG13_Recycle_PowerObj
StartGame	CG13_Recycle_Start
ResetGame	CG13_Recycle_Reset
Recycle	CG13_Recycle_BinObj

All the required objects have been created.

World variables allow information to be shared across all objects in the game. Normally, each game object has access only to the information that belongs to it. World variables are used when information needs to be shared across all objects in a game. This game requires seven world variables.

To create world variables, click the New Var button in the Object Editor, as shown in Figure 13.18. The Variable Editor dialog box is displayed. Carefully enter data into this dialog box using information provided in Table 13.5. Again, variable names are case sensitive; the game may not work with incorrect variable names.

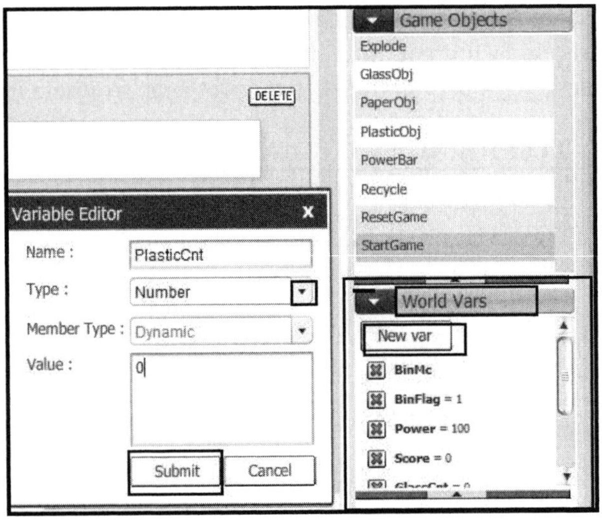

FIGURE 13.18
World variables initialized.

TABLE 13.5 WORLD VARIABLES

Variable Name	Variable Type	Member Type	Value
BinMc	Object	Dynamic	{}
BinFlag	Number	Dynamic	1
Power	Number	Dynamic	100
Score	Number	Dynamic	0
GlassCnt	Object	Dynamic	0
PaperCnt	Object	Dynamic	0
PlasticCnt	Object	Dynamic	0

The seven variables are visible under the World Vars section shown in Figure 13.18.

After you've created the seven world variables, click the Save button found at the top of the Object Editor screen. Don't skip this important step. A message box displays the message `Save complete`. Close the box by clicking the OK button. You can then minimize the Object Editor window using the standard Microsoft Windows Minimize button found in the top-right corner of the Object Editor window. That brings you back to the Build Objects screen that also displays the message `Game ready to build`, as shown in Figure 13.19. Click the OK button to continue the game creation process.

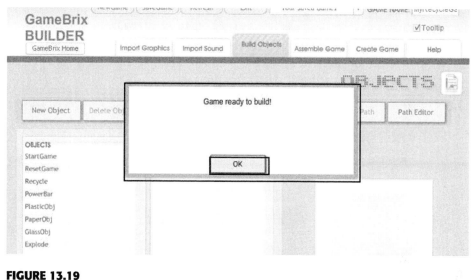

FIGURE 13.19
`Game ready to build` screen.

Assembling the Game

Now that all your objects are ready, it's time for the fun part of assembling the game and testing it. Click the Assemble Game tab. This screen has several buttons and fields. The area on the left labeled Levels lists all the levels that you have created. `Level1` is always created by default.

Level Description

The Objects area lists all the objects that you have created. These are the toys you get to play with in the Assemble Game tab. In the center is the Game Assembly Area. Figure 6.12 in Chapter 6 describes all areas of the Assemble Game tab.

This game has three levels: a title screen, the game screen, and endgame screen.

ASSEMBLING LEVEL 1

Assembling the title screen with a Start button is simple. First change the name of the level to `title`. Then change the width and height of both the Level and View Size areas to 800×600. Select `CG13_RecycleStartGame` as the background by clicking on it from the Backgrounds list. Click and drag the object named `StartGame` onto the area displaying the `Click Here To Play` message from the `title` graphic. Click on `StartGame`, and resize it to completely overlap the `Click Here To Play` message displayed in the `title` graphic. The `StartGame` object hides the Play message. The `StartGame` object is not visible when the game starts, but it has all the intelligence for a Start button. This creates a nice illusion; when the player clicks on the Start button area visible on the title page background, he is actually clicking on the `StartGame` object. The Start button for the game, title, room size, and background used are shown in Figure 13.20. That completes the Level 1 assembly process.

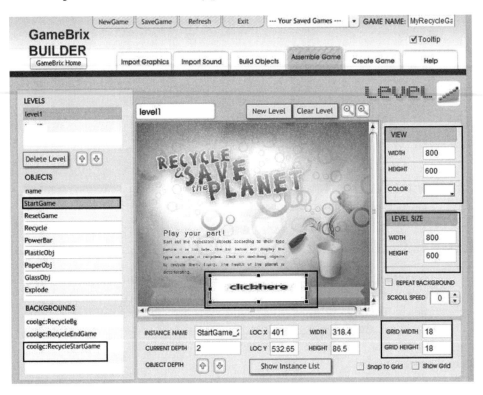

FIGURE 13.20
Level 1 assembled.

ASSEMBLING LEVEL 2

Create a second level by clicking the New Level button. This level houses the actual game. Name the level gamelevel, and set both the Level and View Size areas to be 800×600.

Click the background labeled CG13_Recycle_Bg, and place it in the Game Assembly Area, as shown in Figure 13.21.

Click and drag an instance of the object named PlasticObj to the top-left corner of the level. Create three rows of seven objects of each category that are to be recycled in the game as shown in Figure 13.21. Place one instance of the bin object Recycle at the bottom along with the PowerBar object in the right-corner of the level. That completes assembly of the gamelevel.

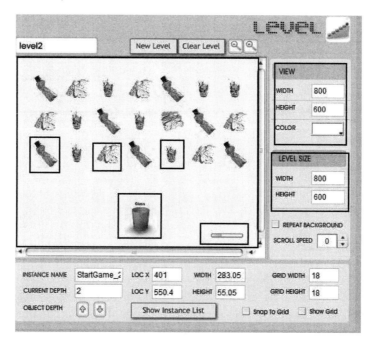

FIGURE 13.21
The complete game room assembled.

ASSEMBLING LEVEL 3

Create a third level by clicking the New Level button. This level houses the last level of the game. Name the level Lastlevel, and set both the Level and View Size areas to be 800×600.

Click the background labeled `CG13_RecycleEndGame`, and place it in the Game Assembly Area, as shown in Figure 13.22.

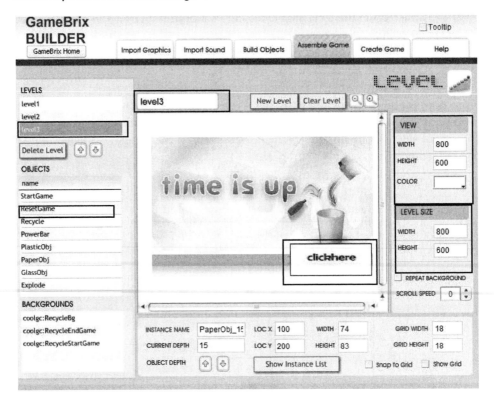

FIGURE 13.22
Level 3 assembled.

Click and drag an instance of the object named `ResetGame` onto the area displaying the `Click Here to Play` message. Resize it to completely overlap the Click Here to Play message displayed in the `LastLevel` graphic. The title, room size, and background used are shown in Figure 13.22. That completes the Level 3 assembly process.

CREATING THE GAME

Next, click the tab labeled Create Game, and then click the Preview button. You are prompted with a screen that asks for the game name and instructions for playing the game. Provide this information in the text area as deemed appropriate, and then click the Save & Play button at the bottom right of the Save Game pop-up window that appears to test the game. The game opens in a new window. Make sure your pop-up blocker is turned off so you can see the game.

Congratulations! You have built a game that encourages players to go green and save the environment!

BUILDING THE GAME USING THE PUBLISHER'S APPROACH

The second method to build this banner game is to use a black-box approach and buy the complete source for the game. The game source is kept in the GameBrix system as a GDF file. Click on Store, and search for `CG13_RecycleBin`. Then change the asset type to GDF. In the search results, look for the file owned by coolgc, and add this asset to your shopping cart. Then click on the My Cart tab. After you have loaded the shopping cart, scroll down and click the button labeled Buy Now. When the transaction is complete, this GDF file is added to your inventory. When you load GameBrix GameBuilder, the GDF file appears in the section Your Saved Games. Open this file and build it directly from the Create Game tab. The game builds (complete in all its glory) in one step. You can customize it by clicking the Build Objects tab and modifying each object.

SUMMARY

In this tutorial, you used the GameBrix Builder to create a recycling game. The game provides a scaffold for creating a more elaborate game that can be a fun and entertaining experience for game players. You are now ready to set up a game studio by forming a group with your friends and publishing games that are fun, entertaining, and educational at http://www.gamebrix.com or hosting them on your Web site.

Appendix: GameBrix Reference

In This Appendix

- Describe GameBrix States
- Define GameBrix Tasks and Options

This section describes all the important states and tasks that GameBrix Builder supports.

To create a game in GameBrix Builder, you need graphics assets or sprites, objects, states, and tasks that add intelligence to objects. Creating a game in Game-Brix builder is easy; the process can be applied to any type or genre of game. You first need graphics or sprites. These images do not have any behaviors preprogrammed into them, so you also need objects. The programmed codes associated with objects are known as *game mechanics*. Objects are the core of game mechanics. They are what separate passive media from pure entertainment. Objects must have sprites attached to them. To give objects a set of instructions to follow and allow them to behave in a specific way, GameBrix Builder provides states and tasks as well as shareable game mechanics. Game mechanics are the states and tasks contained within an object. The GameBrix portal allows users to share mechanics with each other and collaborate with other creative people to design games.

To build objects, select a graphics asset using the Import Graphics tab shown in Figure A.1. Notice that the Build Objects tab is grayed out when you select graphics.

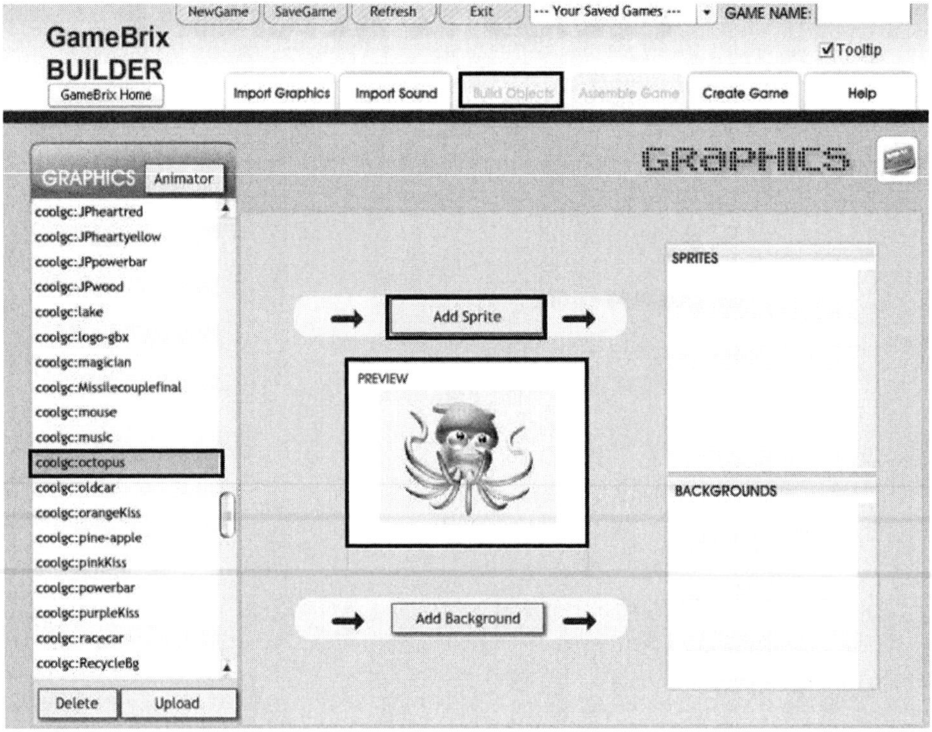

FIGURE A.1
Selecting a graphics asset.

The grayed-out tab Build Objects becomes active as soon as a game sprite is added to the game, as shown in Figure A.2.

Click on the Build Objects tab to open a new user interface, as shown in Figure A.3.

Notice that no objects are shown. Select the New Object tab to build an object. Then select the graphics shown in Figure A.4.

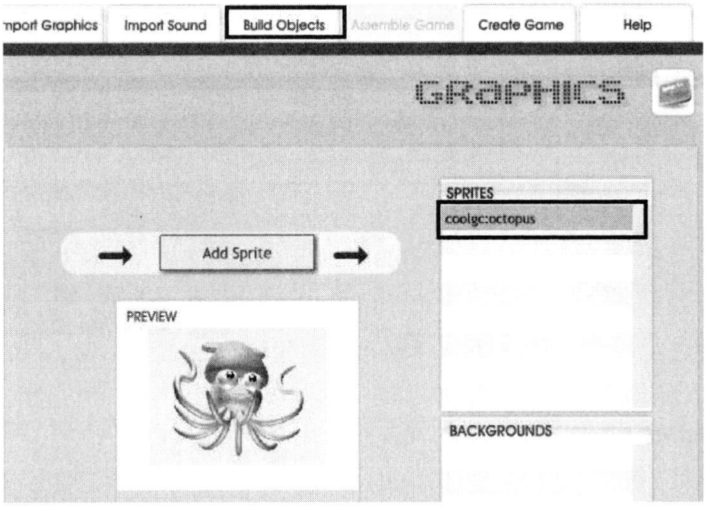

FIGURE A.2
Creating an object.

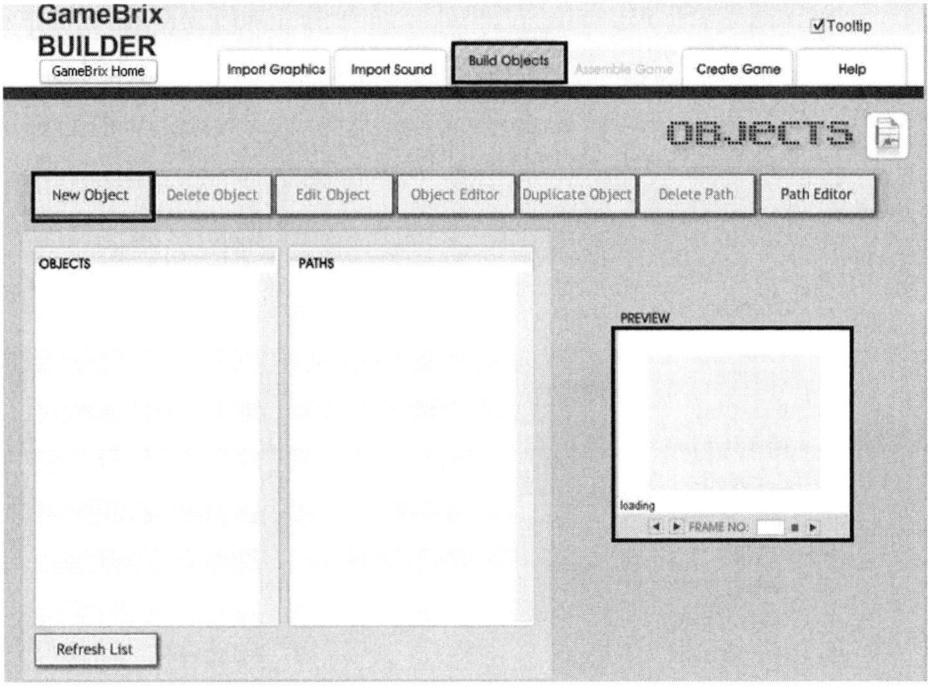

FIGURE A.3
Object Builder menu options.

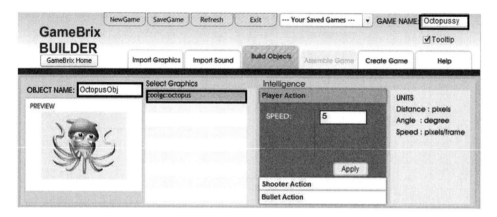

FIGURE A.4
Selecting the sprite.

Provide a name for the object to be created. It is useful to append `Obj` to the name of the sprite, as shown in the figure.

Select the New tab below the Object State menu. This step allows exploration of the available states for any object. GameBrix Builder provides multiple options for states. A sprite is said to be in a certain state when you associate a specific state to the sprite. When a state is assigned to a graphic asset, an object is created.

Using the scroll bar on the right, explore the possible states that can be associated with an object, as shown in Figure A.5.

- Click
- Collision
- Create
- DoubleClick
- DragOut
- DragOver
- GameCycle
- GameEnd
- GameStart
- KeyDown
- KeyUp
- MouseDown
- MouseMove
- MouseUp
- MouseWheel
- NoMoreHealth

- NoMoreLives
- OnEndPath
- OnJoinRoom
- OnLogin
- OnPublicMessage
- OnUserEnterRoom
- OnUserLeaveRoom
- OutsideRoom
- OutsideView
- Press
- ReleaseOutside
- RollOut
- RollOver
- RoomEnd
- RoomStart
- Timer

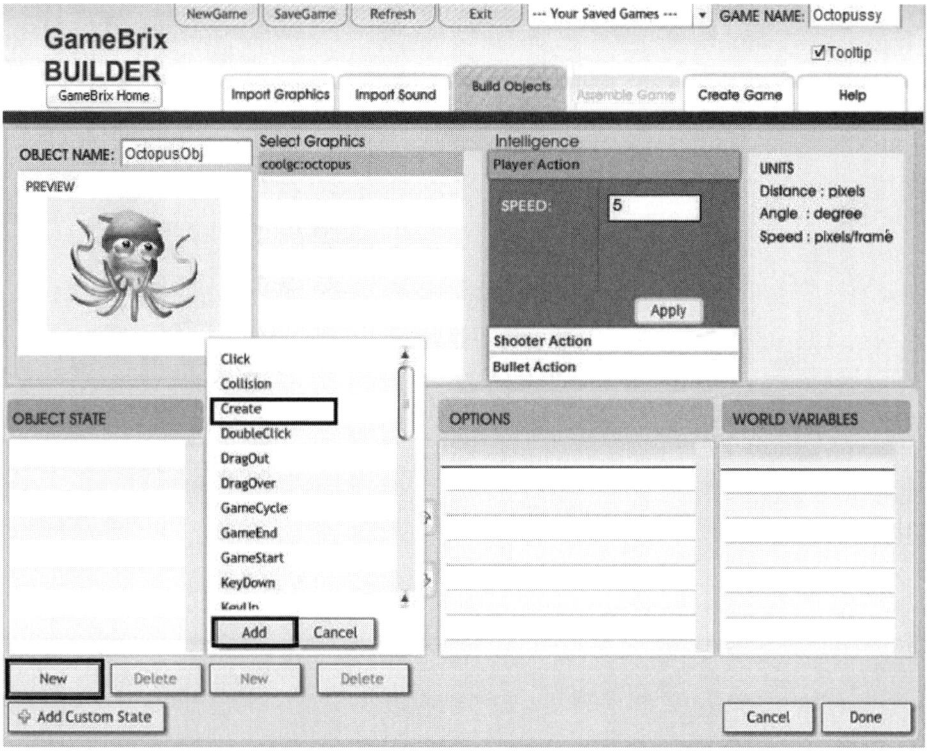

FIGURE A.5
Selecting a state.

DESCRIBE GAMEBRIX STATES

Every object can be likened to a living creature. Objects have a definite lifespan; they are born into the game, live, and die. Along the way, they may be in specific circumstances; they may be clicked or an arrow key may be pressed. GameBrix states are events that occur throughout the course of a game. The terminology state refers to the scenario that the object is in at a certain point in gameplay. An example of a state is the create state. This is similar to when an object is created, when it first appears in the game room. GameBrix states work together with GameBrix tasks to create game mechanics.

CLICK

A standard computer mouse has buttons that are used to click and select objects on the computer screen. The Click state has two options, as shown in Figure A.6. It is standard to use the left mouse-click behavior to select an item or to get game points.

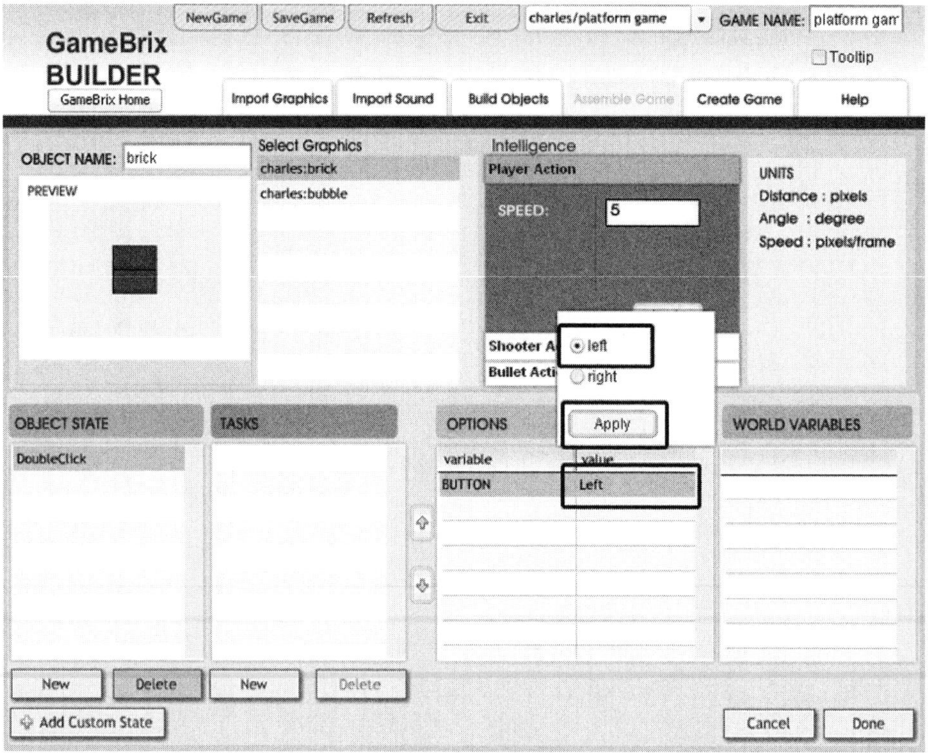

FIGURE A.6
Click state options.

COLLISION

The objects in a game that are in motion most often run into other objects or a wall. The Collision state is useful to specify the behavior of collisions with other objects or boundaries of the game room. You need to create at least two objects to use the Collision state. Select the colliding object from the menu and use the Apply button. You can use the Collision state with a variety of tasks.

CREATE

Create is the state of an object at time t=0 in the timeline. Every object in the world is associated with a timeline. The timeline defines the state when the object is born, the life cycle of the object, and the instant on the timeline when the object is destroyed. When an object is associated with the Create state in a game, it has a choice of multiple tasks. A few tasks that are often used in games are start moving, follow mouse, make scroller, and display message.

The options available to the Create task are described in Table A.1.

TABLE A.1 ADVERGAME FORMATS

Option Name	Value	Description
FOLLOWFRICTION	50	Increase/decrease value as needed
CONSTRAINX	false	If true, instance will move only on X axis
CONSTRAINY	false	If true, instance will move only on Y axis
EASEIN	false	Adds ease in effect to the object movement
DISABLED	false	Disables the existing mouse Follow action

FOLLOWFRICTION defines the lag when following the mouse. If the FOLLOWFRICTION is 0, there is no lag. By using different values of the options, you achieve the desired effect in the game.

DoubleClick

The left mouse button clicked twice within a short time is defined as the state of DoubleClick.

The only option available for the DoubleClick state is the left mouse button. GameBrix Builder provides the option to perform a double-click when the mouse button is pressed twice rapidly without a pause, in half a second intervals. The Mouse Control Panel in an operating system provides options to define the time interval for a double-click. The Builder does not set this. To double-click, move the cursor over a game sprite and press the left mouse button twice rapidly. The DoubleClick state is associated with selection, opening doors in a game, or moving to the next level in a game.

DragOut

The DragOut state allows you to mouse off the object while clicking and holding down the mouse. This state is usable in a line-following game where you must hold down the button on the mouse and follow a line. You lose the game if the mouse leaves the line.

DRAGOVER

The DragOver state is used to mouse off an object by clicking and holding the mouse button.

GAMECYCLE

The GameCycle state is useful to check the value of a variable during gameplay for every cycle in the game. In a game situation, where the game player has a few lives, GameCycle detects whether all the player's lives are used and triggers a Game Over level to be displayed.

GAMEEND

This state represents the end of a game and activates or terminates tasks as the gameplay ends. The GameEnd state commonly triggers levels that display a Game Over message.

GAMESTART

The GameStart state represents the beginning of the game and is used to initialize variables. This state is commonly used to initialize the score, health, and number of lives available to the player.

KEYDOWN

The KeyDown state is used for character movement. It is typically used with the arrow key pointing south, also known as the Down key on the keyboard. The Key-Down state has two options. The All option may be used to associate with any keys on the keyboard. The Press Any Key option is used to select the specific key that you want to be associated with the state. When you perform the specific action on the keyboard, Builder picks up the specific key to be associated with this state.

MOUSEDOWN

The MouseDown state triggers a task when you press a mouse button. You can use this state to make an object change position or start moving when you click a mouse button.

MOUSEMOVE

The MouseMove state triggers a task when you move the mouse. By using this state, you can make an object follow or point toward the mouse.

MouseUp

The MouseUp state occurs when you release the mouse button. As long as the mouse button remains pressed, this state is not reached. This state is useful in conjunction with a task such as making an object stop following the mouse when the mouse button is released.

MouseWheel

The MouseWheel state is triggered when the mouse's scroll wheel is moved. This state is used to scroll or pan across the game view.

NoMoreHealth

The NoMoreHealth state indicates when an object's health reaches 0. You can take specific actions when you detect this state on an object. Typically, when a player has no more health, he goes to the next life cycle if it exists, or a DisplayMessage task indicates that the object has no more health.

NoMoreLives

The NoMoreLives state indicates when an object in a game, such as the player, has used up all the life cycles available. You can take specific actions when you detect this state on an object. Typically, when a player has no more life, the game ends.

OnEndPath

Objects in a game may be restricted to follow a trajectory that the Path Editor specifies. The Path Editor has to create the path. Once the path has been created and named, the OnEndPath state can detect whether the object has reached the end of the trajectory. The selection of the Path Editor is shown in Figure A.7.

On invocation of the Path Editor, a screen is available to draw a path using the mouse, as shown in Figure A.8.

Specify a name for the path, as shown in Figure A.9.

In the Object Editor, an instance of an object in the CREATE state may choose the option of FollowPath, as shown in Figure A.10.

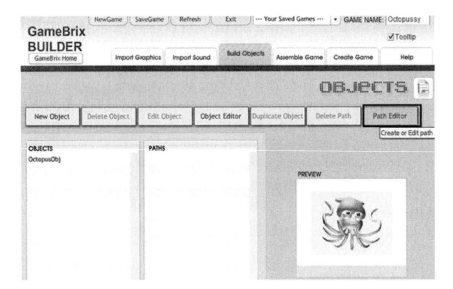

FIGURE A.7
Path Editor in Builder.

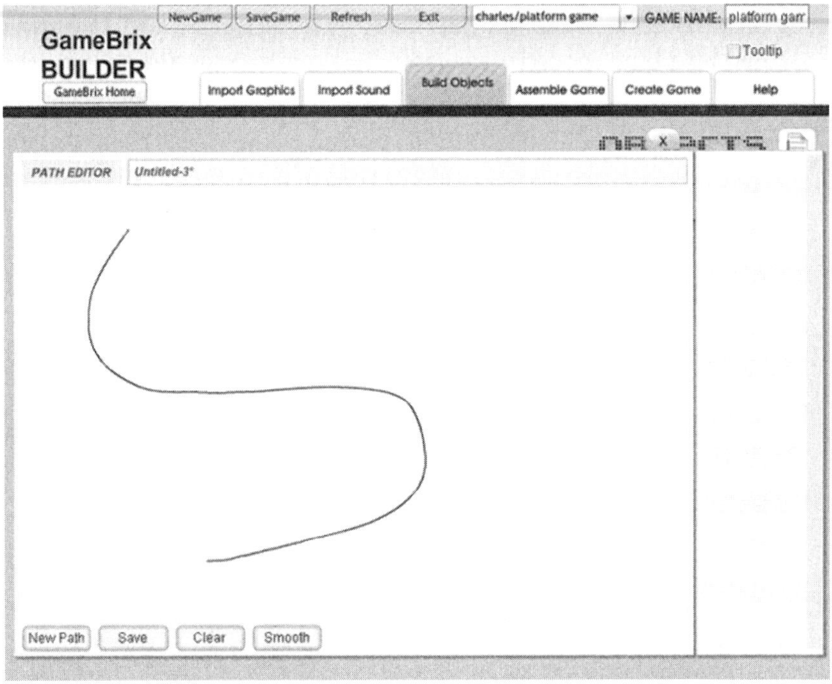

FIGURE A.8
Draw a path in the Path Editor.

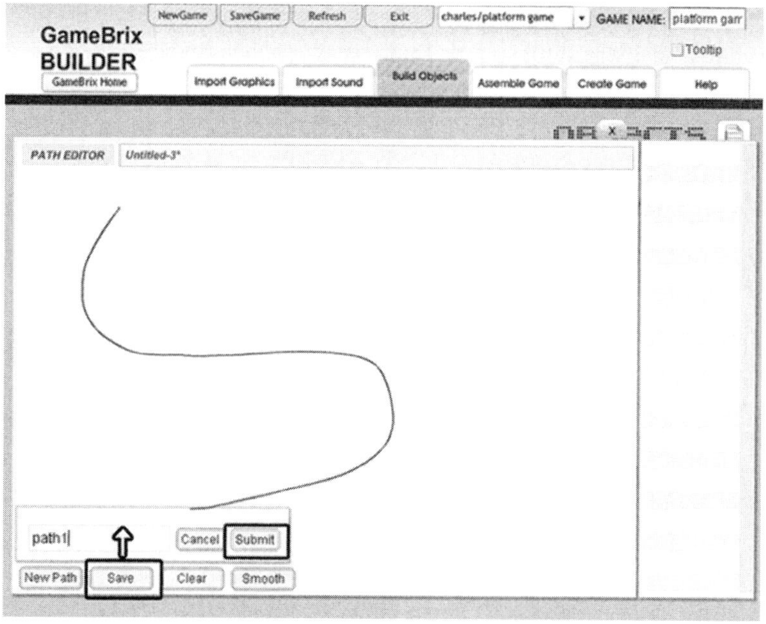

FIGURE A.9
Create a name for the path.

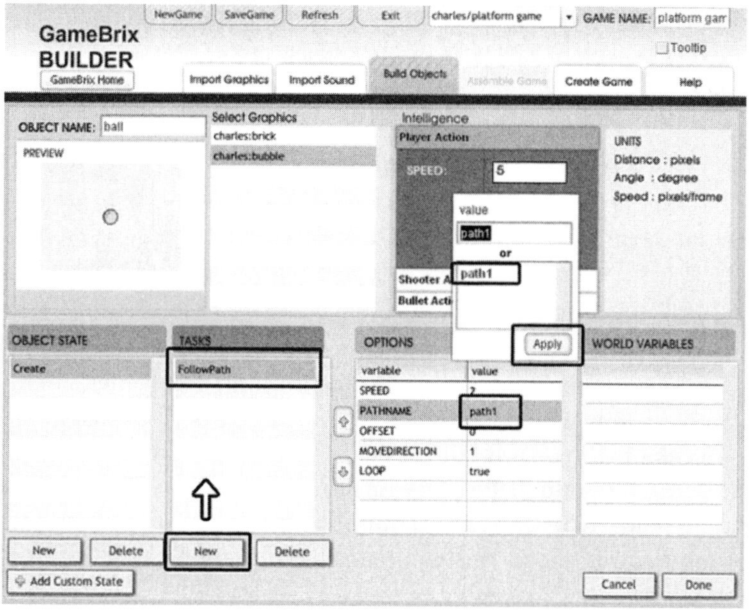

FIGURE A.10
CREATE state with the FollowPath option.

When an object reaches the end of the path, users can define various tasks. The OnEndPath state signals that the object has reached the end state, as shown in Figure A.11.

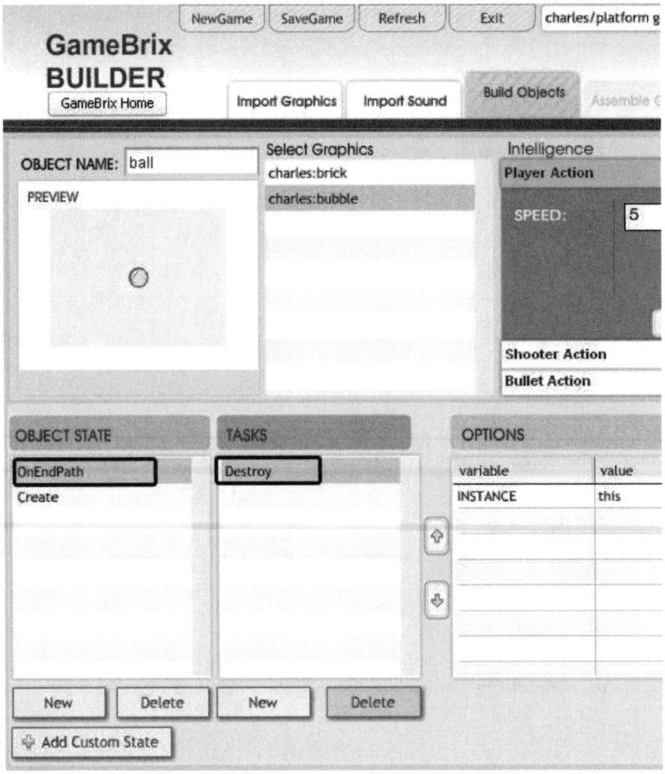

FIGURE A.11
EndPath state.

ONJOINROOM

Using GameBrix Builder, you can create multiplayer games. For a game to be able to handle multiple players, it needs a common game level area for all players or users. A room or lobby is a venue for players to join the game level. Multiple players have to be at login status before they can join a game room. The OnJoinRoom state indicates what to do when users enter a multiplayer room. For example, when a player enters a multiplayer room, this command can be used along with OnPublicMessage to broadcast a public message.

OnLogin

OnLogin is a state that is activated when a person enters a multiplayer environment. This state is useful to load or initialize multiplayer game settings. It is applicable only for the particular user who is logging into that room. This state ensures that players are at login status before joining a room.

OnPublicMessage

The OnPublicMessage state passes a set of instructions to an object or objects when a public message has to be displayed or broadcast. When a message is sent using the SendPublicMessage task, a public message is broadcast to all the users in the room. This state is useful in creating multiplayer games or a chat application.

OnUserEnterRoom

In multiplayer games, individual users may enter or exit a game. The OnUserEnterRoom state detects a new player when he enters the room and assigns tasks that need to be triggered with the new player's entry. This is an advanced option for creating multiplayer games.

OnUserLeaveRoom

In multiplayer games, players have the choice of entering and exiting a game at random. The OnUserLeaveRoom state keeps track of players and assigns tasks as deemed appropriate.

OutsideRoom

OutsideRoom is distinctly different from OnJoinRoom or OnLeaveRoom. The OutsideRoom state tracks objects as they leave the game level. Multiplayer games have rooms that a player can enter or exit from. In a game, each level can be referred to as the game screen or the game room. This sets the bounding limits of the game level. When an object moves off the game level, OutsideRoom can keep track of this object. If objects leave the game level on the right, the OutsideRoom state can trigger a task that makes the objects reappear from the left.

OutsideView

OutsideView is the state that an object is in when it leaves the level size. A game can have a view size and a level size. Sometimes in scroller or shooter games, an object keeps traveling even if it is outside the room. In such cases, instructions can be passed to destroy the object when an object leaves the game view.

PRESS

Press is a state that is triggered when the mouse button is held in a pressed state over an object. This could be to increase the radius of a circle in proportion to the duration of the mouse press or to change the appearance of an object while the mouse button is held down and revert back to the original appearance when the button is released.

RELEASEOUTSIDE

The ReleaseOutside state selects an object with the mouse click and releases the mouse outside the object's frame. ReleaseOutside is used in conjunction with Press.

ROLLOUT

The RollOut state is activated outside the frame of an object. This state is not activated while the mouse stays within the confines of the object's boundary.

ROLLOVER

The RollOver state executes tasks when the mouse moves over the object, without pressing the mouse buttons. A simple game mechanic is to register a score point when the mouse moves over an object.

ROOMEND

The RoomEnd state denotes the end of the game level or room.

ROOMSTART

The RoomStart state specifies the start area of the game level. Game objects can be triggered to start with the RoomStart state.

TIMER

The Timer state, which plays a significant role in game mechanics, is used mostly with the SetTimer task. An example for the Timer task is controlling the time that an object is displayed in a game level. The Timer task has an option that takes values of type numbers or variables. A game may have any number of timers.

DESCRIBE GAMEBRIX TASKS AND OPTIONS

Tasks are associated with object states. Whenever a state occurs, tasks can be performed. For example, if an object has a click state and a start moving task associated with the state, the object will start moving when you click on it in the game. You can combine a multitude of tasks in an object to create new game mechanics. All the tasks in GameBrix Builder and the option will be described in this section.

ARRAYFETCH

Data in games may be stored in arrays. To fetch the data, the array name is specified and the particular element of an array is accessed by specifying the ELEMENTINDEX. An array can also have a variable name that is used to fetch the data and store it as a variable. You can access this by specifying VARIABLENAME. The options available for the ArrayFetch task are described in Table A.2.

See also "CreateArray."

TABLE A.2 ARRAYFETCH OPTIONS

Option Name	Value	Description
ARRAYNAME	arrayname	The name of the array to fetch from
ELEMENTINDEX	0	The element that needs to be fetched from the array is identified by element index
VARIABLENAME	0	The name of the variable that contains the array element

BEGINBLOCK

The BeginBlock task marks the start of a set of instructions to be executed inside a conditional statement. You should use this task along with the EndBlock task.

BOUNCE

The Bounce task describes game mechanics that enable objects to bounce during the collision state. This task is used in many ways to contain objects within the game level when colliding with a solid object.

CALLFUNCTION

To invoke the same type of behaviors from varied objects, it is easier to encapsulate the behavior in a function. The CallFunction task enables the function to be executed with a single instruction. This eliminates writing the same set of instructions multiple times. As an example, in a game with three balloons of different colors that pop when they collide on contact with a projectile, a single CallFunction can be created that emulates the behavior. The CallFunction task options are described in Table A.3.

TABLE A.3 CALLFUNCTION OPTIONS

Option Name	Value	Description
FUNCTION	"customstate"	Function name
ARGS	arg1,args2	Arguments
OBJECT	instancename	Object name

CHANGESPRITE

The ChangeSprite task enables a change of sprite or graphics. This is a useful game mechanic where, during the gameplay, a player object is allowed to change appearances. ChangeSprite allows swapping of images or animations and allows the option of a new object name, as shown in Table A.4.

TABLE A.4 CHANGESPRITE OPTIONS

Option Name	Value	Description
SPRITENAME	0	Object name

CHANGEVARIABLE

Variables store values. The ChangeVariable task options are shown in Table A.5.

TABLE A.5 CHANGEVARIABLE OPTIONS

Option Name	Value	Description
VARIABLENAME	myVariable	Variable name
VARIABLEVALUE	0	Value
EXPRESSION	true	Expression type true/false
RELATIVE	false	Self-add true/false

CREATEARRAY

Arrays enable data to be stored. Tile-based games and puzzle games use the CreateArray task to store information on tile maps or puzzle pieces. The CreateArray task enables the creation of an array. The options available are shown in Table A.6.

TABLE A.6 CREATEARRAY OPTIONS

Option Name	Value	Description
ARRAYNAME	"arrayname"	Array variable name
ELEMENTS	1,2,3	Array elements

CREATEBLUR

The CreateBlur task creates a blur visual effect. It is a useful game mechanic to create visual effects in games. The CreateBlur task and its options are shown in Table A.7.

TABLE A.7 CREATEBLUR OPTIONS

Option Name	Value	Description
XBLUR	5	X blur value
YBLUR	5	Y blur value
RELATIVE	true	Self-add true/false

CREATEINSTANCE

The CreateInstance task creates an instance of an object in the game level. It is important to specify the location of the new instance of the object. The CreateInstance task and its options are shown in Table A.8.

TABLE A.8 CREATEINSTANCE OPTIONS

Option Name	Value	Description
VARIABLENAME	5	Variable name
INSTANCENAME	5	Created instance name
XLOC	0	X position
YLOC	0	Y position
RELATIVE	true	Self-add true/false

CREATEPROJECTILE

Projectiles are a staple in any game. The CreateProjectile task enables the creation of a projectile. The projectile's speed, angle at which it is launched, and special effects like gravity are some of the options available for the CreateProjectile task, as shown in Table A.9.

TABLE A.9 CREATEPROJECTILE OPTIONS

Option Name	Value	Description
SPEED	60	Speed value
ANGLE	60	Angle value
GRAVITY	9.8	Gravity value
YLOC	0	Rotation ability

CUSTOMIZEHEALTH

The CustomizeHealth task enables optimization of a game player's performance index. Health levels are specified in the game using the SetHealth task. The CustomizeHealth task changes the health display appearance set by SetHealth. The options available for this task are shown in Table A.10.

TABLE A.10 CUSTOMIZEHEALTH OPTIONS

Option Name	Value	Description
XLOC	10	X position
YLOC	10	Y position
WIDTH	200	Height value
HEIGHT	30	Rotation ability
FONTSIZE	0x00ffff	Font size value
FONTCOLOR	0x00ffff	Font color value

CUSTOMIZELIVES

The CustomizeLives task customizes the appearance of the text field that displays the life of a player. The options available for the CustomizeLives task are described in Table A.11.

TABLE A.11 CUSTOMIZELIVES OPTIONS

Option Name	Value	Description
XLOC	10	X position
YLOC	10	Y position
WIDTH	200	Width value
HEIGHT	30	Height value
FONTSIZE	0x00ffff	Font size value
FONTCOLOR	0x00ffff	Font color value

CUSTOMIZESCORE

GameBrix, by default, sets the Score field at a specific location. To override the location, font, and size from the default mode, use the CustomizeScore task. The options available for this task are listed in Table A.12.

TABLE A.12 CUSTOMIZESCORE OPTIONS

Option Name	Value	Description
XLOC	10	X position
YLOC	10	Y position
WIDTH	200	Width value
HEIGHT	30	Height value
FONTSIZE	0x00ffff	Font size value
FONTCOLOR	0x00ffff	Font color value

DESTROY

The Destroy task removes or destroys a specified object in the game. The Destroy task and its options are shown in Table A.13.

TABLE A.13 DESTROY OPTIONS

Option Name	Value	Description
INSTANCE	this	Remove instance name

DISPLAYMESSAGE

During gameplay, the players receive many messages. The DisplayMessage task is used to create a message. The options available to the DisplayMessage task are shown in Table A.14.

TABLE A.14 DISPLAYMESSAGE OPTIONS

Option Name	Value	Description
MESSAGE	`'some message'`	Message
EXPRESSION	`false`	Expression type `true`/`false`

DragNDrop

The `DragNDrop` task enables an object to be dragged and dropped. This is an advanced control task that does not require `StartDrag` and `StopDrag` tasks. The `DragNDrop` task and its option are shown in Table A.15.

TABLE A.15 DRAGNDROP OPTION

Option Name	Value	Description
ALLOWTHROWING	`false`	Throw or not

Else

The `Else` task is a component of a conditional statement. For example, an object can be instructed to move toward the mouse if it is red, or move away from the mouse if it is not.

EnableAcceleration

The `EnableAcceleration` task is an advanced macro that facilitates an object to control the acceleration. It is either enabled or disabled using `true` or `false`, as shown in Table A.16.

TABLE A.16 ENABLEACCELERATION OPTION

Option Name	Value	Description
VALUE	`true`	Enabled or disabled

EnableCollision

`EnableCollision` is a macro task that enables objects to collide. It can be enabled or disabled using `true` or `false` options, as shown in Table A.17.

TABLE A.17 ENABLECOLLISION OPTION

Option Name	Value	Description
VALUE	true	Enabled or disabled

ENABLEKEYBOARDACTION

The `EnableKeyBoardAction` task allows or disallows an object to be controlled using the keyboard. It is an advanced task that has specified controls for directional and momentum control. The options for control are shown in Table A.18.

TABLE A.18 ENABLEKEYBOARDACTION OPTIONS

Option Name	Value	Description
SPEEDX	5	Start or stop
SPEEDY	5	X speed
SHAPETYPE	SQUARE	Y speed
KEYLEFT	LEFT	Move shape type
KEYUP	UP	Set key for left action
KEYRIGHT	RIGHT	Set key for right action
KEYDOWN	DOWN	Set key for top action

ENABLEMOUSEACTION

The `EnableMouseAction` task allows or disallows an object to be controlled using the mouse. It is an advanced task that has options for friction and speed, as shown in Table A.19.

TABLE A.19 ENABLEMOUSEACTION OPTIONS

Option Name	Value	Description
VALUE	true	Enable mouse
FOLLOWFRICTION	15	Friction value
SHAPETYPE	SQUARE	Collision shape type

ENDBLOCK

The EndBlock task specifies where a block of instructions ends. This task is always used with the StartBlock task.

ENDGAME

The EndGame task creates the game mechanic for ending the game.

ENDLOOP

The EndLoop task stops the loop of instructions specified in a block.

FOLLOWINSTANCE

The FollowInstance task instructs an object to follow an instance of an object. The options available for this task are shown in Table A.20.

TABLE A.20 FOLLOWINSTANCE OPTIONS

Option Name	Value	Description
VALUE	true	Start/stop
FOLLOWFRICTION	15	Friction value
SHAPETYPE	SQUARE	Movement shape
INSTANCENAME	BirdObj	Instance name

FOLLOWMOUSE

The `FollowMouse` task enables an object to follow the mouse. It can be used to determine the friction, speed, and constraints along the X and Y axis, as shown in Table A.21.

TABLE A.21 FOLLOWMOUSE OPTIONS

Option Name	Value	Description
CONSTRAINX	false	Follow X pos or not
CONSTRAINY	false	Follow Y pos or not
FOLLOWFRICTION	15	Friction value
EASEIN	false	Add ease effect or not
DISABLED	false	Follow or not

FOLLOWOBJECT

The `FollowObject` task instructs one object to follow another. It provides options to set the friction, speed, and constraints along the X and Y axis, as shown in Table A.22.

TABLE A.22 FOLLOWOBJECT OPTIONS

Option Name	Value	Description
CONSTRAINX	false	Follow Y pos or not
CONSTRAINY	false	Follow X pos or not
FRICTION	25	Friction value
OFFSETX	10	X Offset Value
OFFSETY	10	Y Offset Value
DISABLED	false	Follow or not

FollowPath

The `FollowPath` task instructs an object to follow a predetermined path. A path can be created using the Path Editor and an assigned path name. The options available for `FollowPath` are shown in Table A.23.

TABLE A.23 FOLLOWPATH OPTIONS

Option Name	Value	Description
PATHNAME	NAME	Path name
SPEED	2	Speed value
MOVEDIRECTION	1	Direction value
LOOP	true	Number of looping

ForwardVideo

The `ForwardVideo` task cues an Internet video. The option available for this task is shown in Table A.24.

TABLE A.24 FORWARDVIDEO OPTION

Option Name	Value	Description
SECONDS	5	Number of seconds

GetCollisionObject

The `GetCollisionObject` task returns an instance of the last colliding object and allows the execution of additional instructions on the colliding object. The options available are shown in Table A.25.

TABLE A.25 GETCOLLISIONOBJECT OPTIONS

Option Name	Value	Description
VARIABLENAME	myvar	Variable name
GLOBAL	false	Variable scope

GetCurrentFrame

The GetCurrentFrame task is used to get the current frame of an animated sprite. The option available for this task is shown in Table A.26.

TABLE A.26 GETCURRENTFRAME OPTION

Option Name	Value	Description
VARIABLENAME	getFrame	Variable name

GetInput

The GetInput task displays a dialog box that has a text field. The position of the dialog box along with the variable name and value to be displayed can be controlled with the options shown in Table A.27.

TABLE A.27 GETINPUT OPTIONS

Option Name	Value	Description
VARIABLENAME	name	Variable name
VARIABLEVALUE	0	Variable value
XLOC	0	X position
YLOC	0	Y position

GetInstanceByName

The GetInstanceByName task gets a specific instance of the object in a game level. This task allows the use of variables for the instance name. The options available for this task are shown in Table A.28.

TABLE A.28 GETINSTANCEBYNAME OPTIONS

Option Name	Value	Description
INSTANCENAME	0	Instance name
VARIABLENAME	name	Variable name
EXPRESSION	true	Expression type `true/false`

GETINSTANCEPROPERTY

The `GetInstanceProperty` task provides a property value of an instance in a variable. The options available for this task are shown in Table A.29.

TABLE A.29 GETINSTANCEPROPERTY OPTIONS

Option Name	Value	Description
INSTANCENAME	0	Instance name
PROPERTYNAME	name	Variable name
VARIABLENAME	true	Property name

GETKEYCODE

Every key on the keyboard attached to a computer is associated with a specific code. `GetKeyCode` gets the key code of the last key pressed. The options available for the `GetKeyCode` task are shown in Table A.30.

TABLE A.30 GETKEYCODE OPTIONS

Option Name	Value	Description
VARIABLENAME	UserDefinedVariable	Variable name
VARIABLESCOPE	Class	Variable scope type

GETLABEL

The GetLabel task retrieves the text of the label component. The options available for this task are shown in Table A.31.

TABLE A.31 GETLABEL OPTIONS

Option Name	Value	Description
INSTANCENAME	ball	Instance name
VARIABLENAME	varName	Variable name

GETPATHOFFSET

The GetPathOffset task provides the offset position of an object in a path from its starting point. The options available for this task are shown in Table A.32.

TABLE A.32 GETPATHOFFSET OPTIONS

Option Name	Value	Description
VARIABLENAME	path	Variable name
VARIABLESCOPE	class	Variable scope type

GOTOFRAME

The GoToFrame task allows the display of a sprite from a specific animation frame. The option available for this task is shown in Table A.33.

TABLE A.33 GOTOFRAME OPTION

Option Name	Value	Description
VALUE	0	Frame number

GoToLevel

The `GoToLevel` task enables a player to reach a specified game level. The option available for this task is shown in Table A.34.

TABLE A.34 GOTOLEVEL OPTION

Option Name	Value	Description
VALUE	0	Level value

GoToNextLevel

`GoToNextLevel` enables the player to move to the next level of the game. This task does not allow you to go to a previous level.

GoToPreviousLevel

`GoToPreviousLevel` enables transition of the player to the previous level.

IfInstanceCount

The `IfInstanceCount` task counts the number of instances of an object. The options available for this task are shown in Table A.35.

TABLE A.35 IFINSTANCECOUNT OPTIONS

Option Name	Value	Description
VALUE	20	Camper value
OBJECT	ball	Object name
OPERATION	==	Relation operator

IfKeyPress

The `IfKeyPress` task gets the value of a key pressed. The option allows specification of the specific keyboard value, as shown in Table A.36.

TABLE A.36 IFKEYPRESS OPTION

Option Name	Value	Description
KEYCODE	66	Key name

IfObjectPresentAtLocation

The IfObjectPresentAtLocation task checks the existence of an object at a particular location to execute instruction sets as shown in Table A.37.

TABLE A.37 IFOBJECTPRESENTATLOCATION OPTIONS

Option Name	Value	Description
OBJECTTYPE	ObjectName	Object type
XLOC	0	X position
YLOC	0	Y position
RELATIVE	true	Self-add or not

IfScoreHasValue

The IfScoreHasValue task checks the score's value. The options available to this task are shown in Table A.38.

TABLE A.38 IFSCOREHASVALUE OPTIONS

Option Name	Value	Description
VALUE	number	Score value
OPERATION	==	Relation operator

IfVariableHasValue

The IfVariableHasValue task enables checking variable value and the options available for the task, as shown in Table A.39.

TABLE A.39 IFVARIABLEHASVALUE OPTIONS

Option Name	Value	Description
VARIABLENAME	UserDefinedVariable	Variable name
OPERATION	==	Relation operator
VALUE	true	Variable value

IGNOREUSERINPUT

The IgnoreUserInput task instructs an object to ignore inputs from a user. The option available for this task is shown in Table A.40.

TABLE A.40 IGNOREUSERINPUT OPTION

Option Name	Value	Description
DISABLED	true	True/false

INSERTSCRIPT

The InsertScript task inserts ActionScript codes and accepts the script in the form of text. This is an extremely useful task for creating user-generated game mechanics. The InsertScript task enables extending the game mechanics of the Builder with new functionality. The syntax accepted is ActionScript code. It is important to check the syntax of the script for accurate execution. The option for this task is shown in Table A.41.

TABLE A.41 INSERTSCRIPT OPTION

Option Name	Value	Description
TEXT	AnyScript	Your script

JUMPTOPOSITION

The JumpToPosition task allows any object to jump to the specified position through options shown in Table A.42.

TABLE A.42 JUMPTOPOSITION OPTIONS

Option Name	Value	Description
TARGETX	0	X position
TARGETX	0	Y position
RELATIVE	true	Self-add or not

JumpToStartPosition

The JumpToStartPosition enables an object to return to the start position.

KeepInsideLevel

The KeepInsideLevel task instructs an object to remain inside the level at a specific location. The boundaries are specified with the options shown in Table A.43.

TABLE A.43 KEEPINSIDELEVEL OPTIONS

Option Name	Value	Description
TOP	0	Top value
LEFT	0	Left value
BOTTOM	0	Bottom value
RIGHT	true	Right value

LoginMultiPlayer

The LoginMultiplayer task lets a player enter a multiplayer environment. The options available for this task are shown in Table A.44.

TABLE A.44 LOGINMULTIPLAYER OPTIONS

Option Name	Value	Description
USERNAME	username	Username
EXPRESSION	false	Any string or variable

LOOP

The Loop task allows a set of instructions or tasks to run through repeatedly. The options available for this task are shown in Table A.45.

TABLE A.45 LOOP OPTIONS

Option Name	Value	Description
VARIABLENAME	i	Variable name
INITIALVALUE	0	Start value
ENDVALUE	5	End value
CONDITION	<	Relation operator
INCVALUE	true	Increment value

MAKEBOUNCEABLE

The MakeBounceable task enables an object to bounce. The options to set the parameters for the bounce option are shown in Table A.46.

TABLE A.46 MAKEBOUNCEABLE OPTIONS

Option Name	Value	Description
BOUNCEVALUE	1	Bounce value
SPEEDX	5	X speed
SPEEDY	5	Y speed
COLLIDINGOBJECT	ObjectName	Colliding object name

MAKESCROLLER

The MakeScroller task is useful for creating Mario-style platform games. This macro task enables creation of a platform scroller game and allows the camera to follow the direction of the player. It also allows the game view to move with the player. The option available for the MakeScroller task is shown in Table A.47.

TABLE A.47 MAKESCROLLER OPTION

Option Name	Value	Description
OFFSET	200	Distance before the current view area. If the view area is 600 and the offset is 200, the Scroller starts working at 400.

MOVEATANGLE

The MoveAtAngle task makes an object move at a tangent. The options available for the task are shown in Table A.48.

TABLE A.48 MOVEATANGLE OPTIONS

Option Name	Value	Description
ANGLE	60	Move angle value
SPEED	5	Move speed value
RELATIVE	false	Self-add or not

OpenPage

The OpenPage task opens an Internet location in a browser. The options available for this task are shown in Table A.49.

TABLE A.49 OPENPAGE OPTIONS

Option Name	Value	Description
PAGEURL	http://www.cengage.com	URL path
POPUP	true	Pop-up window or not
EXPRESSION	false	Expression type or not

PaintCircle

The PaintCircle task creates circles. The options available for this task are shown in Table A.50.

TABLE A.50 PAINTCIRCLE OPTIONS

Option Name	Value	Description
XPOS	0	X position
YPOS	0	Y position
WIDTH	0	Circle width
HEIGHT	0	Circle height
RELATIVE	false	Self-add or not

PaintLine

The PaintLine task draws a line from one specified point to another. The options available for this task are shown in Table A.51.

TABLE A.51 PAINTLINE OPTIONS

Option Name	Value	Description
XLOCSRC	0	X position
YLOCSRC	0	Y position
XLOCDEST	0	X distance
YLOCDEST	0	Y distance
RELATIVE	false	Self-add or not

PAINTRECTANGLE

The PaintRectangle task creates a rectangular shape with the specified coordinates with options shown in Table A.52.

TABLE A.52 PAINTRECTANGLE OPTIONS

Option Name	Value	Description
XLOC1	0	X position first point
YLOC1	0	Y position first point
XLOC2	0	X position second point
YLOC2	0	Y position second point
RELATIVE	false	Self-add or not

PAUSEVIDEO

The PauseVideo task allows a video that is playing to pause.

PLACEABOVEALL

The PlaceAboveAll task allows the manipulation of an object's depth in a game. PlaceAboveAll specifies that the assigned object's position be above all other objects.

PLAYSOUND

The `PlaySound` task plays a specified sound that has been added to the game, with options shown in Table A.53.

TABLE A.53 PLAYSOUND OPTIONS

Option Name	Value	Description
SOUNDNAME	MP3SoundFileName	Sound name
REPEAT	false	Repeat or not

PLAYVIDEO

Internet video can be linked to a game if it is of the FLV format. The `PlayVideo` task plays a specified video URL. The options available for this task are shown in Table A.54.

TABLE A.54 PLAYVIDEO OPTIONS

Option Name	Value	Description
URL	www.youtube.com	Path of the FLV video or any YouTube video link
YOUTUBE	false	true if the FLV refers to YouTube link; default is false
EXPRESSION	false	Any URL string or variable name

POINTATLOCATION

The `PointAtLocation` task instructs an object to point toward specified coordinates, as specified with options shown in Table A.55.

TABLE A.55 POINTATLOCATION OPTIONS

Option Name	Value	Description
XLOC	0	X position
YLOC	0	Y position
DISABLED	false	True/false

POINTATMOUSE

The `PointAtMouse` task instructs an object to point toward the mouse, with an option shown in Table A.56.

TABLE A.56 POINTATMOUSE OPTION

Option Name	Value	Description
DISABLED	false	True/false

POINTATOBJECT

The `PointAtObject` task instructs an object to point toward another specified object or instance with options shown in Table A.57.

TABLE A.57 POINTATOBJECT OPTIONS

Option Name	Value	Description
OBJNAME	objName	Object name
DISABLED	false	True/false

PULSATION

The `Pulsation` task triggers a pulsating visual effect, with options shown in Table A.58.

TABLE A.58 PULSATION OPTIONS

Option Name	Value	Description
PULSESIZE	15	Pulse size
PULSESPEED	0.2	Pulse speed

REMOVEOBJECT

The `RemoveObject` task removes all instances of an object from the play area, with an option shown in Table A.59.

TABLE A.59 REMOVEOBJECT OPTION

Option Name	Value	Description
OBJECT	this	Object name

RESTARTGAME

The RestartGame task replays or restarts a game.

RESTARTVIDEO

The RestartVideo task restarts an Internet video.

RESUMEVIDEO

The ResumeVideo task resumes the play of an Internet video.

RETURN

The Return task fetches a specific value with a query option, as shown in Table A.60.

TABLE A.60 RETURN OPTIONS

Option Name	Value	Description
TEXT	0	Variable or value

REWINDVIDEO

The RewindVideo task rewinds an Internet video. The option available for this task to specify the time interval for rewind is shown in Table A.61.

TABLE A.61 REWINDVIDEO OPTION

Option Name	Value	Description
SECONDS	15	Set time for video rewind

SendPublicMessage

The SendPublicMessage task sends a message to all players in a multiplayer environment. The option available for this task is shown in Table A.62.

TABLE A.62 SENDPUBLICMESSAGE OPTION

Option Name	Value	Description
MESSAGE	Hello World!	Any message

SetAcceleration

The SetAcceleration task sets an object's acceleration. The options for this task are listed in Table A.63.

TABLE A.63 SETACCELERATION OPTIONS

Option Name	Value	Description
VALUE	0	Acceleration value
DIRECTION	0	Direction value
RELATIVE	true	Self-add or not

SetAccelerationXY

The SetAccelerationXY task specifies the momentum of an object in a specific direction. This task is used when an object's direction is specified between a set of coordinates, with options as listed in Table A.64.

TABLE A.64 SETACCELERATIONXY OPTIONS

Option Name	Value	Description
ANGLE	0	Acceleration angle
SPEED	0.2	Acceleration speed

SetCollisionObject

The SetCollisionObject task specifies the object to collide with options, as listed in Table A.65.

TABLE A.65 SETCOLLISIONOBJECT OPTION

Option Name	Value	Description
COLLIDINGOBJECT	playerObj	Object name

SetFooter

The SetFooter task allows customization of the game footer. The option available to this task is listed in Table A.66.

TABLE A.66 SETFOOTER OPTION

Option Name	Value	Description
MESSAGE	Game sponsored by www.Cengage.com	Message

SetHealth

The SetHealth task enables setting of health values. The option available for this task is listed in Table A.67 and determines the value of health in gameplay.

TABLE A.67 SETHEALTH OPTIONS

Option Name	Value	Description
VALUE	0	Health value
RELATIVE	true	Self-add or not

SetHorizontalSpeed

The SetHorizontalSpeed task allows setting the horizontal speed of an object. The options available for this task are listed in Table A.68.

TABLE A.68 SETHORIZONTALSPEED OPTIONS

Option Name	Value	Description
HSPEED	0	Horizontal speed value
RELATIVE	false	Self-add or not

SETINSTANCEPROPERTY

The SetInstanceProperty task allows you to set object properties such as size, visibility, and position. The options available for this task are listed in Table A.69.

TABLE A.69 SETINSTANCEPROPERTY OPTIONS

Option Name	Value	Description
INSTANCENAME	BlueKissObj	Instance name
PROPERTYNAME	BlueKissProperty	Property name
PROPERTYVALUE	True	Property value

SETJUMPACTION

The SetJumpAction task enables an object to jump with parameters for the jump specified, with options listed in Table A.70.

TABLE A.70 SETJUMPACTION OPTIONS

Option Name	Value	Description
COLLIDINGOBJECT	BirdObj	Collide object name
KEYCODE	SPACE	Key name
GRAVITY	0.5	Gravity value
FRICTION	0.8	Friction value
JUMPHEIGHT	8	Jump height value
MOVE	4	Move value

SETLABEL

The SetLabel task allows objects to retain a text label. The text displayed for the object is specified using SetLabel. The options available for this task are listed in Table A.71.

TABLE A.71 SETLABEL OPTIONS

Option Name	Value	Description
TEXT	TEXT	Label message
SIZE	14	Font size
COLOR	0x000000	Font color
EXPRESSION	false	Expression type or not

SETLIVES

The SetLives task allows you to set the number of lives for a player. The options available for the task are listed in Table A.72.

TABLE A.72 SETLIVES OPTIONS

Option Name	Value	Description
VALUE	0	Live value
RELATIVE	true	Self-add or not

SETMASK

The SetMask task allows an object to be used to mask another object. SetMask specifies that the current instance will be masked using the specified instance, with options listed in Table A.73.

TABLE A.73 SETMASK OPTIONS

Option Name	Value	Description
INSTANCENAME	Object Name	Masked instance name
EXPRESSION	false	Expression type or not

SetObjectPosition

The SetObjectPosition task specifies the position of an object in the game level, with options listed in Table A.74.

TABLE A.74 SETOBJECTPOSITION OPTIONS

Option Name	Value	Description
XLOC	1	X position
YLOC	1	Y position

SetScore

The SetScore task specifies the global score. You can use it to increase or decrease the value of the score, with options listed in Table A.75.

TABLE A.75 SETSCORE OPTIONS

Option Name	Value	Description
VALUE	0	Score value
RELATIVE	true	Self-add or not

SetTimer

The SetTimer task initializes a timer, with options listed in Table A.76.

TABLE A.76 SETTIMER OPTIONS

Option Name	Value	Description
TIMERNO	0	Timer ID
DELAY	1000	Timer delay time
REPEAT	true	Repeat or not

SetVariable

The `SetVariable` task allows you to set variables associated with an object. The options available for the `SetVariable` task are listed in Table A.77.

TABLE A.77 SETVARIABLE OPTIONS

Option Name	Value	Description
VARIABLENAME	GameScore	Variable name
VARIABLEVALUE	0	Variable value
EXPRESSION	true	Expression type or not
VARIABLESCOPE	Class	Variable scope type
RELATIVE	false	Self-add or not

SetVerticalSpeed

The `SetVerticalSpeed` task sets the speed of an object in a vertical plane using the options listed in Table A.78.

TABLE A.78 SETVERTICALSPEED OPTIONS

Option Name	Value	Description
VSPEED	0	Vertical speed value
RELATIVE	false	Self-add or not

SetVideoBufferTime

The `SetVideoBufferTime` task allows you to set the buffer time duration for video download. The option available for this task is shown in Table A.79.

TABLE A.79 SETVIDEOBUFFERTIME OPTION

Option Name	Value	Description
SECONDS	0	Number of seconds

SETVIDEOPOSITION

The SetVideoPosition task specifies the position in the video component to be displayed. The options available for this task are listed in Table A.80.

TABLE A.80 SETVIDEOPOSITION OPTIONS

Option Name	Value	Description
XLOC	0	X location
YLOC	0	Y location

SETVIDEOSIZE

The SetVideoSize task determines the dimensions of the video component, with options listed in Table A.81.

TABLE A.81 SETVIDEOSIZE OPTIONS

Option Name	Value	Description
WIDTH	300	Width value
HEIGHT	200	Height value

SETVIDEOVOLUME

The SetVideoVolume task determines the volume of the video being played, with an option listed in Table A.82.

TABLE A.82 SETVIDEOVOLUME OPTION

Option Name	Value	Description
VALUE	0	Sound volume

SHOWCAMERA

The ShowCamera task allows live video from a Web camera to be included in a game. ShowCamera gets input from the camera and displays it in the specified area. The options available for this task are listed in Table A.83.

TABLE A.83 SHOWCAMERA OPTIONS

Option Name	Value	Description
VIDEOCLIPID	objectID	Video clip ID
XLOC	0	X location
YLOC	0	Y location
WIDTH	300	Video width
HEIGHT	200	Video height
SAVEFRAMES	false	Save frames or not
SAVEFRAMESINTERVAL	200	Save frames interval seconds
VIDEOPLACEID	VideoSurface	Video placed ID

SHOWVIDEO

The ShowVideo task displays an Internet video. The options available for this task are listed in Table A.84.

TABLE A.84 SHOWVIDEO OPTIONS

Option Name	Value	Description
URL	www.youtube.com	Video URL path
YOUTUBE	false	Play with YouTube or other
EXPRESSION	false	Expression type or not
WIDTH	300	Video width
XLOC	0	X location
YLOC	0	Y location
WIDTH	300	Video width
HEIGHT	200	Video height

StartBlock

The StartBlock task specifies the start of a block of instructions. It is similar to BeginBlock.

StartDrag

The StartDrag task specifies when you can drag an object. The options available for this task are listed in Table A.85.

TABLE A.85 STARTDRAG OPTIONS

Option Name	Value	Description
OBJECT	this	Object name
LOCKCENTER	true	Make mouse center or not

StartMoving

The StartMoving task specifies when an object starts moving. Options available for this task are listed in Table A.86.

TABLE A.86 STARTMOVING OPTIONS

Option Name	Value	Description
DIRN	0	Direction value
SPEED	10	Speed value

StartMovingXY

The StartMovingXY task instructs an object to start moving in a specified plane. The plane is described as X and Y coordinates. The options available for this task are shown in Table A.87.

TABLE A.87 STARTMOVINGXY OPTIONS

Option Name	Value	Description
SPEEDX	5	X speed
SPEEDY	5	Y speed
SHAPETYPE	SQUARE	Moving shape type

STOPDRAG

The StopDrag task ends the drag sequence of an instance.

STOPFOLLOWINGMOUSE

The StopFollowingMouse task stops an object from following the mouse.

STOPMOVING

The StopMoving task stops the movement of an object.

STOPMOVINGXY

The StopMovingXY task stops the movement of an object that has started moving with the StartMovingXY task.

STOPSOUND

The StopSound task stops a sound that is currently being played. An option is shown in Table A.88.

TABLE A.88 STOPSOUND OPTION

Option Name	Value	Description
SOUNDNAME	MyMusic	Sound object name

StopTimer

The StopTimer task stops a timer that has been triggered. The option available for this task is shown in Table A.89.

TABLE A.89 STOPTIMER OPTION

Option Name	Value	Description
TIMERNO	0	Timer number

StopVideo

The StopVideo task stops the play of an Internet video.

Trace

The Trace task displays a message in debug mode. This is particularly useful to test a game during runtime. The options available for this task are shown in Table A.90.

TABLE A.90 TRACE OPTIONS

Option Name	Value	Description
MESSAGE	Game Over!	Message or value
EXPRESSION	FALSE	Expression type or not

TransformObject

The TransformObject task transforms an object's attributes, such as size, position, rotation, and visibility. The options available for this task are shown in Table A.91.

TABLE A.91 TRANSFORMOBJECT OPTIONS

Option Name	Value	Description
ALPHA	0	Opacity value
HEIGHT	0	Object height
WIDTH	0	Object width
ROTATION	40	Object rotation
VISIBLE	true	Show/hide
XSCALE	0	X scale
YSCALE	0	Y scale
RELATIVE	false	Self-add or not

TriggerInstanceEvent

The TriggerInstanceEvent task triggers an event of an instance. The functionality of the TriggerInstanceEvent is similar to a call function, which initiates a function. The options available for this task are shown in Table A.92.

TABLE A.92 TRIGGERINSTANCEEVENT OPTIONS

Option Name	Value	Description
INSTANCENAME	Object name	Instance name
EVENTNAME	Event name	State name that needs to be triggered

ChangeDirection

The ChangeDirection task changes the direction of a moving object. The options available for the ChangeDirection task are shown in Table A.93.

TABLE A.93 CHANGEDIRECTION OPTIONS

Option Name	Value	Description
XCOMP	1	X value
YCOMP	1	Y value

CHANGEDIRECTIONKEYS

ChangeDirectionKeys is an advanced task that specifies which direction to change when a specified key is pressed. The options available are described in Table A.94.

TABLE A.94 CHANGEDIRECTIONKEYS OPTIONS

Option Name	Value	Description
KEYLEFT	37	Key code
KEYUP	38	Key code
KEYRIGHT	39	Key code
KEYDOWN	40	Key code

SETFORCE

SetForce is an advanced task that specifies the force of an object. It is particularly useful for games where projectiles are used. The options available with the default values are shown in Table A.95.

TABLE A.95 SETFORCE OPTIONS

Option Name	Value	Description
FORCEX	1	Force X
FORCEY	1	Force Y

SETSPEED

SetSpeed is an advanced task that sets the speed of an object. You can also use it to control the directional speed of an object within an X-Y coordinate plane. The options and the default values are shown in Table A.96.

TABLE A.96 SETSPEED OPTIONS

Option Name	Value	Description
SPEEDX	5	X speed
SPEEDY	5	Y speed

WAVEMOTION

The WaveMotion task enables an object to follow a trigonometric sine wave movement. The wave height, speed, and axis are options that need to be specified for this task, as shown in Table A.97.

TABLE A.97 WAVEMOTION OPTIONS

Option Name	Value	Description
WAVEHEIGHT	15	Wave height
WAVESPEED	0.2	Wave speed
WAVEAXIS	x	Change wave axis

SUMMARY

The GameBrix Builder allows users to add user-defined game mechanics that are sharable between the GameBrix communities of game developers. This appendix provides a concise description of the states and tasks available to build new, innovative Flash games. GameBrix enables a collaborative approach to Flash game creation with videos and graphics. Multiplayer games require advanced skills and have not been covered in this book, although you can use concepts from this book to create them. Today, the game arena has expanded globally. Building innovative games with GameBrix allows new developers to produce games without the need for complex code.

Index

Note: Page numbers referencing figures are italicized and followed by an "*f.*" Page numbers referencing tables are italicized and followed by a "*t.*"

Note: Page numbers referencing figures are italicized and followed by an "*f.*" Page numbers referencing tables are italicized and followed by a "*t.*"

Note: Page numbers referencing figures are italicized and followed by an "*f*." Page numbers referencing tables are italicized and followed by a "*t*."

Note: Page numbers referencing figures are italicized and followed by an "*f.*" Page numbers referencing tables are italicized and followed by a "*t.*"

Note: Page numbers referencing figures are italicized and followed by an "*f.*" Page numbers referencing tables are italicized and followed by a "*t.*"

Note: Page numbers referencing figures are italicized and followed by an "*f*." Page numbers referencing tables are italicized and followed by a "*t*."

Note: Page numbers referencing figures are italicized and followed by an "*f.*" Page numbers referencing tables are italicized and followed by a "*t.*"

Note: Page numbers referencing figures are italicized and followed by an "*f.*" Page numbers referencing tables are italicized and followed by a "*t.*"

Note: Page numbers referencing figures are italicized and followed by an "*f.*" Page numbers referencing tables are italicized and followed by a "*t.*"

Note: Page numbers referencing figures are italicized and followed by an "*f.*" Page numbers referencing tables are italicized and followed by a "*t.*"

Note: Page numbers referencing figures are italicized and followed by an "*f.*" Page numbers referencing tables are italicized and followed by a "*t.*"

Note: Page numbers referencing figures are italicized and followed by an "*f*." Page numbers referencing tables are italicized and followed by a "*t*."

Note: Page numbers referencing figures are italicized and followed by an "*f.*" Page numbers referencing tables are italicized and followed by a "*t.*"

Note: Page numbers referencing figures are italicized and followed by an "*f.*" Page numbers referencing tables are italicized and followed by a "*t.*"